TESTING AND MEASUREMENT IN THE CLASSROOM

TESTING
AND
MEASUREMENT
IN THE
CLASSROOM

Dale P. Scannell / D. B. Tracy
University of Kansas

HOUGHTON MIFFLIN COMPANY · BOSTON

Atlanta · Dallas · Geneva, Illinois
Hopewell, New Jersey · Palo Alto · London

The "Wizard of Id" by Brant Parker and Johnny Hart on page 1.
By permission of John Hart and Field Enterprises.

Editorial cartoon on page 102 by Pat Oliphant.
Copyright The Denver Post.
Reprinted with permission of Los Angeles Times Syndicate.

Printed in the United States of America
Library of Congress Catalog Card Number: 74-14142
ISBN: 0-395-18608-0

CONTENTS

Appendix / 267

PREFACE

Testing and Measurement in the Classroom has been written to guide present and future teachers through the processes of testing, grading, and reporting students' achievements. We have deliberately limited the topics to measurement theory, technology, and issues that have a direct and immediate bearing on the teaching–learning process and the measurements teachers must and should make of their students. We omitted topics included in general measurement texts if we deemed them to have little or no usefulness to classroom teachers. Further, we included only those techniques and processes that are practicable for teachers in terms of the amount of time they can spend on their measurement programs.

All too often teachers have equated measurement with testing and testing with assigning grades and as a result have relegated classroom measurement to a rather low priority among the demands made on their time. The premise reflected throughout this book is that classroom measurement practices should provide reliable data to help teachers and students make classroom decisions and simultaneously should influence the teaching–learning process in a positive, constructive way.

Effective teaching requires that students and teachers constantly monitor learning progress and make frequent decisions on strategies to realize optimal student achievement. These decisions are based on observations of students' abilities to assimilate new material, develop skills, and apply knowledge to the performance of curricular tasks. The teacher makes many observations casually, but he should plan some activities specifically to provide an opportunity to measure achievement. Classroom assessment techniques should be formal, effective, and efficient extensions of informal observations teachers constantly make. If teachers carefully plan formal measurement procedures, they can enhance the learning process and gather valuable insights—without compromise. Improvement in measurement techniques will result in the collection of better data that will make more useful contributions to the teaching–learning process.

This book is organized into an introductory chapter and three parts comprising topics from initial planning of instruction through use of data to improve teaching and testing. Chapter 1 is an overview of the ways classroom measurement fits into a complete teaching strategy and helps improve the teaching–learning process; it also introduces some basic measurement concepts. Unique features of educational measurement are described with specific attention to the ways measurement of achievement differs from the physical measurements we all use constantly.

Part I contains suggestions for the planning and preparation that are needed if measurement and instruction are to be effectively related. Teaching should be based on explicit instructional goals, statements describing the changes in student capabilities that should result from effective instruction. Chapter 2 discusses the formulation of goal statements—objectives—that provide foundations for teaching and measurement. Chapter 3 focuses on factors that teachers should consider in formulating plans for both the total assessment program and the individual test.

Part II emphasizes ways evidence can be collected on the learning occurring in the classroom. Chapter 4 describes how to develop and use free-response tests—tests in which the examinees supply the answers—and includes essay, short-answer, and completion tests. The next two chapters discuss choice-type tests—tests in which examinees select answers from among the options presented. Chapter 5 discusses true-false and matching exercises, and Chapter 6 considers multiple-choice tests and two variations of the traditional multiple-choice format. Chapter 7 presents some useful test and nontest methods for collecting evidence of the noncognitive development of students.

Part III focuses on the use of the data teachers collect in the classroom. Chapter 8 presents simple classroom quantitative methods, treatment of test scores required for classroom purposes, and use of test data for improving tests. Chapter 9 considers reporting test results to examinees to help the teaching–learning process and also some of the issues concerning marking systems.

The list of objectives that begins each chapter should provide structure and guidance to students as they proceed through the chapter. The exercises at the close of each chapter relate to the objectives and allow students to test their accomplishments. Answers to most of the exercises are presented in the Appendix.

This is not a general measurement text and therefore makes only passing reference to measurement theory, standardized tests, and measurement procedures that are not under the direct control of a classroom teacher. This text deals with issues of concern to a teacher, addressing ways measurement can be used in harmony with various teaching strategies and learning theories. We have not taken a dogmatic position or presented a cookbook approach because we believe that dedicated teachers will use appropriate, understood measurement techniques and that when they are presented with crucial issues and various opinions on controversial topics, teachers will make decisions resulting in a consistent approach to teaching and assessment.

We express our gratitude and acknowledge our indebtedness to our former teachers, to our colleagues whom we have met seldom and read frequently, and to our students who have helped to fashion the philosophy and approach this book represents. We also express our deep appreciation to our patient and forbearing wives.

D.P.S.
D.B.T.

THE WIZARD OF ID

by Brant parker and Johnny hart

Chapter 1

BASIC CONCEPTS OF CLASSROOM MEASUREMENT

As a result of studying this chapter you should be able to:

1. *Describe the interrelationships among measurement, testing, and evaluation.*

2. *Distinguish between formative and summative evaluation in terms of the goals of the processes and a teacher's responsibilities in the processes.*

3. *Identify ways measurement can assist in formative evaluation in your teaching field.*

4. *Give reasons why most classroom measurement in your teaching field is of necessity indirect and incomplete.*

5. *Describe the concepts of validity and reliability as they pertain to classroom measurement.*

6. *Describe the effect of indirect and incomplete measurement on the validity and reliability of classroom measurement.*

The importance of measurement within the teaching–learning process has long been recognized, and texts describing measurement techniques have been available for teachers' libraries since the early 1900s. Even so, a mild revolution has occurred in recent years concerning the importance of monitoring individual pupil progress for the purpose of planning instruction.

All too often teachers and pupils have viewed classroom testing as a necessary evil prior to the assignment of marks. Students have regarded tests as hurdles, and teachers have used testing in ways that caused students to view tests as punishment or at least as a threatening and noxious experience. Although it is true that tests provide an objective and reliable basis for assigning marks and thus for describing level of achievement, proper application of sound measurement practices can minimize the threatening aspects of taking tests. A complete measurement program emphasizes the supportive aspects of testing within the teaching–learning process.

Many aspects of teacher training and teaching practices reflect models that include assessment of pupil status, prescription of a learning strategy for each pupil, application of the strategy, and assessment of the effectiveness of the efforts. This last step, assessment of effectiveness, can represent the beginning of the sequence, the assessment of pupil status, in the next phase of the continuous teaching–learning process. Figure 1.1 depicts the process graphically.

Measurement plays an integral role in the total teaching–learning process; only when the teacher and learner are aware of the progress being made at various points in time can they plan and implement appropriate activities. A conscientious teacher acts as an adviser for each pupil in determining his learning needs and as a guide in establishing the activities that will be conducive to accomplishing his goals.

Role of Classroom Measurement

The role of classroom measurement can be divided into two major parts running along one continuum: first, the role of analysis during the learning process and, second, the role of describing the level of achievement at the close of a semester or academic year. In present-day parlance the first is called *formative evaluation* and the second, *summative evaluation*. Classroom testing and mea-

FIGURE 1.1

The continuous teaching–learning process

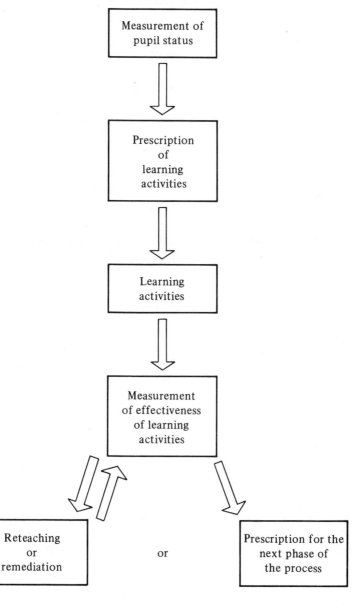

surement will be presented in these twin roles throughout this text.

Although the term "evaluation" is often used in close conjunction with "measurement," the two terms should not be used interchangeably. *Evaluation* may be defined in several ways, but here it means the process of judging the degree of adequacy or value in, for example, a person's performance, a set of teaching procedures, or curricular materials. The process of determining the degree of adequacy may rely heavily on information obtained by formal measurement, but other kinds of information, such as informal observations, school records, health histories, or parent-teacher conferences, can often be used.

Evaluation should occur at the beginning, middle, and end of a unit of instruction. In all cases the process includes the collection of relevant data—measurement—and a comparison of that data against established standards or expectations—evaluation. The purpose of evaluation will be different at various stages during instruction, and the action taken as a result will be different also. The following examples will help clarify these concepts.

Prior to beginning instruction, the teacher's evaluation of the students' present achievements, interests, and attitudes should serve as the basis for selecting objectives and content and planning appropriate learning experiences. For example, in an elementary school unit on map reading, the teacher might assess what the pupils know of map symbols and related skills and what their interests are in various geographic regions and types of maps. These steps would provide clues for deciding what amount of review and basic knowledge to cover and what material would appeal to the interests of the class.

In the course of a unit of study, periodic evaluations allow feedback to the students and parents about each student's progress, and the teacher may use this information to alter the teaching–learning plan. Should the plan prove more effective than anticipated, the teacher may be able to accelerate or enrich the students' program or circumvent certain parts of the teaching–

learning plan. On the other hand, an ineffective plan can be revised or even abandoned if necessary. For example, if the results of quizzes and exercises revealed that pupils could spell most of the words in their spelling lists, the teacher might accelerate the pace of the class through the lists, add more complex words, or decide to reduce the time devoted to spelling and increase the time devoted to topics that the class had not mastered so well.

At the end of a unit of study, evaluation gives students and parents information about each student's achievement in terms of the goals and objectives. At this point, the teacher may use evaluation to assign grades or certify that the student is ready for the next major step in the school program. This evaluation will also tell the teacher how effective his instruction has been in helping students toward their objectives. For example, the evaluation of language development at the end of a semester could provide the basis for reporting to the student and his parents how well the student has progressed in usage, diction, and punctuation. In addition, by pooling information about all students, topic by topic, the teacher might find that progress in one or more areas was generally below expectations, indicating a need to revise instructional plans in these areas.

Formative Evaluation

Using measurement to clarify a task, provide helpful guidance for a learner, and help the teacher adjust teaching strategies is part of formative evaluation. Constructive use of measurement can facilitate an effective teaching–learning environment by enhancing the teacher's ability to react to individual student needs and by guiding students through a learning task.

One well-established tenet of learning theory concerns the effect of knowledge of results on learning processes. Research has shown that less than optimal learning occurs when the learner lacks knowledge of his progress. It seems that a student cannot proceed effectively through new steps of a learning sequence without an indication of how well he has accomplished the earlier steps. Research suggests that the lack of this knowledge is associated with slower subsequent learning, with incomplete learning, and with poorer retention of what has been learned.[1]

Teachers use many different techniques to inform students of their progress. A simple verbal reaction to a student's effort is effective, fits into the normal interaction pattern between teacher and student, and certainly should be included in a measurement program. Each time a teacher asks students to submit written assignments, themes, or lab reports, he has an opportunity to measure student progress and report that assessment to the student. This is done most often by writing comments on the papers returned to the students.

In both procedures the assessment should focus on the learning process and the report should be as supportive and provide as much guidance as possible. Specific errors should be regarded in terms of how they affect the total learning process within the unit being considered, and the report should suggest methods the student can use to correct his problems. These procedures may seem to be merely part of effective teaching, but that is precisely the point—classroom measurement can and should be used to facilitate the teaching–learning process and should be viewed as one of the tools of good teaching.

Other types of measurement that occur less frequently in classrooms but nonetheless provide avenues for feedback to students are periodic quizzes and unit examinations. If these are spaced throughout·a semester at appropriate intervals, students will receive more formal assessments of their abilities to apply material studied previously, which will help them structure their own attempts to remediate problem areas and build on strengths.

Measurement used in a formative evaluation process can also help improve student motivation. It is well established in research literature that the effectiveness of learning and retention relate to

---

[1] For a review of research on this topic see A. J. Edwards and D. P. Scannell, *Educational Psychology* (Scranton: International Textbook Co., 1968), pp. 168–177.

the degree the learner is motivated to accomplish the task.[2] Educational psychologists also refer to the desirability of intrinsic as contrasted with extrinsic motivation—that is, learning for its own sake rather than learning to achieve a reward controlled by someone else.

Tests can help establish desirable student motivation in several ways; students can become intrinsically motivated more easily if they know precisely what the task or learning problem is. Measurement that clarifies the task opens the way for intrinsic motivation to occur, and conversely teachers can hardly expect learners to be self-motivated in school activities when the purpose and goals are unclear. Tests also provide students with knowledge of their achievements that can be rewarding and thus instill or maintain a level of motivation. Students will naturally participate with some enthusiasm in activities that promise satisfaction from accomplishment and success.

Classroom measurement can provide a way for student self-motivation to occur if teachers use data prudently and observe some important corollaries. First, challenges provided by tests and other measurement tools must be within the range of students' competencies—that is, measurement should not be an experience of predominant or overwhelming failure for a learner. Teachers must sense what their students' capabilities are and adjust their tests accordingly. Second, since tests can influence the direction of student motivation, it is critical that they represent desirable learning goals. If tests consistently represent accomplishments students should be making, they can provide guidance and impetus to progress toward the central goals of schooling. Conversely, if measurement includes trivia or misrepresentations of the real goals, measurement will distract learners from what is important and be counterproductive. Since the nature of the classroom measurement program is under the direct control of

---

[2] For a review of the research on motivation, see Edwards and Scannell, *Educational Psychology*, pp. 127–144.

teachers, this will not happen if the teacher is knowledgeable about a subject and sees how it relates to the total development of students.

Summative Evaluation

The information obtained during the school year from the measurement of achievement will be used in a formative evaluation process to guide decisions on subsequent instruction and learning activities. In addition, though, it is necessary periodically for teachers to describe succinctly, objectively, and accurately the level of progress achieved by individual students. Using measurement data in this way can contribute to a summative evaluation.

Describing a student's level of achievement is an important use of classroom measurement data, and the teacher should not take this responsibility lightly. Reports of achievement of which grades or marks are only one form are useful to students, their parents, and all those who have a role in their education.

Students need to know their level of achievement and what this means in terms of their own plans and aspirations. Knowledge of capabilities and achievement is essential to developing an accurate self-concept and planning realistically for the future. If a student is contemplating a college program in premedicine, he needs to know how well his achievement in relevant courses has prepared him for that particular curriculum. Inaccurate descriptions of his level of accomplishment may encourage or discourage him falsely. If a student is contemplating an apprenticeship in the electrical trades, he needs to know whether his talents, skills, and achievements in relevant courses support a prediction of success in that field.

If parents are to assist their children in educational and vocational planning, they need to be told of the achievements their children have made.

One role of school counselors is to help students plan their programs of study on both a short-term and long-term basis. Information on interest patterns, as expressed by students and measured by tests, evidence of abilities, and measures of achievement all influence decisions about course and curriculum selection. In planning instruction, teachers need to consider the level of readiness students in the class have for the topics to be studied, and measures of prior achievement are valuable in this process.

The summative use of classroom measures need not interfere with or detract from the formative uses. A major theme throughout the following chapters will be the development of an effective relationship between the two major uses of classroom measurement data.

Defining Objectives

Although concerted efforts are being made in preservice and inservice teacher education to help teachers learn how to specify the objectives of a course in behavioral and thus measurable terms, the goals in most classes still remain somewhat vague to students. By calling attention to those elements that compose and relate to objectives, measurement helps define for teachers and students the real meaning of an objective.

An objective such as "Understands the concept of supply and demand" may take on entirely different meanings in different classrooms. In one classroom, for example, the teacher may expect students to learn the data concerning production in various industries during the twentieth century, but in another classroom the teacher may emphasize the effects on society of different patterns of supply and demand levels. "To understand Ohm's Law" may mean to learn the formula in its various forms, or it may mean to develop the ability to compute resistance in the branches of a complex electrical circuit.

Objectives are often stated in laudatory terms, emphasizing the loftier aspects of understanding important concepts and generalizations and the ability to apply the appropriate techniques to new situations, while in fact the teaching and measurement reflect such pedestrian activities as memorizing lists and learning definitions of terms. In spite of the nature of the stated objectives, students will study and prepare for the types of tests and papers they expect the teacher to use or assign.

Each time a test or quiz is given to a class, the true meaning of the objectives becomes more apparent to students. An understanding of the nature of the skills and knowledge required provides a much clearer definition of an objective than a formal one-line statement. Because tests and other measurement tools provide definition and guidance for students as they attempt to accomplish the objectives of a course, it is essential that these tests reflect the important and permanent learning that should occur.

Instruction Evaluation

Measures of student achievement not only shed light on individual and class accomplishments, but they also provide a good source of information for a teacher's self-evaluation of instructional effectiveness. Even though precise standards or expectations usually cannot be expressed, most teachers have sufficient knowledge of the subjects being taught and the capability of class members to establish a general level of class achievement that can be reached if instruction is effective.

Analysis of test results helps teachers identify the topics that students have mastered fairly well and those they have not mastered satisfactorily. This information in turn is a basis for identifying areas where teaching has been satisfactory and those where improvement should be sought. For example, if an analysis of test results shows that students in a class have performed at a generally high level on exercises covering mathematical skills—that is, simple operations with numbers provided—but have performed poorly on thought and word problems, the teacher will know that some adjustment in teaching is necessary to strengthen instruction in the area of quantitative reasoning.

When measurement data reveal areas or topics in a unit of instruction that students have not mastered satisfactorily, a teacher can take immediate action to remediate the problem. He can reteach the same material or use a different but complementary approach to the topics. When summative measures at the close of a unit reveal areas of deficiency, the teacher should note the topics and modify the instruction before he teaches the material again.

Analyses of test results can also be used to evaluate the test itself. Student answers to test items may provide important clues to ways in which the test can be improved for use with subsequent classes. A somewhat random pattern of answers would suggest that the question seemed ambiguous to the class. In other cases an analysis might suggest that a question was too difficult or too easy to provide useful information about differing levels of achievement. Methods of test analysis will be considered in a later chapter.

Experienced teachers know that teaching is an evolutionary process, and they will seldom teach a course or unit in the same way twice. Changes evolve from information accumulated from previous experience, and analyses of measurement data provide one of the best sources of information for teachers who are continuously seeking ways to improve instruction.

Tests as Measuring Instruments

Everyone is familiar with measurement in the physical world. Most children are interested in their physical development, so the height and weight of their own bodies are important to them. Adults too are interested in weight and waistlines. In addition, many purchases are made by quantity: gasoline is purchased by the gallon or liter, milk by the quart or liter, and meat by the pound or kilogram.

Measurement is a process by which numbers are assigned to objects according to a set of rules established for the purpose of representing the amount of an attribute possessed by those objects. For example, volume is an attribute of a milk carton which can be expressed in quarts or liters, length is an attribute of a piece of cloth which can be expressed in inches or centimeters, and weight is an attribute of a piece of meat which can be expressed in pounds or kilograms. We are able to measure the attributes of volume, length, and weight because units of measurement, quarts, inches, and pounds, have been defined, and we have developed methods and instruments such as standard-size measuring cups, rulers, yardsticks, and scales.

Most of the common physical measurements are concerned

with attributes that can be perceived directly and completely through the senses. Classroom measurement, however, usually concerns human attributes that cannot be perceived directly or completely, such as abilities, aptitudes, and values. The teacher needs this information to plan effective learning experiences for a class and to determine at appropriate stages whether or not, or to what extent, the learning he has planned has actually taken place. He can make some of these measurements by using standardized tests, inventories, and scales; but he will base many important decisions on measurements made by his own tests.

Length and volume can be sensed through the eyes, and weight can be sensed by lifting, but the attitudes, abilities, aptitudes, interests, and values which are the main concern of classroom teachers cannot be seen or felt. That people differ in the amount of these attributes they possess can be inferred only from observation of their behavior.

A teacher cannot look inside a student to see or feel his ability to solve arithmetic problems, but he can present a set of arithmetic problems and observe the speed and accuracy with which the student solves them. From these observations the teacher can infer the degree of ability the student has for solving arithmetic problems. Then the teacher can administer the same set of arithmetic problems to all the student's classmates and determine how the student has performed in relation to all the others in his class. The teacher can infer that the student's relative standing in problem-solving ability is the same as his relative standing in the number of problems solved.

The number of problems solved is not in itself problem-solving ability, but it is an outward expression of that ability. When the measurement of an attribute cannot be made directly but must be inferred from outward behavior or performance, the measurement is *indirect*. Virtually all educational measurement is indirect measurement.

A wide variety of behaviors may relate to a single psychological attribute, and student ability related to a single objective may be manifested in many ways. A student may demonstrate arithmetic computation by solving an almost infinite variety of numerical exercises and written problems. It is usually not possible to include every conceivable type of question on a test; instead, items which will elicit important behaviors are included in sufficient number to produce a reasonable sample of the examinee's ability. Such measurement is *incomplete* because the entire range of behaviors is not measured. Often behaviors that are considered so basic as to be mastered by virtually every examinee or so difficult as to be mastered by almost no one are excluded from an examination in the interest of brevity and efficiency. The measuring instrument is trimmed to fit the job. Just as a carpenter uses a long folding rule rather than a twelve-inch ruler and a draftsman uses a ruler rather than a yardstick to measure the lines on a blueprint, arithmetic tests for first graders do not include problems in long division, and eighth-grade tests do not include exercises such as "2 + 2 = ?".

Most measurements obtained in a classroom must be regarded as samples of behavior and not as complete measures of traits. Because of the indirectness and incompleteness of classroom measurements, students and teachers need to be assured that test performance reflects the trait of interest and that the single performance observed is typical of what would have been observed if a different test measuring the same trait had been used. The teacher must be sure that the test score reflects the trait of interest and not some other factor, and that the particular sample of items used is representative of those that are possible, important, and relevant. Because questions such as these surround all measurements of human traits, the concepts of *validity* and *reliability* are of central importance to educational measurement.

Validity

A measurement is considered *valid* to the extent that it represents what it is intended to represent and nothing else. That is, the differences among the scores or numbers resulting from measurement are related to real differences among the persons or objects being measured in the amount of the trait or characteristic the test was intended to measure, and, conversely, the differences in the scores are not due to irrelevant factors or traits that the test was not intended to measure.

To someone familiar with physical measurements, validity may seem an unnecessary concept. Certainly, when the width of a doorway is measured to determine whether one can move a refrigerator through it, there is no question about the validity of the measurement. It is obvious that a foot rule measures the width of the doorway and not some irrelevant factor such as the amount of light the doorway admits. Because most educational measurements are indirect and incomplete their validity is not obvious. Validity is composed of two separate qualities, relevance and consistency.

A test cannot be valid unless the behaviors it calls forth are relevant to and made possible by the traits to be measured. The relevance of a test refers to the tasks required by the test and the situation in which the tasks are performed. For example, it is assumed that the student who can solve arithmetic problems required in determining the amount of concrete needed to build an imaginary patio could solve a similar problem if he were actually building a patio. Conversely, a student who could describe verbally the proper procedure for serving a tennis ball may not be able to follow that procedure in practice. A test requiring a verbal description of a process may not indicate at all well the ability of the student to perform the task.

Consistency of measurement has been given a special name, reliability. *Reliability* refers to the extent to which the student's test score precisely represents his capability in the area tested. A teacher would prefer to have a student's test score remain the same were he to take the test on another day or if he were to answer an alternate set of items; such consistencies would be evidence of reliability. Reliability will be considered in detail in the next section and in chapter 8.

There are two general approaches to establishing the validity of tests. One approach is statistical or empirical and the other is rational or logical.

Empirical validity is established by relating the scores on a test to the results of other tests or other criteria of performance. Empirical validity is seldom applicable to classroom testing and therefore this book will not deal with methods for determining it.

Logical validity is established by comparing the actual exercises of a test with a logical criterion of what the test should contain. For a classroom test this requires careful consideration of the *content* a teacher wishes to cover and the kinds of *processes* that are included in the achievement of objectives. As a general rule, the content and processes should be organized into a testing plan, and test items should be designed specifically to fit them.

Suppose the content of a course in physics included Ohm's law. In planning a test, the teacher would need to select the proper process—that is, the situations in which students should be able to apply Ohm's law. He might ask them merely to state Ohm's law, or he might require them to apply Ohm's law to determine the proper amperage of a fuse to be used in an electrical circuit. Although the content would be the same for both situations, the processes would be different.

Teachers can build content and process validity into classroom tests by carefully specifying the content and processes they wish to measure with their test, interrelating them in an organized plan, often called a *table of specifications,* and writing test items which call for the content and processes specified. Detailed explanations of these procedures are given in the chapters on planning the test and writing objectives. If the items of the test are clearly related to the important course objectives, and if all objectives are represented in a balanced plan that gives proper emphasis to each, then when a student does well on the test he is showing that he can do more than "just pass tests." He is demonstrating that he has acquired important skills and understands important concepts.

Face validity is the degree to which the test looks valid to the examinee and perhaps to his parents. When a test looks valid, or fair, to the examinee, he is likely to accept the score as an important indication of his abilities. Sometimes a teacher is tempted to use novel material in a test as a "challenge" to examinees. This is likely to turn the test into a quiz game or "intelligence test" rather than a test of what the examinee has acquired in the course. There is a place for novel material, but such material should be used with caution. In addition, tests composed preponderantly of petty details not within the mainstream of the subject matter also lack face validity. Such tests lead students to feel, justifiably, that an understanding of the subject is unimportant while memorization is paramount.

Reliability

An analysis of the content and processes included in a test helps determine what the test measures and provides a basis for deciding how relevant the test is for measuring achievement toward classroom objectives. Test validity is a function of both relevance and consistency. Even if every item on a test is closely related to an instructional objective, the scores derived from the test will be valid only if the test thoroughly samples all the achievements included in the course objectives and if student performance on the test accurately represents the students' capabilities. The degree to which these characteristics are met determines the *reliability* of the test scores. The reliability of a test can be quantified; and methods for doing this will be described in chapter 8.

Reliability can be thought of as the precision of a set of measurements. The more reliable a set of scores is, the more confident the teacher and his students can be of the accuracy of the data and the more confidence they will have in basing plans or conclusions on the data.

All measurements are subject to some imprecision, and instruments used for physical measurements are constructed according to the amount of imprecision that can be tolerated. A medical thermometer, for example, is built to have more precision than a back porch thermometer. A laboratory scale is built to yield more precise measurements than a bathroom scale. Similarly, a test used to select medical students is probably more precise than a unit quiz in a history class. It should be noted that even though precision varies from instrument to instrument, there is some imprecision associated with all instruments, even the most sophisticated.

Teachers should strive to obtain classroom measurements that are reliable—that are as precise as practicable and as precise as the use to be made of the measurements requires. Even though imprecision cannot be entirely avoided, an understanding of the factors affecting the reliability of classroom data will point to ways of planning, developing, and scoring tests to minimize imprecision.

The score on a test reflects a single observation of a student at one point in time under one set of conditions. The validity of a classroom test can be improved by using a *test plan,* an analysis of content and process, as a guide in the development of the test. This procedure has a desirable effect on reliability because it assures that the sample of items on the test faithfully represents the achievement domain the test is designed to measure. Thus, another test prepared as thoroughly from the same test plan would give comparable results for the same students.

The length of a test is obviously related to its effectiveness in sampling the domain of achievement defined by the objectives. In general, the longer a test the more reliable will be the scores. A one hundred-word vocabulary test should provide a more reliable indication of students' use vocabularies than a ten-word test.

The type and quality of individual items on a test also affect reliability. If the items are either very difficult or very easy, the scores on the test will not be so reliable as they will be if the test is composed of items of moderate difficulty. Similarly, a true-false test is not so reliable as a multiple-choice test with the same number of items.

An important source of errors in classroom measurement is the teacher, the person who scores tests and themes and observes student behavior in the classroom. If the teacher does not follow a carefully prescribed set of standards and procedures, consistency of measurement will suffer. In that case, scores on tests and themes may reflect fleeting moods and reactions to irrelevant factors, such as penmanship, rather than the achievement demonstrated by the students' exposition.

If classroom measurements are to provide information that is valuable and useful to teachers and students as they plan instructional activities and describe level of achievement, the instruments used must be relevant and the data they yield must be reliable. Most of the topics to be covered in subsequent chapters affect directly or indirectly the quality of the data that can be collected by teachers in the classroom.

Five Principles for Establishing Classroom Measurement Programs

1. *Classroom measurement should be developed and implemented as part of the total instructional program.*   Exposure to assessment should be a learning experience in itself, and the results of the assessment should facilitate the planning of effective future activities by teachers and students.

2. *Formal assessment should be designed to complement the data teachers collect in observing students' day-to-day progress.* Teachers are constantly monitoring student activities, and measurement is a tool for assisting in that process.

3. *Decisions affecting the learning environment in the classroom should be made on the basis of the best data teachers can collect.*   Judgments are inherent in teaching, and it is extremely tempting for teachers to react to the student behavior that stands out in their memory, whether the incident was typical or not. Formal assessment provides a better basis for judgment than do casual and subjective reactions.

4. *The assessments made in the classroom should be closely related to the important goals of instruction.*   Tests and other forms of assessment should help clarify the real nature of goals and bridge the gap between learning exercises and the use of the achievements that have been made.

5. *The measurement program includes the interpretation and use of data.*   Both the assessment process and the use of data should be approached constructively in view of their value in enhancing student progress toward the goals of education.

The topics considered in subsequent chapters will suggest ways in which these principles may be implemented in a classroom.

Summary

The primary goal for teachers is to help students develop toward the academic objectives which society, students, teachers, and parents have established. Measurement is an aspect of classroom activity that occurs continuously, and it can either contribute to or detract from the accomplishment of the teachers' responsibilities. Measurement programs that are well-planned and used effectively can contribute in a formative way to student progress. The data obtained from observation and tests can provide students with knowledge of their strengths and weaknesses, can help clarify the objectives of the course or unit, and can be a positive factor in the development of student motivation. Measurement also provides important information for teachers as they evaluate student progress toward instructional objectives, and when properly used the summative aspects of evaluation need not contravene the formative values. Finally, test data can help teachers evaluate their own instructional effectiveness.

Tests teachers construct form a major part of the classroom measurement program, and if they are to provide useful information they must be valid and yield reliable scores. Tests should faithfully represent the content and processes inherent in instructional objectives, and sources of error in classroom measurement should be minimized.

Exercises

1. What is the correct order of the processes of measurement, testing, and evaluation from most to least inclusive? How does the most inclusive subsume the other two and how does the second include the third?

2. Select a key topic from your teaching field. How can classroor measurement contribute in a formative way to enhancing stu dent development on that topic?

3. In the situation of exercise 2, what are your minimum respon sibilities as a teacher in assuring that formative evaluation has beneficial effect?

4. Given the following examples, tell whether each is more likel to be used for formative or summative evaluation.

    a. A spelling test is given at the beginning of a unit.

    b. A nine-week test covering the Civil War is given prior to th end of a reporting period.

    c. A ten-minute quiz is given over the topics included in discussion period.

    d. The pages in a workbook are reviewed, and the student i allowed to begin the next section of the workbook.

    e. A child is required to demonstrate the way he breathes whil doing an American crawl.

    f. A child is required to swim across and back in the shallov end of a swimming pool prior to beginning a unit on divinj from a low board.

5. Given the following procedures that might be used in develop ing and administering a test, tell whether the action taker would most likely improve or decrease the reliability of the dat; obtained from the procedure. If the effect cannot be predictec with confidence, write "unknown."

    a. Reduce a fifty-item vocabulary test to twenty-five items.

    b. Identify the major categories of vocabulary words and selec five words from each category.

    c. For an essay test, prepare in advance a list of the conten that should be included in an outstanding answer.

    d. Base the number of items covering each major topic in the unit on your careful, subjective appraisal of the importance of each topic.

e. Replace all the easiest items from last year's test with slightly more difficult items.

5. To measure the objective that students use commas correctly in compound and complex sentences in their own exposition, a teacher presents ten sentences for students to punctuate. In what ways would the score on the test be incomplete? In what ways is the test indirect?

Suggested Readings

BLOOM, B. S., HASTINGS, J. T., and MADAUS, G. F. *Handbook on Formative and Summative Evaluation of Student Learning.* New York: McGraw-Hill, 1971. *Pages 5 to 8 and 12–17 give an overview of measurement as part of the teaching–learning process. Pages 61 to 84 and 117 to 138 give a discussion of summative and formative evaluation with differences noted in terms of relationship to teaching and test development strategies. Students should read these pages selectively.*

EBEL, R. L. *Essentials of Educational Measurement.* Englewood Cliffs, N.J.: Prentice-Hall, 1972: 29–52. *An excellent discussion of issues each teacher must face in developing a personal philosophy of teaching and testing.*

EBEL, R. L. "Measurement and the Teacher." *Educational Leadership* 20 (1962): 20–24, 43. *Ten principles of measurement are considered as they apply to classroom programs. A provocative article.*

NOLL, V. H., and SCANNELL, D. P. *Introduction to Educational Measurement,* 3d ed. Boston: Houghton Mifflin, 1972. *Chapter 1 provides an overview of the role of measurement in education and some basic features of educational measurement. Pages 134 to 141 discuss validity and pages 142 to 146 discuss reliability.*

POPHAM, W. J., and HUSEK, T. R. "Implications of Criterion-Referenced Measurement." *Journal of Educational Measurement* 6 (1969): 1–10. *Considers implications of a criterion-referenced measurement approach on planning and developing tests and using results of measurement.*

SCHULTZ, R. E. "The Role of Measurement in Education: Servant, Soul-mate, Stoolpigeon, Statesman, Scapegoat, All of the Above, and/or None of the Above." *Journal of Educational Measurement* 8 (1971): 141–146. *A consideration of the various roles measurement may be asked to serve in schools.*

PART I

Planning for the Assessment of Learning

Basic to any effective approach to accomplishing a goal or developing a product is a clear understanding of the nature of the goal or product. If the purpose of education is to assist children to develop intellectually and academically, teaching should be based on a clear conception of the changes in student capabilities that should occur as the result of curricular experiences; and if the purpose of classroom measurement is to measure the extent to which instructional goals are being accomplished, tests must reflect the same objectives that have guided the teaching.

Chapter 2 will consider the issues associated with the formulation of educational objectives and make some suggestions regarding ways these objectives can be conceptualized and stated. Although the roles of a course or grade level are generally established by the policies of a school system or school faculty, teachers usually have considerable latitude in, and the responsibility for translating the general expectations into immediate objectives and specific curricular experiences. The topics in this chapter deal generally with the development of instructional objectives.

When measurement is viewed as an integral part of the total instructional program, the general planning of measurement complements curricular plans. Chapter 3 will present some basic questions that should receive the teacher's attention as he is planning the measurement program. Within the general program each test must be planned and developed. If this task is treated casually, too often tests will be superficial or nonrepresentative of the instructional goals they should reflect. Good tests require adequate planning, and planning requires attention to the major issues that are considered in Chapter 3.

Chapter 2

EDUCATIONAL OBJECTIVES

As a result of studying this chapter you should be able to:

1. *Define educational objectives.*

2. *Distinguish between various levels of educational objectives.*

3. *Distinguish between affective and cognitive objectives.*

4. *Distinguish between objectives for norm-referenced and criterion-referenced tests.*

5. *Write acceptable objectives in your own field for norm-referenced and/or criterion-referenced tests.*

6. *Translate nonbehavioral objectives into behavioral terms.*

Most teachers today are familiar with the verbal commitment given to the importance of establishing educational goals and objectives. Many hours have been spent by people at all levels of education—national, state, and local—in formulating lists of educational objectives for the schools. Unfortunately, few of these lists have had an important impact on classroom teaching. One might say facetiously: "Never before in history have so many done so much and accomplished so little." In many cases, the lists have consisted of very general statements that can be endorsed almost unanimously by large committees and public bodies. Such lists, if they serve a purpose, provide a general direction for education as a whole, but the classroom teacher finds them of little value in guiding teaching and testing activities. Such an objective as, "To develop each child to his fullest potential," appeals to basic, decent instincts, but how teachers are to accomplish the "developing" or find out whether or not they have done so are mysteries indeed.

Nature of Educational Objectives

In light of the limited utility of many committee-produced lists of objectives, the teacher may well wonder whether it is worth his while to select, develop, and write out educational objectives. Formulating objectives is a time-consuming process, and it is certainly possible for teachers to teach and for students to learn without formal lists of objectives. More and more, though, parents, legislators, and others interested in improving education want to know exactly what teachers are trying to teach and what students are learning. The teacher, by expressing his educational objectives in understandable, written form, can communicate his educational intentions to students, parents, and other concerned persons. When objectives are not expressed, little evidence is available one way or the other about what students know, how effective teachers are, or what the teacher's intentions were.

Essentially, the teacher's objectives appear to students to be whatever is contained in tests. Therefore the teacher would do well to base his tests on well-planned educational objectives rather than spur-of-the-moment ideas that occur to him the night before the test. Stating in advance explicit objectives for instruction will improve the quality of tests by making them reflect more accurately the teacher's true instructional intentions.

Educational objectives are statements describing the characteristics and specific skills that the teacher intends students to develop through instruction. Objectives act as the teacher's guide or blueprint for both effective teaching and effective testing. Educational objectives are not methods to be used by the teacher, or activities to be performed or content to be covered by the teacher. Educational objectives pertain to *student* skills, knowledge, and attitudes.

For example, "The student can solve linear equations with one unknown" is an educational objective because it describes a skill of the student. "To cover the solution of linear equations through the discovery method" is not an educational objective because only the intended teacher activity is stated with no reference to student performance.

Sometimes what teachers hope to develop in students are visible and specific *skills*, such as typing, swimming, or calculating. The possession or lack of the ability to perform discrete tasks which demonstrate skills can be fairly evident, and procedures for observing the extent of a student's skill can be straightforward and direct. For example, the objective "Given an unfamiliar piece of written material, the student will type the material for ten minutes at the rate of at least fifty words per minute, making no more than five errors," is a statement describing a very specific task the student must be able to perform. Perhaps the teacher knows that the student must be able to perform at least that well to obtain a job as a typist. The objective states: (1) the kind of behavior that is desired, (2) the conditions under which the behavior is to occur, and (3) the criteria for acceptable performance. The objective implies clearly the kind of testing necessary to measure the achievement.

Often, instead of the ability to perform specific tasks, teachers hope to develop in students *internal* characteristics that are not directly observable, such as "understanding," "appreciation," or "comprehension" of material. Such internal characteristics are evident to the outsider only through the behavior of the individual who "understands," "appreciates," or "comprehends." The teacher who wishes students to develop these internal characteristics must ask himself, "How can I tell if a student really understands the material? What kind of behavior is related to understanding the material? What kind of behavior will I accept as evidence that a student understands?"

Educational objectives related to internal student characteristics should describe how students will demonstrate the degree to which they have acquired the characteristics. Because such verbs as "know" and "understand" describe internal states and have different meanings for different teachers, some specialists advise that objectives be stated only in *behavioral* terms, terms which describe only the external behavior as evidence that the internal characteristic exists. For example, the objective "The student comprehends the meaning of written material" does not describe what the student does when he "comprehends." An objective that more clearly specifies how the student is to manifest his comprehension would be, "The student can identify the main ideas in written paragraphs." Identifying main ideas is a specific behavior that can be observed, but it is not particularly important in itself, except perhaps as an outlining skill. Identifying main ideas is an indicator, an outward sign of the internal ability to comprehend written material.

One danger in identifying only the specific behaviors or outward signs of internal abilities without first identifying the internal characteristics is that the outward behaviors may seem trivial by themselves. Being able to put a set of historical events in chronological order seems in itself a trivial outcome, but if the ability is regarded as evidence of the internal state of "knowing how important historical events in different parts of the world are related to one another in time," the ability to put events in order takes on more importance. Another danger of identifying only specific behaviors without relating them to internal characteristics is that many important internal characteristics may be overlooked because specifying behaviors related to the characteristics is difficult.

Classification of Educational Objectives

In the 1950s a committee of college and university examiners attempted to develop a classification system or *taxonomy* for the categorization of educational objectives according to the kind of skill or student characteristic described by the objective. The committee agreed that educational objectives can be classified into three broad categories, which they called domains. The *cognitive domain* includes those objectives that "deal with the recall or recognition of knowledge and the development of intellectual abilities and skills." The *affective domain* "includes objectives which describe changes in interest, attitudes, and values, and the development of appreciations and adequate adjustment." The *psychomotor domain* includes "observed voluntary actions or action patterns."[1]

The taxonomies of educational objectives divide their respective domains into hierarchical categories generally ranging from the simple to the more complex types of behaviors. The taxonomies provide models for writing objectives and suggest types of objectives which the teacher may have neglected. The many examples, illustrative items, and objectives provide ideas that should help the teacher formulate his own objectives and develop tests and other evaluation approaches.

The cognitive and psychomotor domains are described briefly in this chapter, and the affective domain is described in chapter 7. Nevertheless, teachers should explore the taxonomies themselves in order to understand and use them in the development of objectives and measurement procedures.

The taxonomy of the *cognitive* domain identifies six levels of objectives. The least complex level is *knowledge.* Ranking above knowledge in order of increasing complexity are five cognitive skills: *comprehension, application, analysis, synthesis,* and *evaluation.*

Knowledge includes recall or recognition of ideas, materials, or phenomena in essentially the same form in which they were

---

[1] The following handbooks contain detailed descriptions of the three domains of objectives and a wide variety of examples: B. F. Bloom, ed., *Taxonomy of Educational Objectives: The Classification of Educational Goals. Handbook I, Cognitive Domain* (New York: David McKay, 1956); D. R. Krathwohl et al., *Taxonomy of Educational Objectives: The Classification of Educational Goals. Handbook II, Affective Domain* (New York: David McKay, 1964); and A. J. Harrow, *A Taxonomy of the Psychomotor Domain* (New York: David McKay, 1972).

originally learned. Being able to recall the names and functions of each branch of the federal government would be one example of knowledge.

Comprehension is the ability to understand and use oral or written communications and may include the ability to translate a communication into other terms, rearrange the ideas in a communication, or give the implications of a communication. For example, the ability to follow a set of printed directions would require comprehension.

Application is the ability to use a theory, principle, or method to solve a problem without being told which theory, principle, or method to apply. The ability to solve word problems in arithmetic is an example of application.

Analysis is the ability to break down materials into their essential parts and to find the relationships among those parts. The abilities used to discover the techniques used in a piece of propaganda, the devices used in a musical composition or poem, and the assumptions underlying an argument involve analysis.

Synthesis is the ability to put together ideas, materials, and phenomena to form a new whole. This ability is necessary to compose English themes and term papers and to write educational objectives and test items.

Evaluation is the ability to make judgments on the value of ideas, methods, or materials. This ability is used in such things as detecting fallacious logic in arguments, selecting the most important set of educational objectives from a longer list, and comparing the evidence supporting conflicting theories.

In the cognitive domain each level is presumably more complex than the preceding level. Evaluation is the most complex skill because it requires the application of knowledge and all the other lower skills. An objective should be placed at the highest level of skill that is called for. Most objectives call for some knowledge, and the application of the correct principles to solve a word problem in arithmetic requires first the comprehension of the message contained in the written problem. A brief analysis of the teacher's own objectives will soon reveal whether many are above the knowledge level.

The taxonomy divides the *psychomotor* domain into six major classification levels: *reflex movements, basic-fundamental movements, perceptual abilities, physical abilities, skilled movements,* and *nondiscursive communication.* Again the taxonomy stresses the dependence of higher-order skills on the previous development of lower-order skills.

Reflex movements are actions brought about without the volition of the person, such as involuntary eye blinking. Reflex movements are not the basis of any educational objectives because they are not developed through training, but proper reflex movements form the foundation of more complex movements.

Basic-fundamental movements are combined reflex movements and form the basis for more complex skilled movements. Some examples of basic-fundamental movements are walking, hopping, bending, finger manipulation, and gripping.

Perceptual abilities are the interpretations of visual, auditory, and tactile stimuli and the adjustments of movements to the environment. Following instructions, dodging or catching a ball, determining texture through touch, and jumping rope are some examples of perceptual abilities.

Physical abilities include the strength and stamina needed to develop highly skilled movements. Activities which require sustained effort, muscular exertion, agility, or wide ranges of joint movement require physical ability.

Skilled movement is a degree of efficiency, grace, and skill in performing complex tasks requiring movement and physical abilities. The movements required in athletics and dance are examples.

Nondiscursive communication is communication through bodily movements ranging from facial expressions and gestures to complex choreographic movements. The movements in ballet and modern dance are examples.

It is often difficult to classify an objective in the correct domain. Some complex skills may involve several domains. In addition to the categories listed for the cognitive and psychomotor domains, each category has several subcategories in which objectives may be classified. Fortunately, the classroom teacher need not be overly concerned with fitting objectives into their precise categories. The value of the taxonomies is the wide range of educational objectives which they reveal.

Formulating Objectives

Once the teacher has decided to write out objectives, he should begin by considering what kinds of student skills and characteristics his course will help develop. Some factors to consider in choosing proper outcomes are: (1) level of maturation and past experience of the students, (2) present needs and interests of students that the course should try to meet, (3) possible contributions of the course to meeting the future or adult needs of students, (4) contribution of the course to meeting the needs of society, and (5) recommendations of specialists in the subject-matter field.

Knowledge of the student's level of maturation will help the teacher plan realistic course objectives which will be attainable to some degree or will allow the formulation of individualized programs of study that set realistic goals for each student. Some tasks cannot be mastered before a certain level of maturation has been reached. In other cases, although a skill or concept can be learned at an early age, it may be acquired more easily later. Knowledge of child development is essential to planning objectives for the early school years.[2] The particular skills and characteristics that students have acquired prior to instruction in addition to other experiences they have had should also help determine educational objectives. Much of this information can be gained through school records and direct contact with parents, previous teachers, and the students themselves. Sometimes pretesting is helpful. The experienced teacher can anticipate the maturation level of most students.

If the course is designed to meet present needs and interests

---

[2] For a review of the importance of maturation and readiness in development see Robert J. Havinghurst, *Developmental Tasks and Education*, 3d ed. (New York: McKay, 1972).

of students, these needs and interests may serve as a basis for specific objectives. For example, a high school course in marriage and family relations might include some objectives dealing with adolescent dating, personal appearance, or relationships with parents and teachers. Such objectives might be highly interesting to students, meet their present needs, and also serve as motivating factors.

The future needs of the student must also be considered. A course intended primarily for college preparation would have different objectives from a course intended for terminal students. In mathematics, for example, a college preparation course might include trigonometric functions, but a terminal course probably would not.

The very existence of public schools is based on the proposition that education meets certain needs of the whole society. The well-informed citizen who can make rational judgments is considered a necessity in a democratic society. In choosing objectives, the teacher must consider these demands, as well as the personal goals of students.

In using the recommendations of subject-matter experts, teachers must consider the context in which these recommendations were made. Recommendations the College Entrance Examination Board made, for example, would be directed to college-bound students and would not be appropriate for students in terminal programs. In addition, subject-matter experts sometimes operate in isolation and do not consider that some material is extraneous to the student learning that subject. Subjects should not be taught in isolation. The total educational mission of the school must be considered.

Levels of Educational Objectives

It is useful to distinguish among three levels of objectives: school objectives, departmental objectives, and course objectives. *School objectives* include characteristics and skills students should attain by completing a school program or some major division of it, such as elementary school, secondary school, or college. *Departmental objectives* represent characteristics and skills students should develop by completing a series of courses. *Course objectives* represent the results that students are expected to attain by completing a single course.

These three levels of objectives tend to differ in degree of specificity: School objectives are broad and general, while course objectives are narrow and specific. In addition, course objectives are generally *behavioral*—that is, they specify the kind of student behaviors which indicate whether students have acquired the desired internal characteristics or skills. School and departmental objectives tend to be stated in terms of the desired internal characteristic rather than in terms of specific behavior. Since several kinds of behavior might be indicative of a single trait, a number of course objectives might be related to one departmental or school objective.

For example, a school objective might be, "The student can maintain his health and safety." The science department might base several departmental objectives on this school objective—for example, "The student understands the relationships between diet and physical health," and "The student recognizes safety hazards in his environment." The physical education department and the home economics department might also formulate departmental objectives related to the school objective. In a general science class several course objectives—such as, "When given a list of foods, the student identifies those high in vitamin A," or "The student describes the nutritional contribution of proteins"—might relate to the departmental objective of understanding the relationship between diet and physical health.

School objectives can be formulated by teacher committees, but they ought to draw on the opinions and desires of students and laymen as well. Departmental objectives should be formulated by the department faculty, who should make sure that their objectives are derived from and related to the school objectives. In general, individual teachers or groups of teachers are responsible for course objectives and must pay attention to both departmental and school objectives. Close articulation among the three levels of objectives will reduce unnecessary duplication and also insure that all school and departmental objectives are covered somewhere in the curriculum.

Criterion- versus Norm-referenced Objectives

In an influential work on writing objectives, R. F. Mager urged teachers to specify a *criterion* of acceptable performance when writing objectives.[3] Mager urged that the objective specify not only what the learner must do, but how well he must be able to do it before his performance is judged acceptable. For example, the objective, "Given fifty, two-digit multiplication problems, the student solves at least forty correctly within a period of one hour," not only specifies the desired student behavior but also the standard of performance required to "pass." In stating that the student "solves at least forty correctly," the objective specifies the criterion of acceptable performance. Presumably, the student who solves fewer than forty items must go back to remedial work in two-digit multiplication' problems, and the passing student may proceed to more complex arithmetic topics or to some kind of enrichment experience.

Although the idea of specifying in advance a criterion of minimal acceptable performance struck many teachers as revolutionary, it was not a completely new idea. The concept of a *mastery test*, a test covering vital essentials of a course, was already a well-recognized part of educational testing practices. A mastery test contains items representing the essentials the student must know to move to the next level of instruction. The student must demonstrate that he has "mastered" certain basic objectives by scoring at some predetermined level on the mastery test before he

---

[3] R. F. Mager, *Preparing Instructional Objectives* (Belmont, Calif.: Fearon Publishers, 1962.) (Originally entitled *Preparing Objectives for Programmed Instruction.*)

attempts new objectives. The mastery test concept contrasts with *discriminatory tests,* which are designed to differentiate as much as possible among students who have reached different levels of achievement. The purpose of the mastery test is to distinguish between students who have and students who have not mastered the minimal essentials, while the discriminatory test is designed to identify accurately different levels of student achievement.

Mager's recommendation led many to advocate that predetermined criteria of performance be specified for all tests and that tests become *criterion-referenced* rather than *norm-referenced.* Norm-referencing is the practice of comparing a student's performance to the class or school average rather than to some predetermined criterion. The criterion-referenced approach appeals to an increasing number of advocates. Specifying an acceptable level of performance in advance, they argue, does away with comparisons among children and makes it possible to compare each child's performance with a predetermined criterion without regard to the class average. In addition, with no need to refer to the relative achievement of other students to interpret performance, criterion-referenced tests facilitate instructional models which allow each student to proceed at his own pace thus making instruction more flexible in meeting students' needs.

The criterion-referenced approach was developed along with *programmed instruction.* In programmed instruction, the student is tested after each small unit of new material has been presented, and a decision is made either that he has sufficiently mastered the material and may proceed to new material or that his mastery of the material is insufficient and he must be given remedial materials. In the latter case, when he has studied the remedial materials, he is tested again, and then can proceed either to new or to more remedial materials. A programmed or criterion-referenced instructional model is illustrated in Figure 2.1.

Many modern teaching models are based on the principles of programmed instruction. Although these models differ considerably in specific details, all spring from the concept that students are different primarily in the speed with which they can learn rather

FIGURE 2.1

A criterion-referenced teaching model

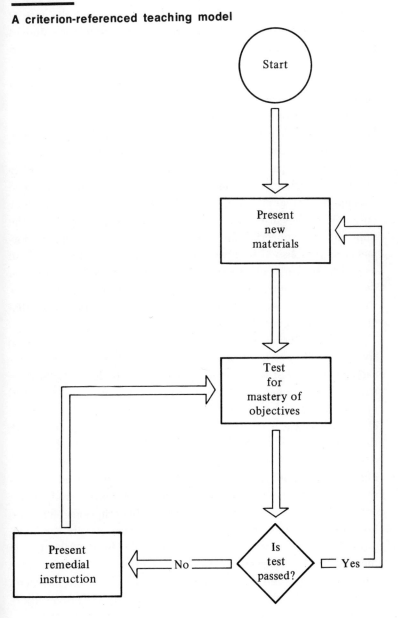

than in the amount they can learn. Therefore, the amount that is learned in a classroom is fixed for all students, but the rate of learning is allowed to vary. In the programmed model, one student may study a concept for a day before passing on to the next concept or to enrichment materials, while another student may spend weeks or months on the concept before he masters it sufficiently to advance.

The norm-referenced approach to classroom organization allows the amount learned to vary greatly from student to student, but requires all students to proceed through the subject matter at about the same pace. Of course, "slow" students are supposed to "keep up" by homework and extra study assignments, and more accomplished students are given additional assignments for depth or enrichment. Because all students are not expected to learn the same amount, no criterion level for a minimum passing performance is established in advance, and the purpose of testing is to make the students' test scores reflect accurately the differences in the degree to which students have acquired the characteristics stated in the objectives. The norm-referenced approach is diagrammed in Figure 2.2.

If the criterion-referenced model is used, it is necessary to specify a criterion level of minimum acceptable performance for each objective, but with the norm-referenced model no criterion is necessary. Proponents of the programmed or criterion-referenced model point out that it does away with unfair comparisons among children because it compares the performance of each child with the criterion only. They argue that the traditional, norm-referenced model dooms some children to failure by decreeing that a proportion of the students must be failed administratively. Proponents of the traditional, norm-referenced model point out that criteria established in advance by criterion-referenced tests are often arbitrary, and that although theoretically it may be possible to determine a level below which the ability to function at the next level of instruction would be impaired, there are few cases where criteria based on experiential evidence have actually been developed. Also, although in some areas, notably arithmetic, there

FIGURE 2.2
_____

A norm-referenced teaching model

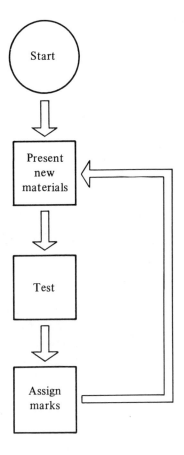

is a logical sequence for presenting materials, this sequence is not at all clear in many other courses. Does it really matter, for example, whether a student knows the structure of county government before he begins to learn the structure of state government? In some ways, the criterion-referenced approach resembles the system of assigning letter grades according to an arbitrary percentage of correct answers. Under such a system the teacher often adjusts the difficulty level of his test so that not too many students fail. A teacher who finds that a large percentage of his class does not meet his criterion will be tempted to change his criterion or his objective. All standards tend to be somewhat relative.

Both the criterion- and the norm-referenced models probably have a place in contemporary education, and for some courses one model might work better than the other. Administrative constraints sometimes preclude the use of some educational models. The teacher should consider his own approach to teaching, his philosophy of education, the nature of his subject matter, and the administrative constraints upon him, and then fit his objectives and testing to his teaching and learning model.

Writing Behavioral Objectives

Course objectives tend to be much more specific than either school or departmental objectives. Generally, course objectives should be stated in terms of student behavior because in order to be measurable, an objective must describe something that can be observed. If the teacher wants his students to "know the major provisions of Woodrow Wilson's Fourteen Points peace plan," he must describe what students must do to demonstrate their knowledge. For example, students could "list the fourteen points of Woodrow Wilson's peace plan" or "identify from a list of thirty which statements were included in Woodrow Wilson's Fourteen Points peace plan." The last two objectives describe what the student can do to show what he knows.

A teacher should not despair if he cannot immediately put all his course objectives into behavioral terms. To abandon an objective for that reason might lead to the discarding of some of the most important course objectives. No matter how nonbehavioral, each objective should be written down, and efforts should be made later to state it in behavioral terms. Sometimes the question, "What kind of behavior will I accept as evidence that this objective is being met?" will help the teacher select observable behaviors for translating the objective into behavioral terms. Sometimes, if the teacher will ask himself how he is presently observing or measuring whether the objective is being met, the relevant behavior will become apparent. An examination of his tests with the question in mind, "Why do I want students to be able to answer these questions?" will often lead the teacher to identify his course objectives.

If the teacher were going to use the objectives only for himself, it would matter little how they were expressed, for he would probably attach his own meanings to the nonbehavioral terms he had used. Because the teacher must communicate his objectives to others, especially his students, he must write them in a form that can be readily understood. The verb is of utmost importance in making course objectives behavioral. Whenever possible, concrete verbs should be chosen to describe student behavior. Avoid vague verbs, such as "understand," "realize," "appreciate," and "know," which describe assumed internal states of the individual but not the behavior that is the clue to the internal state. A few examples of verbs that are useful in describing behavior are listed in Table 2.1.

The more immediate the objective, the more specific it becomes. Objectives for daily teaching and short-term testing should be more detailed and specific than other objectives. End-of-the-unit and end-of-the-term examinations require more generalized, global objectives. Because the teacher must be able to make a decision on whether each student has or has not met each objective, criterion-referenced tests require detailed objectives and statements of standards or criteria of acceptable performance. Norm-referenced tests require less specificity in objectives than criterion-referenced tests because whether or not the student has adequately attained the objectives sampled by norm-referenced tests is a matter of degree—not an all-or-none situation.

TABLE 2.1

Illustrative behavioral verbs

add	dissect	outline
analyze	divide	play
assemble	draw	predict
bisect	explain	produce
build	extract	prove
calculate	extrapolate	record
choose	factor	rewrite
compare	graph	sing
construct	identify	solve
contrast	interpret	subtract
correct	itemize	summarize
criticize	list	support
define	locate	tell
describe	make	translate
diagram	measure	weigh
disassemble	multiply	write

Examples of Objectives

In the following examples, the first statement in each group is not phrased in behavioral terms, the second is a behavioral objective, and the third is a criterion-referenced version of the behavioral objective. These examples are intended as illustrations and should not be interpreted as necessarily appropriate for any particular course.

NONBEHAVIORAL
     To know the vital organs of the human body.

BEHAVIORAL
     Given a drawing of the interior of the human torso, the student can correctly identify the vital organs.

CRITERION-REFERENCED

Given a drawing of the interior of the human torso, the student can correctly identify at least 80 percent of the vital organs.

NONBEHAVIORAL

To know the current health problems of elementary school children.

BEHAVIORAL

The student can list the most common health problems of children in the six- to twelve-year age group.

CRITERION-REFERENCED

The student can list at least four of the five most common health problems of children in the six- to twelve-year age group.

NONBEHAVIORAL

To acquire skill in musical production.

BEHAVIORAL

The student can play a simple tune on the musical instrument of his choice.

CRITERION-REFERENCED

The student can play a simple tune on the musical instrument of his choice, making not more than one error.

NONBEHAVIORAL

To use correct English grammar.

BEHAVIORAL

Given sentences containing grammatical errors, the student will rewrite each sentence correctly.

CRITERION-REFERENCED

Given sentences containing grammatical errors, the student will rewrite correctly at least 80 percent of the sentences.

The following objectives are from the affective domain. The criterion for acceptable performance could be applied to the whole class rather than an individual student, and the teacher is interested more in the effectiveness of his teaching than in individual student performance.

NONBEHAVIORAL
Students will develop a positive self-concept.

BEHAVIORAL
The student indicates that he would feel confident if he were hired to do a job requiring considerable use of the arithmetic skills he had studied in school.

CRITERION-REFERENCED
When asked on a questionnaire how confident they would feel if they were hired to do a job requiring considerable use of the arithmetic skills they had studied in school, at least 75 percent of the class respond "confident" or "very confident."

Summary

Written educational objectives that are derived from knowledge of the present and future needs and interests of students and from the needs of society serve as a basis for improved teaching and testing. Such objectives also allow the teacher to identify and concentrate firmly on his teaching goals and to communicate those goals clearly to others.

The classroom teacher should develop his course objectives logically from school and departmental objectives, and he should express his objectives whenever possible in terms of student behavior. Objectives so stated will have maximal usefulness as a basis for planning teaching and learning activities and for developing valid tests of student achievement. The exact form and degree of specificity required for teacher objectives depend on the teacher's teaching and testing model.

Exercises

1. What is the difference between educational objectives and course content?

2. What are the three levels of educational objectives? Give an example of each from a teaching area of interest to you.

3. What is the difference between affective and cognitive objectives? Give an example of each from a teaching area of your own interest.

4. What is the difference between norm-referenced and criterion-referenced tests? How does this difference affect the way objectives should be written for each? Or does it?

5. Write three objectives for a field of interest to you. Write each in two versions, one appropriate for a norm-referenced test and the other for a criterion-referenced test.

6. For each of the following broad objectives, write at least one behavioral objective.

   a. appreciates classical music

   b. understands the United States Constitution

   c. appreciates the relationship between supply and demand

7. Locate a curriculum guide for a school (preferably the school where you teach), and write two or three course objectives for your own field appropriate to each of at least two of the school objectives. Alternately, formulate at least two school objectives of your own and write two or three course objectives for your own field based on each.

Suggested Readings

BLOOM, B. S., HASTINGS, J. T., and MADAUS, G. F. *Handbook on Formative and Summative Evaluation of Student Learning.* New York: McGraw-Hill, 1971. *Chapter 2 discusses educational objectives.*

BLOOM, B. S. ed. *Taxonomy of Educational Objectives: The Classification of Educational Goals. Handbook I, Cognitive Domain.* New York: David McKay, 1956. *A system for classifying cognitive objectives.*

GRONLUND, N. E. *Stating Behavioral Objectives for Classroom Instruction.* Toronto: Collier-Macmillan Canada, 1970. *A 58-page book designed to assist teachers in writing objectives. Contains a check list for evaluating objectives and a list of illustrative verbs.*

KRATHWOHL, D. R., and PAYNE, D. A. "Defining and Assessing Educational Objectives," pp. 17–45 of *Educational Measurement*, 2d ed., ed. R. L. Thorndike. Washington: American Council on Education, 1971. *Discusses both affective and cognitive objectives and their place in instruction.*

KRATHWOHL, D. R. et al. *Taxonomy of Educational Objectives: The Classification of Educational Goals. Handbook II, Affective Domain.* New York: David McKay, 1964. *A system for classifying affective objectives.*

MAGER, R. F. *Preparing Instructional Objectives.* Belmont, Calif.: Fearon Publishers, 1962. (Originally titled *Preparing Objectives for Programmed Instruction.*) *A programmed text for writing behavioral objectives.*

POPHAM, J. W., and HUSEK, T. R. "Implications of Criterion-Referenced Measurement." *Journal of Educational Measurement* 6 (1969): 1–9. *Examines some of the differences between criterion-referenced and norm-referenced tests.*

Chapter 3

PLANNING THE CLASSROOM MEASUREMENT PROGRAM

As a result of studying this chapter you should be able to:

1. *Describe the factors that should be considered in planning the content and timing of a measurement program for a total course.*

2. *Compare the virtues and weaknesses of using less than the most direct approach to measuring progress toward goals.*

3. *Describe the justification for using multiple approaches to measuring a specific goal in a unit of instruction.*

4. *Develop a table of specifications for a test in an area of your expertise.*

5. *Outline a method for estimating a reasonable length for a test in your area.*

6. *Describe the limitations affecting the development and use of criterion-referenced classroom tests.*

7. *Compare measurement programs for sequential and nonsequential courses.*

The teacher needs to consider two aspects of planning in developing a classroom measurement program: (1) as part of planning activities for a semester, he should develop an overview of the measurement requirements that will complement other instructional activities; (2) he should plan each major test or examination in advance. Both aspects of planning for measurement should be treated with the same care that is given to the planning of instruction and preparation for lessons or units. Because of the interrelationships between instruction and measurement, simultaneous attention to both processes will yield extra benefits that will improve the total instructional program as well as the measurement program.

Planning the General Measurement Program

The nature and timing of all aspects of a testing program cannot be planned with complete precision before the semester begins. Just as instructional plans must be complete but have enough flexibility to accommodate the needs of students as those needs become apparent, measurement plans should reflect a consideration of the kind of data to be collected and when within the instructional sequence data should be collected. It is neither possible nor necessary to plan the program in terms of the times and dates for each measurement session, and careful preplanning will help the teacher be flexible when he applies measurement principles.

During preplanning, several factors deserve attention because they affect the types of measurement tools that can be used and the time to apply each part of the measurement program. Only when these factors have been considered, alone and in relationship to one another, can an effective instructional program be planned.

Methods

Developing precise objectives for a course or subject area will guide and structure teaching and learning and, important for the teacher's purposes, provide a basis for monitoring a student's progress and describing the level of achievement he reaches. The general goal in a classroom measurement program should be to measure student progress toward objectives as directly (validly) as possible within the constraints imposed by time and the nature of the objectives.

Many objectives can be measured effectively and validly by the common types of paper and pencil tests, and the material in the following sections will describe ways tests can be developed to accomplish these purposes. Some objectives, however, must be measured by other methods: for example, an objective relevant to a student's ability to prepare a research paper obviously requires an assignment that includes both library research and the writing of a paper; an objective that relates to some performance, such as a laboratory skill, typing ability, or construction of a wooden end table, requires an assessment of a process or a product; and an objective that relates to student attitudes, interests, or values might require questionnaires or a project out of class. Although these product and performance measurements differ from classroom paper and pencil tests, many principles of good measurement practice may be applied to them with slight modification, and planning is just as important.

Teachers should plan their measurement programs so that each goal is measured directly, in sufficient quantity, and with as much precision as possible. The general approach should be planned in advance, and the teacher should tell students early in the semester or unit how their progress will be assessed. The frequency of quizzes, assignments to be handed in for assessment, major tests, and projects should be announced as part of the unit assignment.

In planning the total measurement program, a balance must be struck between the most apparently direct or valid approach possible and the efficiency and reliability that should characterize data used for important decisions. Some of the techniques and strategies of measurement that provide the most direct observation of progress toward objectives may not be efficient or practicable and may produce results of limited reliability. For example, the preparation of a research paper may directly and completely represent some goals of an English class, but the project would be too complex to grade in an objective and reliable way. In addition, in completing assignments outside of class, students may have drawn on papers written by former students or may have received assistance from a friend or parent. It is advisable sometimes to use a less direct measurement approach with greater scorability and about which there can be no doubt in how the work was completed. For example, some aspects of writing a research paper can be covered adequately on an in-class test. Facts can be presented with the sources indicated, and students can be asked to write a theme of assigned length based on this information and including the proper footnotes. Such an approach allows the teacher to measure skill of organization, clarity of presentation, ability to footnote, and a variety of other skills related to the development of a research paper.

Timing

Measurement of student progress toward instructional goals can enable both student and teacher to take steps that will facilitate student development toward objectives if the measurement is made at appropriate points in the instructional program. The teacher must determine where these points are in a particular class and consider certain guidelines in planning the measurement program.

In any course where sequential learning is important—that is, classes where later content builds on earlier achievement—it is extremely important for progress to be assessed frequently. Mathematics, science, and language courses are good examples. Much time and effort can be saved and frustrations, boredom, or failure avoided when the teacher and student are aware of the progress being made. Students experiencing difficulty may need extra help or a different set of learning exercises to help them cross a hurdle. If students are allowed to persist without succeeding, they may become discouraged and turn their attention to more satisfying activities. Conversely, if a student can make rapid progress through an exercise, he may become bored by the lack of challenge; to avoid this problem, he should be permitted to enrich his learning by studying the topic in greater depth or by studying topics not included in the basic course of study for the class.

Measurement used primarily for a formative purpose—that is, to ascertain whether learning is adequate and, in case difficulties are found, the nature of the difficulty—should be administered with relative frequency. The measurement can take the form of simple tests or quizzes or may include review of assignments, lab reports, or work sheets. Regardless of the technique used, the general nature and timing of the assessment should be planned in advance. A skillful, knowledgeable teacher should be able to anticipate those topics and skills that require frequent measurement of progress.

Of great importance in advance planning is the teacher's decision on what to do with the information obtained from periodic assessment. Measurement may have value in the learning process, but much of its impact will be lost if the data are not used in some constructive way—to reinforce successful learning, to plan remedial activities for individuals, or to ascertain what type of reteaching is required for the class. It is difficult to conceive of measurement that would not be used by teachers and learners to improve the instructional process; and it is equally difficult to conceive of instructional plans that would not include optional activities for students who had reached different levels of achievement from instruction. A skillful teacher should anticipate the problems that may occur and thus be able to project in advance the timing of measurement that would provide useful data to assist in the decision-making process on appropriate activities for individual students.

Quantity

Although formal marking systems have been the focus of intense criticism during the past few years, most school systems retain some form of grading and some system of reporting student progress. Regardless of the nature of the grading and reporting system, as long as schools retain a semblance of their present

organization and structure, teachers will be required to describe
the level of student achievement in a form that is meaningful to the
students, parents, subsequent teachers, counselors, and others
who have a vested interest in the students' progress and the right
to be informed of it. There is nothing unimportant about assigning
a grade or otherwise describing student achievement, and a measurement program should be planned with the definite goal of
obtaining information for the precise purpose of describing level of
achievement.

Frequent measurement is desirable for instructional purposes,
particularly in sequential courses. For purposes of assigning marks,
particularly in sequential courses, there are good arguments for
placing the greatest weight on measurements obtained near the
end of instruction, for a student's performance on a final examination will reflect with some certainty the achievement made
throughout the semester, and of course performance at the close of
the semester built on achievement made throughout is more
important than the interim demonstrations of achievement. This
fact suggests that periodic, interim measurement should focus on
the aspects of learning that will provide the greatest assistance to
instructional planning, and that for grading purposes greater emphasis should be placed on later assessment and the final examination.

Some courses do not have a sequential structure and the units
within a semester may be highly independent. In these courses
achievement in the final unit may not depend on the level of
achievement in prior units, and if a semester grade is to reflect
accurately the achievement for the semester, reliable measurements must be obtained at the close of each major unit of study.

As a general rule of thumb, three hours of in-class testing are
necessary to produce data for decision-making without major errors. This guideline is based on a reasonable estimate of the
reliability of classroom tests and a definition of major error that
minimizes errors of more than one category on a five-point (A to F)
grading system. This point of view will be developed more
thoroughly in Chapter 9. The classroom measurement plan should

reflect the importance of assessment for grading purposes, and the semester or year-long program should include major examinations that reflect instructional goals and allow students to demonstrate how well they have assimilated the various bits and pieces of the major instruction units.

Duplication

Different objectives will require different forms of assessment, and a teacher should plan the measurement program so that all major instructional objectives are assessed. A teacher should not ignore an objective merely because it is difficult to develop a technique for measuring student achievement toward that objective. If progress toward a goal is not measured, the goal becomes only a hope rather than a real target for instruction. It is true that some objectives are elusive, but if they are important enough to be included in instructional plans, they must be important enough to justify an effort to discover whether students are making progress toward achieving them.

In the attempt to measure all objectives as directly as possible, it is likely that measurements will overlap with respect to some objectives. Repetitious measurement of a goal is not completely undesirable, particularly for those goals that are complex or critical in the subject being studied. In common practice, however, the objectives measured in multiple ways are all too often those that can be measured easily. Repetition or duplication of measurement should not occur by chance; when it occurs, it should be deliberate. A teacher may wish to measure the ability of students to recognize examples or definitions of terms. A short-answer or completion exercise might be used, and the same test might also include multiple-choice items. The most efficient use of this format would be to measure student ability to apply the terms or concepts or to relate them to other concepts. To repeat the recognition of meanings in the multiple-choice format would be a questionable practice.

Frequently teachers will use both choice items (true-false, multiple-choice) and supply-type items (essay, short-answer) in the same test. When different item types are included in a test, too often the same topics are covered and the same goals are measured by the different types of items. Since testing formats are differentially effective in measuring different kinds of achievements, the measurement plan should identify types of tests that will be used to measure each objective; the repeated measurement of one type of achievement should be included in the plan only when the importance or complexity of the objective justifies the duplication. The caution given here extends beyond paper and pencil tests to include all aspects of measurement—daily assignments, lab reports, or papers. If lab skills or use of instruments can be measured satisfactorily by observation or lab reports, they need not be demonstrated again in paper and pencil tests, but if the ability "to apply a principle" includes some features best measured with both essay test questions and multiple-choice items, the amount of duplication likely to occur might be justified because of the complex nature of the objective.

Planning the Test

The process of planning each test will be simplified greatly by first planning the general measurement program. Even so, individual tests should be given adequate attention and planned sufficiently in advance so that there will be no last-minute rush to prepare the materials needed. Six aspects of planning, six steps that bring the teacher to the point of writing actual test questions, should be considered.

Identifying the Course Objectives

If an instructor has developed a set of objectives prior to covering a unit with a class, whether or not the objectives have been stated formally, some set of goals will have guided the teacher and the class through the material for which a test is to be constructed. If the objectives have been explicated, then the major task in identifying the goals for the test plan is deciding what emphasis the test should give to each of the objectives to be measured. If the goals have not been stated formally before instruction, it is advisable, if not necessary, for the teacher to do so as part of planning the test.

The development of objectives has been discussed in Chapter 2, but it should be noted again that to be useful for purposes of test development, objectives should focus on the achievements of students—that is, the changes in student capabilities that are expected because of the instructional activities students have experienced. Test questions focus on student capabilities, and precise, behaviorally-oriented objectives are required to guide the teacher in developing a balanced, relevant test.

Many course objectives are included in more than one and sometimes in all the units that compose a course. This is particularly true for skills that pervade the subject being studied. Some objectives relate to only one unit, and general goals for a course may generate subgoals specific to a unit. Whether the objectives for the material to be covered on the test are specific to the unit or more generic to the course, the first step in planning a test is to identify all the objectives the test should measure.

The objectives a test should cover should be the same as those that guided and influenced the instruction, with the exception of objectives which have been measured satisfactorily through non-test means. In planning the test, the teacher must make a deliberate decision on the emphasis to be given to each objective. In the final analysis this decision will be subjective and reflect value judgements, but some factors can help in the decision. If an objective is unique to the material being taught, it should receive somewhat greater emphasis than if it were being taught in several units. The amount of time devoted in class to meeting the objectives should also guide the decision. However the decision is reached, the plan for the test should include the percentage of items that will measure each of the objectives, and the distribution of emphasis should reflect the teacher's analysis of the relative importance of the various objectives for the unit.

Identifying the Content Topics to be Measured

It may seem obvious that the topics to be measured by a test need to be identified as part of the planning, but many classroom tests have omitted important topics when good test items proved difficult to develop. In the press of meeting a deadline for a test, some topics difficult to measure may be overlooked or underrepresented unless the teacher is following a test plan to guide the development of items to represent those topics.

Subject-matter content may be outlined by broad topics, such as "novels," "short stories," and "poetry" for an English class, or by extremely narrow topics that reflect virtually every five minutes of class activities. This general principle should be followed in outlining content for the purpose of planning a test: *Each aspect of content that must be covered on a valid test should appear in the content outline.* The corollary of this principle is that subtopics should be grouped into a more inclusive topic when any of the subtopics would be sufficient for test coverage. In other words, if test validity in terms of goals can be achieved by covering some limited number of several related topics, then these topics should be collected into a broader topic. For example, if a chemistry unit included a goal related to student ability to predict the reaction of an acid with another type of compound, the topic might be "reactions of acids" rather than separate topics for "reactions of H_2SO_4," "reactions of HNO_3," and "reactions of HCL."

If the content of a unit in American literature included contemporary political novelists, authors such as Knebel, Wallace, and Drury might be studied. Then the content outline might include either each author listed separately or merely a topic for "contemporary political novelists." The decision on which approach to use would depend on whether test validity required at least one question on each author, in which case each author would appear as a topic, or whether items covering any one or a combination of these authors would be sufficient, in which case the category of political novelists would suffice.

For most if not all units of content, it is impossible to include in a test all the questions that could be asked on every discrete topic of importance. The test must be developed selectively in order to represent adequately the important subject-matter topics. This fact suggests that some individual topics can be collected under more general labels or categories central to the purposes of the course. No hard and fast rules can be given concerning the number of elements or categories a content outline should include, and there is certainly a limit to the number that a classroom test can cover, but the test must include a sufficient number of items to measure the topic reliably. Between eight and twelve content topics in the test plan would be reasonable for most classroom unit exams, or in other words, about five minutes of testing time should be allowed per topic.

Relating Goals and Content

To reflect faithfully the purposes of the learning it is intended to measure, a test must be balanced, with proper emphasis placed on each objective and subject-matter topic. In planning a test a teacher should devise some procedure to insure that it will be balanced. Since content and goals define the achievement domain of interest, and since these two aspects of instruction are interactive rather than independent, the test plan must provide a way for goals and content to be handled simultaneously during the development of test items.

The purposes of instruction are described in the objectives, which focus on the changes in student capabilities that should occur as a result of instruction. In some courses content is virtually irrelevant except as an avenue for achieving the objectives. For example, the sentences used in studying a particular form of punctuation are of no importance intrinsically and students are not expected to remember them. Skill in using punctuation effectively is the target behavior. In other courses the content may have some value in itself, but the emphasis is still on the objectives; there is a broad field of choice from which the actual content is selected. An example is the study of Shakespearean tragedy, in which any of several plays could be used. And in still other courses, the specification of objectives virtually dictates the content, which has great intrinsic value. For example, in an algebra course the objective of factoring binomials establishes the class of content to be studied. All this suggests that the writing of test items derives most directly from objectives and that the attention given to specific content varies with the type of class. A teacher should decide where his particular course or unit falls on the continuum and should develop test items accordingly.

Since the vast majority of courses will fall somewhere in the middle of the continuum, there is usually the need to relate content and objectives in a way that will guide test construction effectively. One of the most widely recommended procedures for this purpose is the preparation of a *table of specifications* or a *test blueprint,* which is a two-way chart showing the objectives along one side and the content topics along the other. The percentages derived earlier for each objective and each content topic, with each dimension totaling 100, are entered next to the marginal entry.

An example of a table of specifications for a test covering a literature unit is shown in Figure 3.1. Four objectives and three

FIGURE 3.1

Table of specifications for a literature test

Objectives	Content		
	Short story (40%)	Essay (30%)	Drama (30%)
Understanding meanings in context (35%)	14%	10.5%	10.5%
Understanding literary devices (30%)	12%	9%	9%
Identifying main ideas (20%)	8%	6%	6%
Identifying author's purpose (15%)	6%	4.5%	4.5%

types of content are identified. Next to each marginal entry the percentage of emphasis is entered in parentheses. The teacher has decided that 40 percent of the questions should cover short stories and that 35 percent of the items should require the student to demonstrate ability to understand meanings in context. The percentages of emphasis were derived by reviewing the amount of material covered and the emphasis given during instruction. The values entered in the cells were obtained by multiplying the marginal percentages for the row and column intersecting the cell. For example, the number for "identifying main ideas" in the essays—6 percent—was obtained by multiplying 20 percent by 30 percent. The values in the cells total 100 percent. To determine the number of items for each cell the instructor multiplies the total number of items the test is to contain by the appropriate percentage. If a fifty-item test is planned, three items (6 percent of 50) should deal with main ideas of essays.

A table of specifications provides guidance for a teacher by calling attention to the kinds of items needed for a balanced test. As each item is developed, it can be coded in terms of the cell of the table that it represents. Either numbering or lettering the cells will facilitate this step.

Although a table of specifications provides a general guide, the teacher may be justified occasionally in modifying the cell percentages. The two-way table is based on the assumption that all objectives apply equally to all categories of the content outline, and for some tests this assumption will be in error. When alterations are justified for educational reasons, the teacher should make them before he starts to develop items. A teacher should not modify a table of specifications only because he experiences difficulty in developing items for some cells. Frequently the most important achievements are the most difficult to measure and these should not be underrepresented on the test. In fact, using a table of specifications is an effective way to minimize the erosion of noble ideas by the press of producing an instrument.

Figure 3.2 is another example of a test plan. In this plan the major periods studied head up the three columns. The rows are a

FIGURE 3.2

Table of specifications for a social studies test

	1800–1820 (30%)	1820–1840 (30%)	1840–1865 (40%)
Identify contributions of leading figures			
Political (10%)	3%	3%	4%
Social (5%)	1.5%	1.5%	2%
Business (5%)	1.5%	1.5%	2%
Explain importance of key events			
New industries (10%)	3%	3%	4%
Social crisis (10%)	3%	3%	4%
New federal laws (20%)	6%	6%	8%
Important dates			
Industrial innovations (5%)	1.5%	1.5%	2%
Key elections (10%)	3%	3%	4%
Discoveries (5%)	1.5%	1.5%	2%
Explain relationships among social and industrial changes (20%)	6%	6%	8%

combination of goals and topics, such as "Identify contributions of leading figures." The row and column percentages and the cell values were obtained as for Figure 3.1. If a hundred-item test were developed from this table, some decisions would have to be made concerning the adjacent cells with entries of 1.5. Obviously half an item is not possible, and the teacher should decide whether to have two items in the 1800–1820 column and one in the 1820–1840 column, or the reverse.

Selecting Types of Items

Deciding on the type or types of items to use on a test is an important part of test planning. The nature of the achievement defined by the table of specifications should have a major influence on the teacher's choice. Tests emphasizing the recognition of terms, dates, or ideas should comprise items that measure these achievements efficiently and validly. If the test plan calls for organization of ideas, a free-response format is probably the best. Tests requiring application, prediction, explanation, and understanding of concepts in new contexts should be composed of items that measure those achievements directly and efficiently.

In general, there is little virtue in using a variety of item types on a test merely to give examinees a change of pace or to keep them motivated. The quality of a test, not the types of items used, will be the major factor influencing examinee motivation. The decision to use more than one type of item on a test should be based on the assumption that efficient, valid measurement requires the use of several item types.

Teachers can learn to develop and use all types of items effectively. The quality of classroom tests rests primarily on the knowledge the teacher has of the subject and its relationship to the total educational development of students. Teachers must be knowledgeable and creative in finding valid questions that require examinees to demonstrate important achievements. Nearly all teachers have a preference for a certain type of test, whether it be essay or multiple-choice, and there is a natural tendency to use the preferred format, but every teacher should develop the competence to produce several kinds of tests and should then select the most direct and efficient form for a given purpose.

For short, periodic assessment of student progress, the completion, true-false, and short-answer items will often be preferable to essay and multiple-choice tests. The time required to develop multiple-choice items and to score essay items may prevent their use in the formative types of tests. Essay and multiple-choice tests are useful for major examinations that require students to organize and present careful exposition or to interpret, apply, relate, or deduce concepts.

Determining Test Length

Two aspects of test length must be considered: how much time can be devoted to administering the test, and how many items students can complete in the time available. The time available for the test usually depends on the length of a class period or the number of class periods to be used. In the elementary grades tests should be short enough to avoid tiring pupils or exceeding the attention span of the age group. Generally a test should not last more than twenty or thirty minutes. In junior and senior high schools tests are usually of class-period length, from forty to fifty minutes.

The number of items that students can complete in a given length of time depends on the nature of the material and the types of items used. Items based on recognition or recall of facts need less time on the average than those requiring computation or the application of principles to new material. Similarly, true-false, completion, and matching exercises usually require less time per item than essay or multiple-choice items.

Classroom tests should be planned to allow most examinees to complete all items and have time to review their work. The nature of the achievement to be demonstrated and the teacher's earlier experience in teaching the content will guide him in deciding how many items to include. Generally the short-response types require twenty to thirty seconds per item on the average and the more complex require a minute or even more per item.

Using an Answer Sheet

Some teachers require examinees to use "blue books" or something similar for essay tests. When this is the case, planning must include obtaining the materials or giving directions to students in advance to obtain them.

When choice-type tests or completion exercises are to be used, the teacher must decide whether to have examinees write on the test booklet or to provide a separate answer sheet. Generally an answer sheet is preferred, except for primary school children, and the teacher should plan to obtain or produce the answer sheet needed. Answer sheets will be discussed in detail in Chapters 4 and 6.

Planning the Criterion-referenced Test

Although many of the previous suggestions apply to criterion-referenced (or mastery) tests, there are some unique requirements for these tests that need to be considered in planning. This book emphasizes that all tests should reflect instructional objectives, and in that sense all tests are somewhat criterion-referenced. In fact, it could be argued that a carefully and ingeniously developed test may be the best criterion available for measuring students' achievement.

Criterion-referenced tests are most useful for subjects that can be analyzed into all the essential components of the instructional goals. The goals must be related directly to the skills and capabilities to be developed and must be expressed so that knowledgeable people in the field can agree on the meaning of the expressions. These requirements are more easily satisfied when the achievements can be completely circumscribed, as, for example, in the goal, "the ability to add all two-digit number combinations," than when there are many valid interpretations of a complex goal, such as "can predict what economic changes in the European community would cause a heightening of the Cold War."

Even in subjects that lend themselves to the use of the mastery approach, a major problem remains. At what level of performance can the teacher and student conclude that mastery has occurred or that a satisfactory criterion has been met? How can criteria be established objectively?

The simple example, "adding all two-digit number combinations," can be used to illustrate the problem. How many of the combinations need to be presented on the test to allow the conclusion that the skill has been mastered? It is neither practical nor necessary to present all combinations. Would ten be sufficient? Or five? Or perhaps twenty? If the teacher decides that ten should be presented, must the examinee answer all correctly? If an examinee answered nine correctly, would that represent sufficient mastery or satisfactorily meet the criterion? Such questions would be multiplied many times for subjects with more complex objectives and less tangible content.

The most frustrating aspect of the problem is the lack in most subject areas of any specific, concrete, objective way to seek the answers to such questions. The unique aspect of planning a criterion-referenced test is deciding how many items to develop for a given objective and how difficult to make the items. Before administering a test, the teacher must be able to produce a clearly conceived and expressed description of the behavior that will lead him to conclude that mastery has or has not occurred.

This difficult problem may not arise in some sequential areas, such as mathematics and foreign languages. In these subjects it may be possible to develop an empirical answer to the problem by studying student success from one class to the next above it in the sequence. Because appropriate studies have not been made yet, the most satisfactory approach is careful articulation and communication among teachers of successive classes.

Criterion-referenced tests—those in which test items relate specifically to an essential goal or skill that must be mastered—are important, if not essential, as tools in the teaching–learning process. The assumption is made that students who have mastered the elements or reached a satisfactory level of achievement will answer all, or nearly all, items correctly. Errors are assumed to indicate insufficient learning.

Although unit and final examinations are based on objectives and the items reflect knowledge or skills of ultimate value, these examinations are designed to ascertain how well students can apply mastered concepts to new and challenging situations. In addition, such tests are designed to discriminate, to measure differences in the quality of learning that has occurred or differences in ability to apply previously learned materials. As a result, errors are expected, even by outstanding students, and are due not to insufficient learning but to the challenging nature of the test.

Criterion-referenced tests and discriminatory tests are complementary parts of a complete measurement program. A skilled teacher plans to use each type at the appropriate time and knows how to interpret the results of each type.

Summary

In planning the measurement program for a semester or unit, a teacher should consider (1) the methods to use to collect evidence of learning; (2) the appropriate times to collect data to enhance learning and teaching; (3) the amount of information that will be needed; and (4) the amount of duplication of measurement that is appropriate. Careful consideration of these factors will provide the teacher with the framework of a plan he can modify during instruction when he perceives the need for change.

In planning a test the teacher should (1) identify the objectives to be measured; (2) identify the blocks of content to be covered to provide a useful avenue to the objectives; (3) develop a test plan that relates content and objectives with an appropriate distribution of emphasis; (4) decide on the types of test items to use; (5) decide on the length of the test to be used; and (6) decide whether to use a "blue book" in the case of essay tests or a separate answer sheet in the case of choice-type tests. The criterion-referenced approach to testing requires that the teacher identify the components of a learning task and decide how to determine when mastery has occurred.

Planning is important in both guiding student learning and assessing the quality of learning as it occurs. If both parts of the instructional program are planned in advance, measurement can have the optimal impact on student learning.

Exercises

1. For a course you would teach, is there an objective that could *not* be measured with paper and pencil tests? Why?

2. Is there an objective in your area for which multiple measurement approaches should be used? If so, why? How would it be measured?

3. What would be some of the major differences between a measurement program for a first semester course in a second language and a course in modern authors?

4. The unit topics and unit objectives are shown below with the teacher's assessments of relative importance. Prepare a table of specifications for a test in this unit, indicate percentages for each cell, and in parentheses indicate the number of items over each cell for a sixty-item test.

	Relative importance
Topics	
1. poetry	2
2. short stories	3
3. novels	4
4. popular magazine stories	1

	Relative importance
Objectives	
1. knowledge of facts in the literature read	3
2. evaluation of author's mood and intent	2
3. interpretation of words in context	1
4. identification of main ideas in literature read	4

5. Select a topic in your area for which a criterion-referenced test would be appropriate. What criterion or criteria would be used? How did you arrive at the specification of minimal mastery?

Suggested Readings

EBEL, R. L. *"Essentials of Educational Measurement."* Englewood Cliffs, N.J.: Prentice-Hall, 1972, pp. 97–122. *Discusses thoroughly the planning of classroom tests and relates it to planning an entire program.*

FELDHUSEN, J. F. "Student Perceptions of Frequent Quizzes and Post-Mortem Discussions of Tests." *Journal of Educational Measurement* 1 (1964): 51–54. *Report on a study of the use of frequent quizzes and compares three different methods of discussing test results.*

MARSO, R. M. "The Influence of Test Difficulty upon Study Efforts and Achievement." *American Educational Research Journal* 6 (1969): 621–632. *Report on a study comparing student reactions to tests of various difficulty levels and those students' subsequent achievements.*

MCKENZIE, G. R. "Some Effects of Frequent Quizzes on Inferential Thinking." *American Educational Research Journal* 9 (1972): 231–240. *Report on a study comparing the effect of different kinds of periodic quizzes on subsequent study capabilities. The study concluded that students seem to learn what they experience.*

TINKLEMAN, S. N. "Planning the Objective Test." *Educational Measurement*, 2d ed. Washington, D.C.: American Council on Education, 1971, pp. 46–80. *A thorough and excellent review of the planning necessary to produce a test. The student should skip over the topics that only relate to standardized tests.*

PART II

Collecting Evidence of Learning

To evaluate the effectiveness of instruction and the achievement of individual students, evidence of learning must be collected periodically. Although some evidence will be obtained by nontest means, the major part of the classroom measurement program will be based on the use of tests. A wide variety of testing approaches are available and practical for teachers to use. The topics discussed in the following four chapters include (1) the forms of testing that have the greatest flexibility and utility for measuring classroom achievement and (2) the nontest approaches that can be used to complement formal testing. The grouping of topics into chapters is sometimes arbitrary, but within each chapter the forms discussed are related to one another in terms of the nature of the achievement they measure most effectively and the strategies that can be used in developing the tests.

Although many different item types are used widely in classroom measurement programs, essentially, tests require the student either to select an answer from several choices or compose an answer to a question. This dichotomy has been labeled *objective* versus *subjective, recognition* versus *recall,* or *selection* versus *supply.* Only the last of the three sets of labels is sufficiently useful to be retained, but the erroneous assumptions underlying the first two should be considered because they are related to goals and philosophies of the teacher as test author.

The term "objective" as applied to testing refers to the *reproducibility* of the measurements obtained by a given process. To the extent that measurements are derived objectively from the purpose of a test, qualified observers should be able to concur on the degree of achievement represented by the measures obtained. For example, if a measurement is made of students' achievement in American government, to the extent that the measurements are objective, competent scholars in the field should be able to agree on the relative amount of achievement demonstrated by the students who have been assessed.

"Subjective," in common parlance, usually means that a judgment is a matter of opinion. Critics of free-response tests use the term to signify that grades, or other judgments of quality, depend on the idiosyncratic values and skill of the person who makes the judgment. Implicit in the use of the term "subjective" is an assumption that such approaches to measurement would not produce results on which competent judges could agree.

Many aspects of teaching and testing are subjective, including what goals to measure, how many questions to ask, how difficult to make the questions, what weight to place on various topics and objectives, and how to grade the examinee responses. As a result, choice tests are not entirely objective. Furthermore, every test should be derived directly from instructional objectives and developed so that competent judges could agree on the quality of achievement examinees demonstrate. Some free-response tests faithfully represent instructional goals, and careful planning will result in scoring procedures that are satisfactorily objective.

The "recall-recognition" dichotomy is equally disfunctional. Critics frequently claim that to succeed on choice tests, examinees need only recognize something they have experienced earlier. The implication is that recalling is more important in intellectual behavior than recognition. A review of essay and multiple-choice tests would reveal that many essay questions merely require students to recall terms in the exact form they were studied, while many multiple-choice tests require examinees to recall material and apply it to problems they have never seen before in the instructional process. Well-constructed tests, whether of the free-response or choice type, demand that examinees recall the appropriate information selectively and demonstrate the ability to use it in a new but directly appropriate way. As a result, the recall-recognition distinction is not useful for advancing the state of classroom measurement practices.

Chapter 4 discusses two of the types of tests most widely used, particularly in the lower grades—the short-answer and completion tests. These tests are suited uniquely for measuring student ability to produce answers to questions dealing with facts and verbal-level associations. Short-answer and completion tests share with essay tests the characteristic that examinees are required to compose the answer. Chapter 4 also considers essay tests, probably the form most widely used in classrooms.

Tests that require examinees to choose an answer from options presented on the test are discussed in Chapters 5 and 6. True-false and matching exercises, considered in Chapter 5, are most commonly used to measure student achievement on factual and verbal-level material. The most versatile of the choice types is the multiple-choice test, which can be used to measure virtually all types of achievement that can be measured with paper and pencil. Chapter 6 discusses the multiple-choice test and two variations of this format.

In each of these three chapters the discussion includes a review of the nature of the test form, the particular strengths and limitations of that approach to testing, and suggestions for developing and administering the test. A number of the issues associated with different forms of testing are controversial and are based more on opinions than on empirical evidence. These chapters point out the different views on these issues and encourage teachers to adopt a consistent philosophy toward teaching and testing.

Chapter 7 discusses measurement procedures for skills and affective qualities—that is, achievements that are noncognitive or only partially cognitive. Although parts of many classroom instructional programs are based on objectives related to attitudes and skills, these achievements are frequently ignored or given only passing attention in the measurement program. Suggestions and illustrative approaches are presented in this chapter for the difficult but important kinds of measurement that are needed for a balanced, complete assessment of classroom achievement.

Chapter 4

SUPPLY-TYPE TESTS

As a result of studying this chapter you should be able to:

1. *Edit and improve completion and short-answer items that contain technical flaws.*

2. *Construct for a unit in your teaching field some completion and short-answer items that reflect instructional objectives and are free of technical flaws.*

3. *Describe the factors that limit the measurement qualities of an essay exam, and indicate how these effects can be minimized.*

4. *Develop essay exam questions that can be scored in a global (relative) way and are free of technical flaws.*

5. *Develop essay exam questions that can be scored analytically and are free of technical flaws.*

6. *Develop global and analytical scoring keys for essay answers.*

The free-response or supply tests—those in which examinees must create and supply the answers to questions presented on the test—include the short-answer, completion, and essay types. The distinction between short-answer and essay tests is not always made clear, but here it is based on the length of the required answer and on whether or not organization is an important aspect of the examinee response. Short-answer tests require the examinee to write a word, phrase, sentence, or at most two sentences. By contrast, essay tests require a paragraph of at least three sentences and usually two paragraphs or more, and the organization of the sentences and paragraphs is a factor determining the quality of the answer.

Completion Tests

Completion tests are used widely at the elementary school level and to some extent through college. The tests can be prepared rapidly and with relative ease; they can be scored rapidly and usually "objectively"; and they provide an efficient way to measure achievements related to knowledge of names, dates, terms, and other simple associations. Teachers who use this format effectively as part of the measurement program are able to spend most of the time available for test construction in developing challenging tests to measure more complex accomplishments.

The general form of a completion item is a sentence with a word or phrase omitted, for example:

a. The name of the person who delivered the Gettysburg address is _____.

b. The contact method is used to produce _____ acid.

c. The capital city of Utah is _____.

Six Recommendations for Developing Completion Items

1. *Only important concepts should be selected as the basis for completion items.* The source of completion items may be books, articles, workbooks, lesson plans, or other instructional materials. From this vast assortment of materials, the teacher must choose as test items only those containing information that students should retain over a period of time, and he should be sure that there is justification for holding students responsible for each topic on the test. A test plan based on objectives and content will serve as a useful guide to the significant topics that might be included in the completion test.

2. *Statements should be paraphrased versions of those studied or completely new sentences.*   Even though retention of important ideas is a worthy educational goal, there is usually little merit in holding students responsible for one particular way of stating an idea. A more useful form of achievement is measured when completion items are paraphrased versions of the statements students learned in class, or preferably new statements including the association that was learned. For example, one of the facts statistics students learn quite early—that an arithmetic mean is the sum of all scores divided by the number of scores—could be developed into a completion item in this way:

> The arithmetic mean can be found by dividing the sum of scores by the _____.

But perhaps a more useful demonstration that the concept has been learned would be measured by:

> A sum of scores is equal to the arithmetic mean multiplied by the _____.

Though the same concept is covered in each case, the second item requires the examinee to transpose the idea, demonstrating that his learning has included more than memorizing a collection of words. The two following items illustrate the same point in a different way:

> Voltage equals resistance multiplied by _____.
> If resistance is constant, voltage would increase when there is an increase in _____.

3. *The sentence should be written so that only one response, the one desired, can complete the sentence satisfactorily.*   Careful initial thought and subsequent editing are required to avoid the use of items for which a number of responses could be supplied. If an examinee completes a sentence satisfactorily but with something other than the intended response, the teacher may find it difficult to mark the response wrong. Consider, for example:

> The largest city is _____.

In this item the teacher could avoid unintentional problems by specifying "in the world" or "in the United States," or whatever the frame of reference is. Even when this correction is made, there is still the chance that a perceptive (or misled) examinee might insert "crowded," "cold," "unfriendly," or a variety of other words that could describe the largest city. A better way to state the item would be:

The name of the largest city in western Europe is _____.

In editing test copy, the teacher should make sure that each statement appropriately limits the correct responses.

4. *The word or term deleted should be significant.* When the teacher has selected or prepared a statement that will form the basis for a completion item, he will have many options of which word or phrase to delete. This choice should be guided by the goal of measuring a useful achievement in a realistic way. Consider the statement:

The area of a rectangle is found by multiplying the length by the width.

If the word "area" is deleted, the item measures student knowledge of what is obtained by multiplying length by width. Although the relationship of area to length and width may be worth knowing, seldom will a student be in a situation where he needs to know what is found when length is multiplied by width. Much more often he will need to compute area, and therefore the deletion of "length" and "width" would be preferable.

In the previous example, all of the three terms considered, "area," "length," and "width," are significant to the concept embodied in the statement. The same could not be said of "found" or "by," and if these terms had been selected for deletion, the validity of the item would have been reduced greatly. Consider also:

Current in a circuit is directly related to voltage and inversely related to resistance.

The deletion of either or both of the "related's" from the statement would create an item of questionable value.

The problem described here will occur seldom if items are developed to measure knowledge or understanding of a concept and if the teacher keeps in mind the particular achievement which the item is aimed to measure. Any word or phrase deleted should be significant to the achievement measured.

5. *Deletions should be limited to the central thought of the statement.* In other words, overmutilations of the original statement should be avoided. If a completion item contains nearly as many blanks as words, the item almost certainly measures rote memorization of a statement. In addition, success on overmutilated statements places a premium on the examinee's ability to divine the instructor's intent. Consider an item formed from the previous example:

_____ in a _____ is _____ related to _____ and _____ related to _____.

A student who has memorized the statement should be able to complete the blanks *if* there is enough of the statement remaining to prompt recall of the appropriate sentence, but seldom should emphasis be placed on memorization. Care should be taken to write statements that include an important concept or relationship, and deletions should be made judiciously so that an achieving student can demonstrate the concept he has learned.

6. *Deletions should occur at the end of the statement.* The teacher can exercise great flexibility in preparing completion items, writing or rewriting statements to place key words in almost any position. Usually it is preferable to write statements so that blanks appear near the end. The "message" can be grasped more easily when the blanks occur at the end rather than at the beginning or middle of the statement. Although the validity of individual items may not be affected by the placement of the blank, both the time required for each item and the frustration of

the examinee will be reduced by placing blanks at the end of the main thought. Consider the following item:

A person's _____ income is his gross income minus all deductions.

Many examinees will need to read the item once to determine the general nature of the concept and a second time to decide on the answer. Simple rewording will allow students who know the answer to grasp the concept and determine the missing word in one reading. For example:

A person's gross income minus all deductions is called his _____ income.

In addition to these six recommendations, there are a few additional factors to consider in developing a completion test. Although completion tests can be prepared so that examinees can write their answers directly in the blank of each statement, there are several reasons for preparing a separate answer sheet or providing answer spaces at the edge of the test paper.

One principle of test construction is to avoid unintentional clues to the answer. For example, in a completion test the size of a blank can provide a clue to the length of an answer. The teacher can avoid giving such a clue by making all blanks the same size, putting the item number in parentheses in the blank, and directing examinees to write their answers in the appropriate spaces at the edge of the test page or on a separate answer sheet. Neither the answer sheet nor the answer column would complicate the test-taking process or increase the time required for the test, although the answer column should be used with young children who would have difficulty manipulating a second sheet of paper.

Scoring is easier and less time consuming if an answer column or answer sheet is used. The teacher can prepare a key on a strip with spaces that correspond to those in the answer column. A test page set up for use with a separate answer sheet, the answer sheet, and the scoring key are shown in Figure 4.1. A test with an answer column is shown in Figure 4.2. Note that the spaces in the test where the blanks occur are relatively small, but the spaces pro-

FIGURE 4.1

A completion test

Directions   Read each statement carefully to determine the word or words that will correctly complete the statement, and write your answer in the appropriate space on the separate answer sheet. Be sure to write legibly.

1. The capital of Greece is the city,   (1)   .
2. The mainland of Greece is divided by the Gulf of   (2)   .
3. The peninsula forming the southern part of Greece is called the   (3)   .
4. The port of Athens is the city of   (4)   .
5-6. The three great architectural styles of Greece were the Doric,   (5)   , and   (6)   .
7. The state Church of Greece is the   (7)   .
8. The terrain of Greece is mostly   (8)   .
9. The small political units in ancient Greece that developed into minor kingdoms were called   (9)   .
10. In ancient Greek religion the supreme lord of the skies was the god,   (10)   .

Answer sheet	Answer key
1. _____	1. Athens
2. _____	2. Corinth
3. _____	3. Peloponnesus
4. _____	4. Piraeus
5. _____	5. Ionic
6. _____	6. Corinthian
7. _____	7. Orthodox
8. _____	8. mountainous
9. _____	9. city-states
10. _____	10. Zeus

FIGURE 4.2

A completion test with an answer column

Directions Read each statement carefully to determine the word or words that will correctly complete the statement, and write your answer legibly in the appropriate space at the right edge of the page.

1. The capital of Greece is the city, _____.

1. _____

2. The mainland of Greece is divided by the Gulf of _____.

2. _____

3. The peninsula forming the southern part of Greece is called the _____.

3. _____

4. The port of Athens is the city of _____.

4. _____

5-6. The three great architectural styles of Greece were the Doric,   (5) , and   (6) .

5. _____

6. _____

7. The state Church of Greece is the _____.

7. _____

8. The terrain of Greece is mostly _____.

8. _____

9. The small political units in ancient Greece that developed into minor kingdoms were called _____.

9. _____

10. In ancient Greek religion the supreme lord of the skies was the god, _____.

10. _____

vided in the answer columns are large enough to accommodate a long word or a phrase.

A final comment about completion tests: In general, the

teacher should provide clear, complete directions so that examinees will understand thoroughly the mechanics of the test, including the way responses are to be indicated. Directions for completion tests should include:

1. an indication of the time limits,

2. clarification that each blank will require one word, a phrase, or a combination,

3. the place where answers should be written: in the blank, in an answer column, or on an answer sheet,

4. the degree of accuracy required, if applicable, as in computational problems.

Short-Answer Tests

Short-answer tests are similar to completion tests and some suggestions for writing one kind of test will apply equally to the other. The short-answer format may require the same type of examinee response as a completion test; frequently, the only difference is that a short-answer item presents a complete question rather than a statement with some words omitted. In the following example the same task is presented to the examinee, first as a completion item and then as a short-answer item.

    a. The area of a circle with a 3-inch radius is _____ square inches.

    b. What is the area of a circle with a 3-inch radius?

When the short-answer format requires single words, dates, or other relatively brief responses, an answer column or answer sheet can be used, with a strip key to expedite the scoring. Again, important ideas should be used as the basis of the questions, and only one or a limited number of responses should be possible.

When short-answer items require examinees to respond with phrases or sentences, the scoring process is more complex than for items requiring words or numbers as answers. This fact alone should not discourage the use of short-answer items, but if the same achievement can be measured with multiple-choice items, that format might be preferable. When the short-answer format requires extended answers, the teacher should prepare the key before he administers the test and should specify for his own reference during scoring which answers will be acceptable and which ones will be considered wrong. This process is essential for assuring objective scoring with constant standards for all papers and will help the teacher identify items that might need editing or revision.

Essay Tests

Although the limitations of the essay test have been researched and documented extensively during the past sixty years, it remains perhaps the most widely used form of classroom testing. The apparent values of the essay test are quite convincing: Examinees must recall appropriate material, organize it effectively, and present an answer in a form that communicates clearly. These characteristics seem to parallel many real-life situations, and thus the advocates of essay tests claim that this approach to testing has the greatest validity in measuring students' ability to explain material that they remember.

The potential value of essay testing probably lies somewhere between the exalted claims of proponents and the extreme limitations cited by critics. Many of the documented problems are associated more with misuse than with inherent characteristics, but good results can be obtained from essay tests only when the potential weaknesses are recognized and avoided. The teacher must be skilllful in developing questions and ascertaining the extent to which answers reflect progress toward instructional goals. For a skillful teacher who applies measurement techniques, essay tests can be an effective tool for measurement.

Six Recommendations for Developing Essay Tests

1. *Follow a test plan in selecting topics for the test.* Test plans, tables of specifications, are useful in preparing essay tests and perhaps even more important than for other types of tests. An

individual essay item obviously can cover more content and goals than an individual short answer or multiple-choice item can. At the same time, satisfactory coverage of important goals is difficult to achieve with a test format that can present only a limited number of independent questions in one examination period because of the time examinees need to organize and write their answers.

The coverage of an essay question can be estimated only after a scoring key has been developed for the question. The aspects of the intended answer that will affect the score or mark should be identified and compared with the table of specifications. Then the teacher can note the aspects of the test plan that must be covered by other questions. These steps will guide him in developing an essay test that gives appropriate emphasis to the various content topics and goals included in the test plan. A deliberate effort should be made to develop a test that reflects the instructional content and goals.

2. *Carefully define the task presented in each question.* Tests are designed to reflect instructional expectations. Only if the examinee understands the intent of a question and what is expected of him in the answer will the question assess achievement. If a question is to serve its intended purpose, the task presented should be explicit and precise so that examinees who have made the required achievement can demonstrate their accomplishment with confidence. Consider the item:

> What are the major differences between "representative" and "participatory" democracies?

This question poses a broad challenge to examinees, and the quality of the answer may reflect student ability to divine the instructor's intent as much as or more than reflecting an understanding of the two forms of government.

The question could be modified to call attention to the essential aspects of the intended answer without compromising the quality of the question as a measure of achievement. For example:

> How do "representative" and "participatory" democracies

compare in terms of the process by which laws and major policies are adopted?

With the additional guidance provided by the more carefully defined problem, examinees can respond to the true intent of the question. They will also be less likely to include extraneous, irrelevant material, and this in turn will help the teacher score the critical aspects of the answers.

If essay questions are not properly limited and precisely defined, examinees will experience frustration in deciding how much to write, how many aspects of the problem to address, and what relative emphasis to give each aspect that could be included—processes that waste limited and important examination time.

The following pairs of questions illustrate how imprecisely stated questions can be modified to present a clear task to examinees.

Original: Discuss the factors that led to the establishment of the Marshall Plan.

Revised: What were the three major reasons for establishing the Marshall Plan? Discuss each briefly in correct chronological sequence, and in one paragraph indicate how the three factors were interrelated.

Original: Compare the writing styles of Bret Harte and Mark Twain.

Revised: Compare the writing styles of Bret Harte and Mark Twain in terms of settings, depth of characterization, and dialogue styles of their main characters.

A well-defined question assures that students are all answering the same question and improves the gradeability of responses. In addition, delimited questions facilitate broad sampling of the table of specifications.

3. *Use questions requiring brief answers and include as many questions as practical.* A potential and serious weakness of essay

tests is the difficulty of sampling adequately a table of specifications because of the limited number of items on an essay test. To assess confidently a student's achievement requires giving the student an adequate opportunity to show what he has achieved. All tests include only a sample of the tasks related to the achievement, and if the sample is too small it may represent the whole inaccurately. A test that comprises a few broad questions will not sample a domain of achievement as well as a test that includes a balanced selection of more questions with each covering a carefully outlined area.

The only serious argument against the recommendation that questions should require short answers is that tests of this type will not measure the student's ability to organize and present cogently an extended answer—that is, important demands of real-life writing will be excluded. In response to this argument, an examination period is an extremely poor setting for students to demonstrate their skill in writing carefully edited and polished themes; actually, the best way to assess that skill is to require students to write such themes. Many teachers give an assignment that requires library research, an outline, and a preliminary draft prior to writing a final theme in class. In-class themes also provide a realistic setting and the opportunity for valid assessment of student abilities in written exposition.

It is difficult for one test to measure adequately both comprehension of subject matter and skills of written composition, and it is usually a mistake for a teacher to combine attempts to measure these two elements of achievement. It would be better to use the examination period to measure the comprehension of material, thus sampling a domain of achievement with questions requiring relatively short answers, and then to use theme assignments to measure writing skills. This "division of labor" would improve the measurement of both important aspects of student achievement.

4. *Do not use optional questions.* There are several reasons for this recommendation. First, a test should represent instructional goals, and unless goals differ among students, a common test

should be presented to all examinees. Second, since no absolute standard or common yardstick of measurement can be applied to different questions, the use of optional questions introduces a spurious factor into the score or grade. Third, the mark an examinee receives is dependent not only on the difficulty of the questions and the knowledge he has, but also on the standards of excellence the teacher applies to different questions. For example, a student might receive a higher mark on a question for which he is less sure of his answer if the teacher applies more relaxed standards than he would on an optional question for which he knows the answer but for which the teacher has established rigorous standards. This type of guessing game does not contribute to good measurement.

5. *Allow examinees ample time to answer all questions.*   A common student criticism of essay tests is the amount of writing required in the time available. The teacher's attempt to cover all aspects of achievement as broadly as possible tends to make essay tests unrealistically long. Judging the appropriate length of a test is a difficult task but one that cannot be ignored or taken casually. Examinees must be given time to collect their thoughts, organize their answers, and then do the required writing.

The proper length of an essay test is related to the level of the examinee and the nature of the material covered on the test. Teachers need to determine length on the basis of their experiences with students. As a rule of thumb, a teacher should be able to write complete answers to questions in no more than one third of the time permitted to students. In addition, answers for essay tests should require no more than 800 to 1000 words per hour.

6. *Directions should be thorough and specific.*   How much time the student has to complete the test, how important each question is in relation to the whole test, and what factors will affect grades should be explicit in the directions. Examinees should know how much time they can spend on individual questions and on the total test so that they can arrange their time. To aid their planning, they should also know how much each question will contribute to

the total score. Finally, examinees should be told whether organization, grammar, punctuation, and spelling will affect the scoring.

Scoring Essay Tests

The value of an essay examination for measuring achievement depends largely on the skill of the teacher in assessing the quality of the examinee responses. Research on this point is less than comforting for teachers who prefer essay tests and also seek good measurement of student achievement. Two methods have been used to study teacher scoring capabilities. In one, teachers read and scored a set of tests without marking on the papers. Several days later they rescored the same papers. If the mark assigned on a given day is a valid measurement, the teachers should be able to assign essentially the same marks later. The second approach was to have two or more competent teachers score the same set of test papers. If marks represent more than idiosyncratic and personal standards, competent judges should agree closely on the quality of examinee answers. The results of these studies indicate that teachers disagree with themselves and with other teachers by an amount that seriously affects the value of the measurement.

The inconsistencies in teachers' assessments in repeated scoring of essay papers and the variability among equally competent judges is well enough documented in research literature to establish the potential weakness of essay tests as measurement instruments. Although research has not yet illuminated the reasons for the problem—and there are undoubtedly many—it is reasonable to assume that a major factor is the all too frequent lack of clear-cut, carefully delimited essay questions and a corresponding lack of well-conceived scoring keys. These factors are under the control of the teacher, rather than characteristics of the format, and therefore acceptable standards may be achieved with essay tests if sufficient care is taken in preparing questions and keys.

Two basic methods can be used for scoring essay test answers—the *relative* and the *analytical*—and some proponents of essay tests add a third method—the *absolute*—which involves the elements of analytical scoring.

Relative scoring involves the determination of the rank order of the answers to a given question—that is, the teacher attempts to rank the answers from the best to the least acceptable. In the average-size class the teacher must attempt to accurately rank twenty-five to thirty-five different papers for each question on the test. This task is neither easy nor rapidly accomplished. One reading of the papers is insufficient because the teacher will not be capable of keeping in mind the assessment of all papers. One method to improve the relative scoring of papers is multiple readings. During the first reading the papers are tentatively assigned to three or four qualitative groups—for example, "above average," "average," and "below average." During the second reading the rank order within groups is refined and papers are shifted to another group when necessary. A second reading is certainly an improvement over one reading, and a third would probably add even more precision and accuracy to the ranking. In addition to the problem of obtaining accurate measurement, the whole process is quite time-consuming, but unfortunately no short cut is possible.

After the papers have been ranked, the teacher still must decide on a numerical system to use, including the maximum score for the best answer and the average score across all papers. Teachers should be realistic in assessing their own ability to detect qualitative differences that have some educational significance. The maximum score should reflect the number of meaningful differences in achievement that can be detected with confidence. For example, if only five levels can be determined, the maximum score should be five points. To use an inflated scale, for example twenty points, would add nothing to the measurement process and might encourage the teacher to make distinctions among papers that were not educationally meaningful. Generally, the average score for a question should be the middle score on the scale—for example, 3 on a 5-point scale—and marks should be distributed across the range. Since the numbers used have no absolute meaning, this process should not cause difficulties. An example of a useful process for grading themes is shown in Figure 4.3. Relative scoring does not often produce marks that are highly reliable or easily explained to students, and other methods are preferable when they can be used.

Analytical scoring may be used when the qualities of an outstanding answer can be described before the test is given. To use this system the teacher must list all the factors that will be graded and decide on the relative importance of each. The process of scoring requires determining for each paper how many of the factors are present and adding the points for those factors.

Analytical scoring adds a desirable measure of objectivity to the scoring of essay tests. When this system is used, questions must be stated clearly and completely so that examinees will know what is expected in the answer. Although students will develop answers in different ways, satisfactory answers on a test of useful knowledge and the application of knowledge will contain a large proportion of the same essential components. If teachers *know* what a question is supposed to measure, they should be able to delineate the factors of a complete answer and develop an analytical key to reflect these factors.

The following is an example of a question to be analytically scored:

> Listed below are some changes that could take place in the business activity of a community. For each change, assuming other factors are unchanged, you are to indicate the effect in the community on (a) unemployment, (b) job mobility, and (c) assessed evaluation of property. You should also describe in a brief paragraph why each change should occur, referring to the economic principle involved. You will receive one point for each change correctly described and a maximum of two points for a complete explanation of why the change could be predicted.

In this example each aspect of a perfectly acceptable answer can be anticipated and listed, and papers can be scored with relatively high precision. Even though the teacher may think the answers are so obvious that there is no need to develop a written key, it is

FIGURE 4.3

Procedure for grading themes*

Teachers often differ widely in their ratings of themes. An *A* in one class may be a *B* in another and a *C* in a third. The procedure described here has been used successfully by teachers to increase the reliability of theme grading. The following general distribution must be kept in mind:

Poor   to   Fair   to   Good   to   Very Good   to   Excellent

1	2	3	4	5	6	7	8
(about 15%)		(about 35%)		(about 35%)		(about 15%)	

In reading a theme, the evaluator first has to decide whether it belongs in the upper half (5-8) or the lower half (1-4). The next step is to decide in which quarter the paper belongs—for example, whether it belongs in the lowest quarter (1-2) or the one above (3-4). The third step requires deciding which of the two numerical values in one quarter applies best, for example, 1 or 2.

This procedure prevents the evaluator from giving the "average" grade, such as 5 on a 9-point scale. The practice of regressing toward the mean often occurs when an evaluator is grading a considerable number of papers. With this scale of rating, the evaluator has to determine whether a 4 or a 5 is more accurate for the average theme.

In evaluating a theme, both *content* and *mechanics* should be considered. Content includes the following: how convincingly the assigned topic is discussed, how well the central idea is supported, how well it is organized, how well unified, and how well expressed. Mechanics includes errors in spelling, punctuation, capitalization, grammar, and usage.

---

* Adapted from D. P. Scannell and O. M. Haugh, *Teaching Composition Skills with Weekly Multiple Choice Tests in Lieu of Theme Writing*, Project no. 6–8134 (Washington, D.C.: Department of Health, Education, and Welfare, Office of Education, Bureau of Research, 1968), p. 47.

FIGURE 4.3 (continued)

Procedure for grading themes*

A theme that receives a grade of 8 rates excellent in content and has few if any errors in mechanics. A theme ranked 7 similarly has few if any errors in mechanics but is not quite equal in content to one ranked 8. At the opposite end of the continuum, a rank of 1 denotes a theme that fails completely in both content and mechanics. One ranked 2 is not a complete failure, but it has serious weaknesses.

The two middle groups, 3-4 and 5-6, often present problems in differentiation. Of the two basic divisions, content is considered to be more important than mechanics. A paper would more likely be rated 6 than 5, or 4 than 3, if the content is better than the mechanics. Ordinarily, content and mechanics go hand in hand, but there are occasional papers which seem to be strong in one and weak in the other. If a teacher wants to translate the numerical rating to a letter grade, he could follow a pattern such as $8 = A$; $7 = A-$; $6 = B$; $5 = B-$; $4 = C$; $3 = C-$; $2 = D$; $1 = F$.

advisable to prepare the key and have it available for reference as the papers are being scored. These steps will help the teacher maintain constant standards.

An absolute scoring system is based on the assumption that the teacher "knows" what constitutes an exceptional, good, average, or poor answer, and that these qualities can be ascertained. If these assumptions are correct, a key can be made and analytical scoring can be used. When absolute scoring cannot be outlined precisely, the scoring may rest on hope more than on accurate assessment, and competent judges are not likely to agree closely on the scores.

Six Recommendations for Scoring Essay Tests

1. *Score papers one question at a time.* For example, the teacher should score all the answers to question number 1 before

scoring any answers to other questions. He should not score all the answers for one student and then move on to another student's paper. Maintaining constant standards is difficult under the most favorable conditions and virtually impossible when the teacher shifts from item to item. In scoring one item at a time, he has less to remember and can be more consistent in his evaluation. No increase in total scoring time need accompany the use of these procedures. This recommendation is most important for relative scoring but has merit even for analytical scoring.

2. *Minimize the opportunity to know who wrote the examination papers.* Irrelevant factors frequently influence the scores assigned to a paper, and steps should be taken to eliminate these sources of error. Student reputation is one factor: A teacher may be favorably disposed toward an answer he knows was written by an *A* student and severe in scoring a paper written by a *D* student.

Several methods can be used to conceal student identity. If the school uses student identification numbers, the teacher can direct examinees to write their number on the back of each page. Alternatively, he can pass a page around the class with a column of numbers ranging from 1 to the total number of examinees, directing students to write their name next to any unused number and then to put that number on the back of each examination page. After the tests are scored the teacher can use the page of student names and numbers to identify the author of each exam paper.

3. *If several factors are to be graded, evaluate them separately.* Some essay questions are marked in terms of different factors, such as accuracy, methods used, and correctness of expression. In such cases the accuracy of scoring will be improved if each factor is assessed and marked separately. This method will also have better feedback value for students than a global score would have.

4. *Ignore errors in the mechanics of expression while assessing the quality and accuracy of the answer's substance.* If grammar, spelling, and punctuation are included among the factors to be

assessed, they should be assessed separately. If such factors are not included, teachers should not allow them to detract from their assessment of the quality of the answer but should score the substance only and then call the examinees' attention to the mechanical errors. Recent research has shown that teachers' marks on essay exams are influenced by students' mechanical errors, particularly spelling, even when the teachers have been directed to assess only the substance of the answers. The average mark for a paper with errors has been found to be one half of a letter grade lower than the same substantive answer from which errors had been eliminated. These findings suggest the need for teachers to deliberately ignore mechanical errors that are irrelevant.

5. *Either have examinees start each answer on a fresh page or do not write scores on test papers until all the scoring is completed.* Since teachers may be influenced by the scores on previous answers, it is well to prevent this possibility.

6. *Shuffle test booklets after scoring each question.* The mark assigned to a paper may be affected by whether the paper is read early or late in the sequence and by the quality of the preceding answer. To avoid that possibility papers should be shuffled to vary their positions when different questions are being scored.

Essay tests are quite time-consuming for teachers and they have potential weaknesses. Care must be taken to develop questions that are specific, well defined, and capable of eliciting the desired achievement. Even more care must be taken in scoring answers. However, when steps are taken to avoid and minimize potential weaknesses, this versatile tool can provide measures that meet acceptable standards of accuracy and usefulness.

Summary

Among the types of tests requiring examinees to supply answers, three have utility for classroom use: the completion, short-answer, and essay tests. Items for all three types can be constructed in a relatively short time, and if care is taken to develop items that reflect a table of specifications, these tests can be useful tools in a classroom measurement program. The potential weaknesses of the three formats deserve careful attention, for it cannot be assumed that a test requiring examinees to supply answers is necessarily valid and useful. A classroom measurement program that is carefully developed, complete, and well-balanced usually comprises several different kinds of tests, including the completion, short-answer, and essay types.

Exercises

1. Revise the following completion items to eliminate their technical flaws:

   a. _____ is the tallest mountain in North America.

   b. The King of _____ at the time of the _____ Revolution was _____.

   c. The Law of Supply and Demand is from the field of _____.

   d. The state flower for Kansas is _____.

   e. A _____ is larger than a quart.

2. Construct five completion items in your teaching field that are free of technical flaws.

3. Revise the following short-answer items to eliminate their technical flaws.

   a. For what is Akron famous?

   b. In what field is the Law of Conservation of Matter important?

   c. What was the name of Johnny Tremain's horse?

   d. How is the cost of a product affected by the amount of the product on the market?

4. Either convert the completion items from exercise 2 into short-answer items or construct five different short-answer items.

5. How can an essay exam be developed to enhance the way it covers objectives and content well?

6. Develop a scoring procedure (including key) for the following essay exam question. What would you add to the question to describe the scoring procedure?

   In less than two pages describe the Peace Corps during its early years. Indicate the domestic and international factors that led to its establishment, and indicate how the program responded to these factors. The maximum score for this question is 10 points.

7. For a topic in your field develop one essay question that can be scored analytically, and construct the key for grading answers.

Suggested Readings

CHASE, C. I. "The Impact of Some Obvious Variables on Essay Test Scores." *Journal of Educational Measurement* 5 (1968): 315–318. *Report on a study on the effect of handwriting, spelling, and availability of a scoring key on scores for essay exams.*

COFFMAN, W. E. "Essay Examinations." *Educational Measurement*, 2d ed. Washington, D.C.: American Council on Education, 1971: pp. 271–302. *A thorough review of research and a scholarly consideration of the issues associated with the development and scoring of essay examinations.*

SCANNELL, D. P., and MARSHALL, J. C. "The Effect of Selected Composition Errors on Grades Assigned to Essay Examinations." *American Educational Research Journal* 3 (1966): 125–130. *Report on a study of effect of spelling, punctuation, and grammatical errors on the scoring of essay exams when graders are told to base grade on only the content of the answer.*

Chapter 5

TRUE-FALSE AND MATCHING ITEMS

As a result of studying this chapter, you should be able to:

1. *Develop acceptable true-false items to fit objectives.*
2. *Recognize technical flaws in true-false items.*
3. *Develop acceptable matching sets.*
4. *Recognize technical flaws in matching sets.*
5. *Recognize objectives in your own field (if any) for which true-false or matching items would be appropriate.*

True-false and matching test items that are properly written provide effective means of examining students' knowledge of terms, principles, generalizations, and other important facts. In some instances, true-false items especially can be adapted to test the ability to interpret, predict, and apply principles to the solution of problems. Both forms have the advantage of requiring very little space, and students can usually respond more rapidly to true-false items than to any other form.

True-False Items

In its basic form, the true-false item consists of a statement which examinees must judge to be either true or false. For example:

      T _F_   0. The present capital of the state of New York is
                 New York City.

Several variations of the true-false form are also possible. One form consists of questions which can be answered "yes" or "no." Since the variations do not differ essentially from the basic form, only the basic form will be considered here.

    The true-false item is quite compact, requiring little space on a test and a minimum of reading and response time by the examinee. Its compact form also eases the burden of the item writer because he can concentrate on the formulation of good true or false statements and need not worry about developing a set of alternatives, as in other choice forms. In addition, the true-false item shares with other choice-type items ease, speed, and objectivity of scoring.

Writing True-False Items

When writing any test item, the teacher should begin with the important objectives and content he wishes to test. This is especially true of true-false items, because unless the item writer keeps in mind the central purposes of instruction, the true-false form lends itself all too well to testing trivialities. The item writer should begin by identifying the objectives he wishes to test, and then proceed to develop items that will measure achievement of these facts and principles. For example, a basic principle in test theory is that the more items in a test, the higher the reliability coefficient of the test is expected to be. One could test for an objective calling for recognition of this principle as follows:

      _T_ F   0. Adding more items to a test is expected to in-
                 crease the reliability of the test.

If the objective called for application of the principle by recognizing situations in which reliability would be affected, the following item might be appropriate:

      T _F_   0. If the twenty items with the lowest positive
                 discrimination indexes were removed from a one

                hundred-item test, the reliability of the test
                would be expected to increase.

The first item would probably prove easier, because it merely restates the basic principle. The second item, which requires application of the principle in a novel situation, might appear plausible to the poorly prepared student because throwing out items with low discrimination indexes would seem to be an improvement in a test. Yet even items having low positive discrimination indexes would contribute slightly to the reliability of the test.

    Careful thought must be given to writing false statements. The teacher should not merely insert negatives in true statements to make them false, but should present misconceptions and misunderstandings of basic principles and facts. A good false statement should appeal to the common sense of the intelligent but misinformed examinee. The following would be a poor item:

    T _F_   0. George McGovern was not the nominee of the Democratic Party for President of the United States in 1972.

The examinee might easily misread this item, overlooking the "not," and decide that the item is true. It would be better to make a positive statement:

    T _F_   0. Hubert Humphrey was the nominee of the Democratic Party for President of the United States in 1972.

    True-false items can be adapted to form interpretive exercises by using a picture or bit of written material as a context within which the items may be judged true or false. For example, the following item might have been used in studying current affairs:

Directions Look at the cartoon in Figure 5.1. Judge whether each of the following statements is true or false as it applies to the cartoon.

    T _F_   1. The main figure represented in the cartoon is a former President of Brazil.

FIGURE 5.1

'I DON'T REMEMBER HIM LOOKING LIKE THIS SEVENTEEN YEARS AGO . . .'

T <u>F</u>   2. The artist who produced the cartoon is probably an admirer of Peron.

<u>T</u> F   3. The cartoon comments on the return of the main figure to his country after years of exile.

T <u>F</u>   4. The cartoon is a parody on Moses' crossing of the Red Sea.

The items in this exercise represent behaviors that range from merely knowing that Peron was the President of Argentina rather than Brazil to seeing that the cartoon is based on the second coming of Christ rather than Moses' crossing of the Red Sea. Test writers should be on the alert for materials in newspapers, magazines, or picture files that could serve as bases for test items.

The teacher should be cautious in using interpretive exercises, since they may place too much emphasis on a particular portion of the course content; but the interpretive exercise provides a structure and foundation for judging the truth or falsity of items apart from their absolute truth or falsity as independent statements.

The teacher should avoid writing items that are partly true and partly false because examinees may be confused about which part of the statement is to be judged true or false. This ambiguity occurs most often when compound or complex sentences are used as true-false items. For example:

T <u>F</u>   0. Houston is the location of the Manned Spacecraft Center and is the capital city of Texas.

This item is partly true and partly false, Houston is the location of the Manned Spacecraft Center, but Austin is the capital city of Texas. If both these pieces of information are important, it would be better to use two explicit items instead of one ambiguous item.

<u>T</u> F   0. The Manned Spacecraft Center is located in Houston, Texas.

T <u>F</u>   00. The capital city of the state of Texas is Houston.

A possible exception exists to this rule. Sometimes it is desirable for students to be able to recognize causes for events that are known to be true. True-false items can be written as compound or complex sentences if the part to be judged true or false is underlined and if students are instructed in advance that only the underlined part of the sentence is to be judged. For example:

T <u>F</u>   0. Cigarette smoking is believed by many scientists to be harmful to human health <u>because of the lead content of cigarette smoke.</u>

The student is not asked to judge the factuality of the first part of the sentence, only the reason given. The complex-sentence true-false item expands the usefulness of the true-false item type, but students must be carefully directed so that they are not confused by its somewhat unfamiliar form.

The teacher should avoid lifting sentences directly from textbooks or other sources and using them as true-false items. Such practice emphasizes rote memorization and often results in statements that are neither strictly true nor strictly false. One teacher used the following item after her class had viewed a film on pollution:

<u>T</u> F   0. Lead is the inexcusable pollutant.

This statement is not an absolute fact but a value judgment. The item could have been made strictly true by stating:

<u>T</u> F   0. The film we viewed on pollution stated that lead is the inexcusable pollutant.

Such an item would be trivial, however, as it is hardly important for students to remember the exact adjective used to describe lead. It would be better to write items which would test the students' knowledge of how lead pollution gets into the environment or how lead affects the environment. For example:

<u>T</u> F   0. One source of lead pollution in the atmosphere is exhaust fumes from automobiles.

T <u>F</u>   00. Lead pollution in automobile exhausts comes from the lead used in manufacturing automobile engines.

Words which have precise meanings are to be preferred in true-false statements. It is especially important to avoid vague adjectives—for example:

T F   0. In the four years from January 1, 1965, through December 31, 1968, many people died in the United States from influenza and pneumonia.

At first glance it might appear that indeed "many" persons must have died from influenza and pneumonia during those four years, but the actual rate was 32.4 per hundred thousand men and 21.2 per hundred thousand women. These figures represent 0.0324 percent of the men and 0.0212 percent of the women. These certainly are not large percentages and might cause an examinee to decide that the item is false. It would be better to write the item as follows:

<u>T</u> F   0. More than 57,000 persons died in the United States from influenza and pneumonia in the years from the beginning of 1965 through the end of 1968.

The teacher should take precautions to avoid using words such as "all," "never," "some," and "sometimes" in true-false items. The words "all" and "never" usually indicate that the item is false while the words "some" and "sometimes" usually indicate that the item is true. Experienced examinees recognize these words as clues to the correct answer.

It is generally not advisable to use negatives in true-false items because negatives, which are easily overlooked by examinees, tend to make answering difficult. For example:

T F   0. Pikes Peak is not the highest mountain in North America.

An examinee might respond to this item, "No, it is not," and mark F, or he might fail to read the "not" in the sentence and respond F. It would be better to use items like these:

T F   0. Mt. Whitney in California is higher than Pikes Peak.

or

T F   00. Pikes Peak is the highest mountain in North America.

Arranging True-False Items

True-false items can be answered on separate answer sheets or in test booklets. The teacher can obtain standard IBM answer sheets with provisions for true-false answers; he can make quite acceptable answer sheets with a typewriter and then reproduce them by mimeograph or some other means; or he can use standard answer sheets and instruct students to mark choice A or 1 for true, and B or 2 for false. If an answer sheet is not used, space for responses can be provided on a margin of the test booklet.

Whether separate answer sheets are used or not, instead of requiring examinees to write out their answer, the teacher should have them circle, cross out, or underline the correct choice. Avoiding a written response will facilitate scoring and eliminate the problem of reading student handwriting.

True and false statements should be arranged in a random pattern of responses. Research indicates that false items contribute somewhat more to the reliability of a test than true items, so slightly more false than true items should be used.

Some Criticisms of True-False Items

True-false items are open to two basic criticisms: (1) Since they must be judged unequivocally true or false, they encourage the testing of trivia; and (2) the average score for examinees who know nothing about the material being tested and who guess on every item would be expected to be half the number of items on the test.

The apparent ease of producing true-false items has led item writers to overemphasize verbal knowledge at the expense of other kinds of objectives, and they have used true-false items when other forms would have been more appropriate and effective. One common abuse has been to lift sentences directly from textbooks and use these as true-false items, inserting an occasional "not" or changing a word or two to make some items false. Such practices have the unfortunate consequence of emphasizing the rote memorization of the exact content of textbooks. Additionally, many statements from textbooks represent opinions of the authors or lose their absolute truth when removed from context because the necessary qualifying material has been dropped. Using good item-writing practices, adhering to educational objectives, and following a table of specifications can do much to eliminate trivia from true-false tests.

The second criticism is that an examinee has a 50 percent chance of answering a true-false item correctly, even when he knows nothing about it. Therefore true-false items tend to be low in reliability per item, and the value of true-false items as diagnostic indicators of what the student does or does not know tends to be low. True-false items are unlikely to be of much use in criterion-referenced tests where single items are supposed to indicate achievement or nonachievement of an objective, although several true-false items could be used for each objective. In any case, judging that a student had either attained or not attained an objective on the basis of a single item would be a questionable practice.

Some devices can be used to correct the susceptibility of true-false items to guessing. One method is to require the examinee to correct each statement he marks false—for example:

T <u>F</u>   0. The present capital of the state of New York is <u>New York City</u>.

          0. <u>*albany*</u>

The student who marks this item false must substitute for the underlined word the word or words that make the statement true. An objection to using this form is that it makes the item more difficult to score. Sometimes a short-answer or completion item would be better—for example:

          0. The present capital city of the state of New York is <u>*albany*</u>.

Another device for counteracting the high probability of guessing is special scoring of the responses. The simplest technique is to instruct the examinees that their scores will be the number of items answered correctly minus the number of items answered incorrectly, not counting omitted items:
Thus:

$$S = R - W.$$

where:

    S = score,
    R = the number of items answered correctly,
    W = the number of items answered incorrectly.

This is often referred to as the "correction for guessing" formula. Actually, the formula corrects for guessing only if examinees either absolutely know or absolutely do not know the correct answer to each item, and when they absolutely do not know the answer, they either omit the item or take a random guess. Seldom does this state of affairs exist. When being tested on material in which they have received instruction, well-motivated examinees are likely to respond to items on the basis of partial information or misinformation rather than no information at all. Therefore the "correction for guessing" formula may work to discourage examinees from guessing on items when they are not absolutely sure of their information. The more timid examinees may answer too few items, and bolder examinees may answer too many. The test-wise examinee knows that in the long run it makes no difference whether or not he guesses when he is completely unsure of the response, and that there is an advantage to making "educated" guesses when he is not absolutely sure but has some preference for one response over the other. Correction for guessing may actually work to the advantage of test-wise examinees by revealing differences in test-wiseness and willingness to take a chance rather than in achievement. Other arguments against using the "correction for guessing" device include the additional effort required to score examinations, the increased chance of errors in scoring, and the fact that the practice changes the magnitude of examinees' scores but seldom changes the rank order of those scores significantly.

Various other schemes have been proposed to counteract wild guessing on true-false items—for example, the examinee may be required not only to indicate whether the item is true or false but how confident he is that his answer is correct. A system of weights is then used which gives the greatest number of points to correct answers in which the student expresses the highest confidence, and exacts the greatest penalty for incorrect answers in which the student expresses high confidence. Such a system operates on the theory that it is better for the student to know when he lacks correct information than to hold misconceptions unknowingly.

Systems that require students to rate confidence in the correctness of their response add to the complexity of the true-false item. The mere mechanics of responding to such items demands a test-taking sophistication not required by the basic true-false item. In addition, such items may add an unwanted dimension to an achievement test—that is, they may measure self-confidence as well as actual achievement. Some examinees who are naturally less confident than others may be penalized by an item form that asks them to express their degree of confidence in their answer.

The problem of guessing in true-false tests can be countered best by careful item-writing and by making the tests rather lengthy. These practices should result in more reliable tests and in better coverage of course objectives. Then the effect of chance on a true-false test score may be even less than on an essay test, which would require the same amount of testing time, because of the difficulty of scoring essay tests accurately.

True-false tests are often compared unfavorably with multiple-choice tests because true-false tests are more susceptible to guessing and multiple-choice tests are more reliable per item. R. L. Ebel has shown, however, that although true-false items as individual items may have poorer characteristics than multiple-choice items, half again as many true-false items can be answered by an examinee in the same period of time. The larger number of items will result therefore in a test of about the same reliability for the same amount of testing time.[1]

Matching Items

Matching items are usually presented as a set of terms, names, incomplete statements, phrases, or definitions called *stimuli*, which are placed on the left side of the page, and a set of names, terms, definitions, or pictures called *responses*, which are placed on the right side of the page. Responses are to be matched to stimuli on a specified basis. In Figure 5.2, states are the stimuli and capital cities are the responses.

Matching items provide a very compact means of testing a number of concepts simultaneously. In Figure 5.2, for example, very little space is required to test the ability to identify seven state capitals. Matching items are useful to test student knowledge of definitions, ability to identify objects presented graphically in diagrams or pictorially and ability to translate ideas from one language or set of terms into another.

---

[1] R. L. Ebel, "Can Classroom Teachers Write Good True-False Items?" (Abstract of paper delivered to the National Council on Measurement in Education, April 1974), *NCME Measurement News* 17 (1974): 7.

FIGURE 5.2
_____

A matching exercise

Directions Match the appropriate capital city with each state by placing the letter corresponding to the city in the blank by the state.

State	Capital city
_F_ 1. California	A. Albany
_H_ 2. Florida	B. Columbus
_G_ 3. Illinois	C. Jefferson City
_I_ 4. Kansas	D. Lexington
_C_ 5. Missouri	E. Los Angeles
_A_ 6. New York	F. Sacramento
_B_ 7. Ohio	G. Springfield
	H. Tallahassee
	I. Topeka

Writing Matching Items

Matching items, like other item types, should fit the table of specifications for the test as a whole. Because of their compactness and their presentation as a set of several items, it is tempting to produce too many matching items for a single objective and to overemphasize that objective. Therefore particularly careful attention should be paid to the table of specifications.

Once objectives and content are identified for the matching set, stimuli and response can be written. Care should be taken to make the stimuli and responses homogeneous in content. Matching sets that cover a wide variety of topics—for example, names of persons, dates, and events—often stray from the original objectives. In addition, heterogeneous stimuli and responses often result in items that are unintentionally easy because effective *distractors*, plausible wrong responses, are not available for all stimuli. If there are no plausible but incorrect responses for a stimulus, the correct response will be obvious to an experienced

FIGURE 5.3
___

A heterogeneous matching set

Stimulus	Response
_D_ 1. acromegaly	A. caused by insufficient so-matotropin
_E_ 2. adrenal gland	B. located at the base of the brain
_A_ 3. dwarfism	C. lack of this hormone may result in tetany
_C_ 4. parathormone	D. overdevelopment of the facial bones and extremities
_B_ 5. pituitary gland	E. produces hydrocortisone

student, whether he is informed or not. In the heterogeneous matching set shown in Figure 5.3, there are no effective distractors for item 4, as parathormone is the only hormone in the list. Although acromegaly and dwarfism are both caused by malfunction of the pituitary, the choices do not really require the student to distinguish between the causes of the two conditions because response A deals with a cause and response D describes symptoms of a disease. Likewise, the responses for stimuli 2 and 5, adrenal and pituitary, are heterogeneous because response B is the location of a gland while response E is the function of a gland. A more homogeneous matching set is shown in Figure 5.4. In this set specific diseases or conditions are matched with corresponding hormone imbalances. Each response acts to some degree as a distractor for each stimulus.

It is helpful to the student and test writer to label each set of stimuli and responses as shown in Figure 5.4. Labels help the examinee understand his task by clarifying the basis for matching and help insure the homogeneity of the stimulus and response sets. If the test constructor cannot think of labels which describe all the stimuli and responses in the matching set, the stimuli or responses are probably too heterogeneous.

FIGURE 5.4

A homogeneous matching set

Directions Match the appropriate hormone imbalance with each disease by placing the letter corresponding to the imbalance in the blank by the disease.

Disease	Hormone imbalance
E 1. acromegaly	A. hydrocortisone insufficiency
A 2. Addison's disease	B. hydrocortisone oversupply
G 3. Cretinism	C. insulin insufficiency
C 4. diabetes mellitus	D. parathormone insufficiency
E 5. dwarfism	E. somatotropin insufficiency
H 6. exophthalmic goiter	F. somatotropin oversupply
	G. thyroid insufficiency
	H. thyroid oversupply

Each matching set should be kept relatively short because extremely long sets of matching items require the examinee to spend too much time in searching for the correct answer. A matching set should be limited to a single page to spare examinees the confusion of going from page to page looking for the correct response. A very long matching set will place too much emphasis on the particular objectives to be measured by the matching set relative to other equally important objectives and may upset the balance of the test plan. In addition, extremely long matching sets are likely to be heterogeneous.

Matching sets should contain plausible incorrect responses for every stimulus so that poorly prepared examinees will not be able to identify the correct response just because it is the only one with any plausibility or appeal to common sense. If the correct answer is obvious to the uninformed and the informed examinee alike, the item is worthless in deciding which examinees have achieved the course objectives. For each stimulus there should be at least one distractor in addition to the correct response, and homogeneity of matching sets is an aid in insuring a sufficient number of distractors.

It is good practice to include more responses than stimuli, as in Figure 5.4. This will prevent an examinee who knows all but one of the correct responses from getting that one through a process of elimination. In addition, the extra responses give the opportunity to include a greater number of effective distractors and thus provide more plausible incorrect responses for uninformed examinees.

It is also possible to write matching sets which include some responses that may be used more than once. This technique makes the matching item similar to the key list form of the multiple-choice item, which is described in the next chapter. If some responses may be used more than once, directions should emphasize this fact, for most students are accustomed to matching sets in which each response is used only once. Figure 5.5 is an example of a matching set that allows some responses to be used

FIGURE 5.5

A matching set with reusable responses

Directions In the blank before the number of each invention, write the letter corresponding to the name of the person who invented it. Some inventors' names may be used more than once.

Invention	Inventor
_H_ 1. cotton gin	A. George W. Carver
_C_ 2. electric light bulb	B. Samuel Colt
_C_ 3. phonograph	C. Thomas A. Edison
_B_ 4. revolver	D. Robert Fulton
_F_ 5. sewing machine	E. Benjamin Franklin
_D_ 6. steamboat	F. Elias Howe
	G. Hiram P. Maxim
	H. Eli Whitney

more than once. It would be helpful for the teacher to supplement the written instructions for such sets with oral directions to the examinees to make sure they understand that a response may be used more than once.

Matching items are best suited for the measurement of knowledge, but the measurement of some higher order outcomes with matching items is not impossible. The matching set in Figure 5.6, for example, calls for the ability to make the logical connection between an hypothesis and the data that support the hypothesis.

FIGURE 5.6

A matching set calling for connecting data with hypotheses

Directions In the blank before the number of each datum, write the letter of the hypothesis which tends to be supported by the datum. Some hypotheses may be used more than once.

	Data		Hypotheses
_E_	1. The correlation between the IQ scores of identical twins raised apart is higher than the correlation between the IQ scores of fraternal twins raised in the same family.	A.	Some mental abilities tend to increase after age twenty.
		B.	IQ scores are highly predictive of grades in school.
_C_	2. The correlation between scores on the Stanford-Binet test and scores on the Torrance test is about .00 for a group of children with above-average IQs.	C.	Creativity is essentially unrelated to intelligence.
		D.	High IQ children are low in creativity.

_F_ 3. Tenth-grade black children whose families moved from a rural area to a certain city before the children entered school make higher average IQ scores than do tenth-grade black children in the same city whose families moved to the city after they had entered school.

_E_ 4. The correlation between IQ scores of adopted children and IQ scores of their natural mothers is higher than the correlation between the IQ scores of the same children and the IQ scores of their adoptive mothers.

_A_ 5. Scores on tests of information tend to be slightly higher for groups of forty-year-olds than for groups of fifteen-year-olds.

E. Intelligence is primarily an inherited trait.

F. Intelligence is developed primarily through environmental influences.

G. Creativity is essentially a type of intelligence.

H. IQ tends to decrease with age.

Arranging Matching Items

Traditionally, matching sets have required examinees to indicate their responses by writing in the letter of the response by hand.

The use of most standard machine-scored answer sheets is pre-cluded because most matching sets contain more than five re-sponses, but it would be possible to make separate answer sheets for matching items. An answer sheet for the matching set in Figure 5.5 could be constructed as follows:

1. A	B	C	D	E	F	G	H
2. A	B	C	D	E	F	G	H
3. A	B	C	D	E	F	G	H
4. A	B	C	D	E	F	G	H
5. A	B	C	D	E	F	G	H
6. A	B	C	D	E	F	G	H

With this type of answer sheet examinees could underline, circle, or cross out the letter of the correct response. Scoring would be speeded, and there would be no problems caused by undeciphera-ble handwriting.

Various procedures are possible for ordering the stimuli and responses in sets of matching items. In general, the test writer should strive to avoid arrangements that will give uninformed but experienced examinees a clue to the correct response. A random order of stimuli and responses would be effective, but short stimuli or responses can be arranged in alphabetical order, as has been done in some of the examples in this chapter. Numerical responses such as dates should be arranged from smallest to largest. Such logical arrangements avoid presenting irrelevant clues to the cor-rect response, make responses easier to locate, and shorten the examinees' working time. Clear directions should precede each matching set, and each column of stimuli and responses should be labeled.

The effect of guessing on matching items is difficult to deter-mine because each stimulus probably has a different set of incor-rect responses which function as distractors. The contribution of matching items to good test reliability is probably more a function of the quality of the matching sets than of the item form.

Summary

True-false and matching items provide a compact and easy-to-score means of testing for many important educational objectives. Although they are not so flexible as multiple-choice items, they may be adapted to a variety of testing situations. Care in correlating true-false and matching items with the table of specifications and careful construction of the items will avoid the pitfalls sometimes associated with these item forms.

Both the true-false and matching forms are probably most useful for the measurement of knowledge, but an ingenious item writer can measure some higher level objectives, especially with the true-false item.

Exercises

. Choose at least three course objectives in your own field and write at least one true and one false item appropriate to each, or write one true and one false item appropriate to each of the following objectives:

a. The student can identify the function of the parts of a flower.

b. The student can distinguish among conduction, convection, and radiation of heat.

c. The student can make predictions using the law of supply and demand.

. Identify the fault in each of the following items.

a. T   F   Toads are not reptiles.

b. T   F   Mt. McKinley, which is located in California, is the highest mountain in North America.

c. T   F   Every child in the United States has access to television.

d. T   F   There are five rules to follow in writing true-false items.

3. Choose at least two course objectives from your own field or a field of interest and construct a set of matching items to fit each objective, or construct a matching set for each of the objectives below.

   a. The student can identify the function of the organs and glands in the body.

   b. The student can identify the function of essential vitamins.

4. Identify the faults in the following matching set.

__D__	1. blood	A.	vitamin K
__A__	2. necessary for the clotting of blood	B.	is about twenty feet long
__E__	3. plasma	C.	pulmonary vein
__C__	4. carries blood from the lungs to the heart	D.	tissue that carries oxygen to all parts of the body
__B__	5. small intestine	E.	the liquid part of the blood

5. What objectives in your own field could be measured by true-false items?

6. What objectives in your own field could be measured by matching items?

7. Obtain from a teacher a test in a field you know something about containing true-false and/or matching items (or use an old test of your own), identify the item flaws, if any, and restate the faulty items.

Suggested Readings

EBEL, R. L. *Essentials of Educational Measurement.* Englewood Cliffs N.J.: Prentice-Hall, 1972. *Chapter 7 discusses true-false items and correction for guessing.*

FRISBIE, D. A. "Multiple Choice Versus True-False: A Comparison of Reliabilities and Concurrent Validities." *Journal of Educational Measurement* 10 (1973): 297–304. *This study indicates that true-false tests are less reliable than multiple-choice tests for the same amount of testing time; but students can answer more true-false items in the same time and thus more topics may be covered. True-false tests and multiple-choice tests developed from the same table of specifications can measure essentially the same things.*

WESMAN, A. G. "Writing the Test Item." *Educational Measurement*, 2d ed., Edited by R. L. Thorndike. Washington, D.C.: American Council on Education, 1971: pp. 81–129. *This chapter covers a wide variety of test items, including true-false and matching.*

Chapter 6

MULTIPLE-CHOICE TESTS

As a result of studying this chapter you should be able to:

1. *Recognize and correct technical faults in multiple-choice items.*

2. *Construct multiple-choice items that are free of technical flaws and that reflect instructional objectives in your teaching field.*

3. *Construct key-list and interpretive exercises for topics from your teaching field.*

4. *Describe your reasons for deciding to use or not use an answer sheet for multiple-choice exams in your teaching field.*

5. *Develop a cover sheet, including directions, for a multiple-choice test in your field.*

One of the most versatile and useful assessment tools for teachers is the multiple-choice test. Extremely popular during its early years, this form fell into disfavor in the 1930s as part of a large-scale reaction to tests that emphasized the superficial aspects of educational goals to the neglect of more complex aspects of achievement. After further study of the form as well as developmental efforts by people who believed that multiple-choice tests could reflect important instructional goals, popularity was slowly restored; the form is widely used today both by classroom teachers and in large-scale testing programs which require measurement of important achievements, reliable scores, and high-speed scoring.

A multiple-choice item consists of a stem in the form of a question or incomplete statement followed by a series of possible responses, one of which is correct or clearly better than the other options. Multiple-choice items can measure verbal-level achievement, such as knowledge of dates, names, and symbols, understanding of concepts and principles, the application of formulas, concepts, and principles, and nearly all other achievements that can be measured by paper and pencil tests. The following items illustrate a few of the types of achievement that can be measured with multiple-choice tests.

1. Knowledge of a date

   In what year was California admitted as a state to the Union?

      a. 1845
     *b. 1850
      c. 1855
      d. 1860

2. Knowledge of a fact

   Through which country does the Tropic of Cancer pass?

      a. United States
      b. Brazil
      c. Canada
     *d. Mexico
      e. Argentina

3. Application of a principle

   In which location would water in an open pan boil at the lowest temperature?

      a. On the seacoast of southern California
      b. In a coal mine shaft
      c. In Death Valley, California
     *d. At the top of Mount Rainier
      e. In the Florida everglades

4. Solution of a problem

What is the area of a circle with a 12-inch diameter? (To the nearest tenth of a square inch.)

    a. 18.8
    b. 37.7
  *c. 113.0
    d. 452.2
    e. not given

5. Solution of a problem

When the following equation is balanced, what is the coefficient for HCl?

$$HCl + Ca(OH)_2 \rightleftharpoons CaCl_2 + H_2O$$

    a. 0
    b. 1
  *c. 2
    d. 3
    e. 4

6. Interpretation

In which of the following ways would a *caricature* most likely be used?

    a. To illustrate a high school biology book
  *b. To accompany a political article in a newspaper
    c. To show an example of a great work of art
    d. To diagram the way to install a home appliance
    e. To portray a famous historical event that was not photographed.

7. Interpretation

For a person who believed in respecting and upholding the law, which of the following actions would be *least* consistent with his belief?

    a. Voting against a legislator who proposed a bill the individual opposed

   b. Not voting in an election because he disliked
      all candidates
   c. Publicly disagreeing with a Supreme Court rul-
      ing
  *d. Not buying a required dog license because his
      neighbors did not buy dog licenses
   e. Campaigning for a candidate with views similar
      to his own

8. Translation of a term

   Which statement best illustrates the implication of the
   term, "an interdependent world"?
   a. Most countries are self-governed.
   b. Most countries belong to an international
      organization.
   c. Many newspapers have an international dis-
      tribution.
   d. Rights and freedoms are the same for people in
      different countries.
  *e. Other countries are affected by events within
      one country.

9. Application of a rule

   A procedure requires a student to square a given number
   and then subtract 2. If the number given is 3, what is the
   result?
   a. 0
   b. 1
   c. 2
  *d. 7
   e. none of the above

   As in other forms of testing, the value and quality of an item
depend largely on the teacher's ability to identify important
achievements and on his ingenuity in creating items that will
measure the achievement. A test plan will call attention to general
areas of importance, but for each cell of the table of specifications

the teacher must identify topics that are relevant *and* important. These topics, then, must be cast into items that challenge the knowledge and understanding of students.

Writing Multiple-Choice Items

Three parts of a multiple-choice item contribute to its effectiveness in measuring the achievement of interest in a useful form. An item comprises a stem, a correct answer, and distractors (incorrect responses), each of which will be considered separately.

Item Stems

An *item stem* can be either a question or an incomplete statement, but in both cases the function of the stem is to present the task, to structure for the examinee the achievement that is to be measured. The stem should contain a complete idea in precise and specific terms. After reading the stem an examinee should know what material he needs to recall and consider in order to select the answer.

One of the most important characteristics of an item stem is the reality or naturalness it represents. Questions included on tests should require a knowledge or application that would naturally occur; they should *not* represent an artificial or contrived request for knowledge. For example, for a student to understand how the history of California fits into the flow of United States history, it would be more natural for him to need the knowledge of the date when California was admitted to the Union than to need to identify which state was admitted in 1850. Although there are frequently several ways to test a given idea, the principle to follow is to ask a question that derives from the instructional goals.

Five Suggestions for Developing Item Stems

1. *The stem should pose a problem.*   All too often stems do not include a complete idea and as a result do not define a task for examinees. This happens most frequently when the stem is an incomplete statement—for example:

The Empire State Building
    *a. is 102 stories tall.
    b. was completed in 1917.
    c. is primarily an apartment building.
    d. is located in Chicago.
    e. has the most modern elevators in the world.

The stem in this example asks essentially what is true about the Empire State Building. To use multiple-choice items in this way is to waste the potential value of the items for testing examinee ability to make a useful discrimination. If the knowledge of interest in this item really concerns the height of the building, the stem should call attention to that fact and all the responses should be heights—for example:

How many stories tall is the Empire State Building?
    a. 25
    b. 57
    c. 72
    *d. 102
    e. 114

Incomplete stems can contain a complete idea and in some cases are preferable to questions, particularly when ease of expression and economy of words can be realized. Consider the item:

Which statement best characterizes the first Secretary of the Treasury of the United States?
    *a. A man who wanted a strong central government
    b. A man who remained loyal to England
    c. A man who believed in equality of all people
    d. A man who worked hard to abolish slavery
    e. A man who was born in France

Note the economy when the item is rewritten with an incomplete stem:

The first Secretary of the Treasury of the United States can be described as a man who
    *a. wanted a strong central government.
    b. remained loyal to England.

    c. believed in equality of all people.

    d. worked hard to abolish slavery.

    e. was born in France.

As already noted, a common but unnecessary characteristic of incomplete stems is the lack of a precise task. This problem can be avoided by insuring that the examinee can know after reading the stem the nature of the information needed to answer the question. A second potential weakness of items with incomplete stems is the lack of parallel responses, resulting in some being either grammatically or logically untenable. This topic will be covered in more detail in the discussion of responses.

    2. *Narrowly focused stems help measure examinee understanding.* An earlier example showed an item that was essentially a series of true-false statements. Another, better example, was concerned with a description of the first Secretary of the Treasury; but this item also would test fairly superficial achievement. The responses concern different characteristics, and no great depth of knowledge about the man would be needed to identify the correct answer. Although this type of approach might be appropriate for some purposes, multiple-choice items can be constructed to measure deeper examinee understanding by focusing the stem on a narrower topic or task. For example, the last example given could be altered to:

> Which statement best describes Alexander Hamilton's attitude toward the relative strength which federal and state governments should have?

Then the responses would embody different statements of relative strength for federal and state government. By including in the stem a precise topic that the item covers, greater depth of achievement can be measured.

    3. *Use the terms "why" and "how" rather than "who," "when," and "where."* The last three words suggest items that cover knowledge of names, dates, and places. Although such achievements may be important, many educational goals relate to understanding and the ability to make appropriate use of knowledge. The approaches that include "why does something happen"

and "how can or should something be done" require understanding and application of knowledge.

4. *Do not use definitions as stems.*   The approach that presents a definition and asks for the term it defines is contrived, unnatural, and does not measure a useful achievement. It is far better to give the term in the stem and present alternative descriptions or definitions as responses. Compare the following items:

What is the term for birds moving from one region to another?
      a. immigration
      b. nesting
      c. reproduction
   *d. migration
      e. escalation

What statement describes the process of migration?
      a. invasion of a bird's territory by another species
      b. the process of building a nest
      c. continuation of a species
   *d. movement from one region to another
      e. increasing the level of activity

5. *Do not quote textbook or instructional material.*   Quoting textbooks promotes superficial learning, for the ability to recite or recognize facts as they have been learned does not guarantee the ability to select and apply ideas. Novel test situations, on the other hand, encourage students to understand and integrate the knowledge they have acquired. If examinees have learned material in a useful form, they should be capable of dealing with the content in a new setting.

Keyed Responses

After the stem for an item has been composed, the teacher should develop the *keyed response,* the correct or best answer. Then the other responses, called distractors or foils, should be written. There are at least two reasons for this sequence. First, the test author should be sure that the stem admits to a brief but clearly satisfactory answer; frequently stems need to be modified. Second, the difficulty of an item is affected by the extent to which distractors are written for the purpose of complementing the keyed response.

The purpose of the keyed response in a multiple-choice item is to provide a clear, precise response to the question or task presented in the stem. The keyed response should be the best of the alternatives in the opinion of subject experts in the field, as well as the one most likely to be selected by high achieving students in the class.

Some test items admit to only one response. For example, the question, "In what year was the Battle of Hastings fought?" would require 1066 as the answer. This type of item·has a "correct" answer. Some of the most important learning achievements, however, relate to student ability to discriminate among a number of choices, some of which are tenable but do not contain the most complete or satisfactory response to the question. The best conceivable answer to a question about the meaning of an IQ might require writing a paragraph or even a book, but if the answer provided for the question is acceptable and better than other choices, the item can function validly in measuring achievement. The type of item that does not have only one possible answer is referred to as a "best" answer item.

Four Suggestions for Writing Keyed Responses

1. *Avoid quoting or paraphrasing learning materials.*   Point 5 in the preceding section makes this suggestion in reference to stems, and it is even more important for keyed responses. At a bare minimum, students should be capable of translating concepts and facts into a new form of expression. Useful achievement should always be the focus of tests, and items should ask students to look forward to the use of information, not backward to the learning experience.

2. *Keyed responses should be grammatically and logically consistent with the stem.*   Examinees are susceptible to clues whether they are given intentionally or not, and some examinees

will avoid a misleading response even if they are capable of answering the question correctly. For example, if the question asks for an economic factor, the keyed response must present just that, an economic factor, and not something else, such as a business transaction. If the stem calls for a personality trait of a character in a novel, the keyed response should not describe a physical characteristic, an action by the character, or anything other than a personality trait. Careful editing should eliminate such inconsistencies.

3. *Keyed responses should appear with equal frequency in all response positions.*   Chance should determine the placement of the keyed response in all items which do not require a logical or numerical sequence. Many teachers tend to place the keyed response in a particular position, such as the third position, response *C*. Many teachers unconsciously avoid putting the keyed response in the first or last position. This problem can be avoided by throwing a die, drawing a numbered disc from a hat, or using any other method that allows chance to operate.

A logical sequence should be followed when one is apparent; for example, if an item stem asks for a comparison between two approaches to some task, the responses might be:

a. more than
b. equal to
c. less than
d. insufficient data given to make a comparison

The first three responses could also be presented in reverse order. Another example of an item that suggests a logical sequence of responses is one that asks a question with a "yes" or "no" response combined with an explanation. In such items, the "yes" and "no," responses should be adjacent.

> If the temperature of a saturated solution of ammonia is increased, will more gaseous ammonia dissolve in the solution? Why?
>
>> a. Yes, solubility increases as temperatures increase.

    b. Yes, molecular action of cases increases as temperature increases.

    c. No, volume of the solution will decrease as the temperature increases.

  *d. No, ammonia is more soluble at low solution temperatures.

When responses are single words, an alphabetical approach can be used to randomize the position of the keyed response—for example:

Which of the following countries has the greatest population concentration per square mile?

    a. France
  *b. Netherlands
    c. Norway
    d. Spain
    e. West Germany

4. *Use "none of the above" and "all of the above" only with correct-answer items.* There is a logical inconsistency in an item which calls for the best of a set of responses—for example, the best description of a person or event—and then presents "none" or "all of the above" as a response. This type of keyed response is indefensible.

The "all" or "none" response can be keyed in a correct-answer item, although this should be done sparingly. Research suggests that items with these keyed responses are more difficult than the same items giving a substantive correct answer, perhaps because examinees recognize that teachers tend to use these responses as fillers when they have difficulty in developing a reasonable substantive response.

Distractors

The responses to a multiple-choice item which are not keyed as correct or best are commonly called distractors or foils. Distractors play a major role in determining the effectiveness and difficulty of an item. Their purpose is to provide attractive, reasonable responses for examinees who are misinformed or who lack the required achievement to identify the correct or best response. The complement of this is obvious: students who have made the required achievement should be capable of rejecting distractors on some basis related to the goals of the course.

Distractors should be constructed from misinformation that poorly prepared students might have or conclusions that might be reached by the inappropriate use of knowledge. Distractors should *not* be slightly modified correct statements or be based on false clues that could attract well-prepared examinees. Well-conceived stems, good keyed responses, and attractive but incorrect distractors complement one another in making multiple-choice items valid and challenging intellectual tasks.

Five Suggestions for Developing Distractors

1. *Either three or four tenable distractors should be used in each item.* On any choice-type test examinees can select the keyed response on some items by chance. This is a fact that should be recognized in constructing choice tests and in interpreting test results. On a test which uses four-choice items—that is, a test with three distractors—an examinee who blindly selects a response to an item has one chance in four of choosing the keyed response. If the examinee responds randomly to all items, his expected score, the chance score, is one fourth of the number of items on the test. Similarly, the chance score on a test that comprises five-choice items is 20 percent of the number of items on the test. Choice tests should be developed so that all students who have made reasonable achievement will receive scores well above the chance score. Tests with 20- or 25-percent chance scores leave an ample range for the distribution of scores from the lowest achieving to the highest achieving students. The effective range for three- and two-choice tests is severely restricted, however. It is essential that tests be long enough to provide a desirable range for the distribution of achievers' scores.

Although there is no hard and fast rule that all items on a given test should have the same number of responses, it is good practice to be consistent. Examinees establish a mind set, and variation from four to five, or even three, responses can be unnecessarily distracting. Teachers who devote sufficient time to test construction can produce the number of responses needed for each item.

2. *Distractors should be similar in length, parallel in construction, and equally precise in expression.* Distractors and keyed responses should be indistinguishable with regard to their physical and grammatical appearance. Care should be taken to avoid characteristics that will allow poorly prepared students to eliminate distractors on some basis other than achievement. For example, if a stem requires a plural answer, singular responses can be eliminated automatically. With incomplete stems, a response that does not complete the sentence can be eliminated. If a stem points to a concise correct answer and all the distractors are lengthy, a clue is given to the student. Again, if only one response is stated as technically or precisely as the stem, a clue is presented.

In the following item, two responses can be eliminated because they are not physical characteristics, as required by the stem:

Which physical characteristic described President Abraham Lincoln?

    *a. tall and slender
    b. blond and heavy set
    c. kind and gentle
    d. modest and conservative dresser

The keyed response in the following item stands out among the responses because all the distractors are much longer than the correct answer.

The term migration is most often applied to

    a. animals that sleep through the winter.
    b. animals that live in groups or packs.
    c. people who move frequently.
    *d. birds.

In the following item two of the responses can be eliminated because they are in the plural and the stem requires a singular response:

> The person in the federal government who has the power of veto is
>
>> a. the Supreme Court Justices.
>> b. the Secretary of State.
>> c. the presiding officers of the House and Senate.
>> *d. the President.

When examinees can eliminate some responses on the basis of irrelevance, the amount of achievement needed to identify the keyed response is reduced and the quality of the test is compromised.

3. *Construct distractors from common misinformation and feasible but erroneous conclusions.* When a student who has made the achievement measured by an item has considered the item, he should be able to identify the keyed response. Conversely, a student who is completely lacking in the achievement should not be able to eliminate any of the responses. To realize these idealistic goals the keyed response must be precise and unambiguous, and each distractor must represent a possible answer.

The positions between these two extremes include items for which even highly qualified students are unsure of the answer. On some items an achieving student will arrive at the answer by the process of elimination—that is, he can reject some responses by applying his knowledge. This challenge is quite similar to the "real life" situation in which an individual must select the most tenable option from several that are possible, not knowing which will turn out to be best.

Consider the item:

> In what year was California admitted to the Union?
>
>> a. 1650
>> b. 1776

      *c. 1850
       d. 1910
       e. 1920

An examinee can select the correct answer to this item by one of several processes. He can know the date, eliminate the distractors, or guess successfully. A student with even a superficial knowledge of American history could eliminate the distractors easily because they are untenable. Other distractors, 1830,1840,1860, and 1870, would be more tenable and would function as reasonable alternatives for examinees who know a little but not enough history. Of course, the distractors 1848, 1849, 1851, and 1852 would be even more tenable because they require precise information on the part of the examinee.

In most classroom tests the emphasis is on comprehension and application of information, and the distractors must be based on misconceptions. Usually teachers know what these misconceptions are and can construct distractors to reflect them. Consider the following item:

> If removal of the pituitary gland of a small animal reduced thyroid gland secretion, what conclusion may be drawn about the effect of the pituitary gland?
>
>   a. It probably affects all endocrine glands.
>   b. It controls thyroid gland secretion in all animals.
>   *c. It may affect thyroid secretion in similar animals.
>   d. It is the master endocrine gland.

The distractors in this item are related to erroneous conclusions that ill-prepared examinees might reach, and none of them could be eliminated by nonachievers.

    4. *Distractors should not overlap each other or the keyed response, either semantically or numerically.* The error implied by this suggestion is illustrated in the following items:

> Where is Oslo located?
>   a. north of the Arctic Circle
>   *b. north of the Tropic of Cancer

c. north of the Equator
d. south of the Equator
e. south of the Tropic of Capricorn

The distance from Los Angeles to New York is more than
a. 1,000 miles.
b. 2,000 miles.
*c. 3,000 miles.
d. 4,000 miles.
e. 5,000 miles.

In the first example, *b* and *c* are both correct even though the test
author intended *b* to be the keyed response. This item might
frustrate examinees and reduce their confidence in the test. In the
second item the problem could be eliminated by changing "more
than" to "approximately"; as the item stands, responses *a*, *b*, and *c*
are all correct.

Whenever one response includes another, an undesirable
situation is created. When the correct answer is included in the
overlap, the item is invalidated. When two distractors overlap, the
perceptive examinee will eliminate both on the ground that
neither one could be the keyed response. The problem of overlap
can be eliminated by the careful editing of items. The teacher who
re-reads a test several days after composing it will be able to detect
the problem if it exists and correct it.

5. *Modify distractors to control item difficulty.*   The difficulty
of an item is due partly to the concept covered and partly to the
relative heterogeneity of the responses. As a general principle, the
more alike responses are, numerically or conceptually, the more
difficult an item will be. The earlier example concerning the date
of statehood for California on page 134 illustrates this point. When
the responses are as diverse as in that example, relatively little
achievement is required for an examinee to select the correct
answer. When the responses are made more homogeneous and
therefore more tenable, the difficulty of the item increases.

Many examples of this principle are available in all subject matter fields. On a literature test containing questions concerned with character development, an item can be made more difficult by presenting distractors that are only slightly less descriptive than the keyed response. Conversely, these items can be made less difficult by using distractors that are quite inaccurate descriptions. Would many students who have read Dickens select "kindly, humorous, and good natured" as a description of Scrooge?

Ability to master this principle and use it effectively is central to the construction of a challenging and valid multiple-choice test. The principle applies particularly to tests designed to measure understanding and the ability to apply generalizations.

Variations of Multiple-Choice Tests

Key List Items

A useful variation of the multiple-choice format, one which includes some elements of matching items, is called a *key list* exercise. This approach employs a key or list of responses that is to be used with a series of questions. Here is an example:

In answering items 1 to 3 you are to use the following key. For each item select the letter for the one statistic which satisfies the statement made.
  a. arithmetic mean
  b. standard deviation
  c. correlation coefficient
  d. semi-interquartile range
  e. T-scores

1. If ten points were added to each score of a set, the value for the statistic would be increased by ten.
2. If the lowest score were decreased by five points, the size of the index would increase.
3. This statistic can be found from two points in the distribution.

The second example uses a slightly different approach.

In answering items 4 to 10 you are to use the following key. For each item select the letter for the author of the work listed.

    a. Washington Irving
    b. Edgar Allen Poe
    c. James Fenimore Cooper
    d. Nathaniel Hawthorne
    e. Herman Melville

4. *The Purloined Letter*
5. *The Pathfinder*
6. *Moby Dick*
7. *Legend of Sleepy Hollow*
8. *The Scarlet Letter*
9. *Deerslayer*
10. *The Cask of Amantillado*

Key list items may be of any length, and series of up to ten questions based on one key are quite efficient when the elements in the key are related. Care should be taken to make sure that the elements do not overlap—for example, in a chemistry key list test, the terms "organic compounds" and "aldehydes" should not be used in the same key.

The suggestions and recommendations for constructing multiple-choice items apply generally to key list items. The teacher should be sure that these items aid in sampling the table of specifications for the test.

Interpretive Exercises

An interpretive exercise is a series of multiple-choice items that tests the examinee's ability to evaluate or interpret material such as a passage, diagram, or map. Several advantages are claimed for this approach to testing. First, the presentation of the material about which questions are to be asked guarantees that all examinees have the same information on which to base their analyses. Second, the item is well suited to measuring higher level achievements such as interpreting and drawing conclusions.

Two examples of interpretive exercises will be presented, the first of which consists of written material.

Items 1–3 are based on the following selection:

> Spores serve the same propagative and reproductive function as the seeds of higher plants, but spores are much smaller and simpler in structure than seeds are. Usually spores have one or at most a few cells and do not contain an embryo as do seeds. Nevertheless they germinate and produce new fungus plants with parental characteristics. The conditions required for germination are similar to those for seeds, moisture and appropriate temperature being the most important. Time for germination varies with the kind of spore and the temperature, ranging from an hour to several days.

1. To what does the word "higher" refer as used in the first sentence?
   a. size
   *b. complexity
   c. cost
   d. location
   e. none of the above

2. In what way are spores most different from seeds?
   *a. structure
   b. number of varieties
   c. their inability to produce plants
   d. the conditions needed for germination
   e. length of germination time

3. What does a seed contain that a spore does not?
   a. cell walls
   b. parental characteristics
   *c. embryo

    d. stamen and pistil

    e. stem

In that example the questions are based on a paragraph of material that, while new to the class, refers to terms and concepts included in prior instruction. Ability to respond to the questions reflects achievement in the course.

The second example of this format is based on a fictitious map.

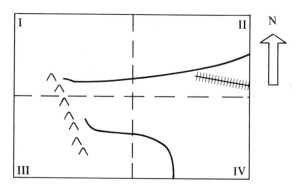

Key: ∧∧∧ mountain range
       ⊞⊞⊞⊞⊞⊞ railroad
       ———— river

1. If the prevailing weather in this region comes from the southwest, which quadrant would receive the greatest rainfall?

    a. I

    b. II

  *c. III

    d. IV

2. In which quadrant would industrial activity probably be the greatest?

    a. I

  *b. II

    c. III

    d. IV

Interpretive exercises can be valuable measurement tools if the selections relate to instructional goals and the items require examinees to draw on previous knowledge. To make efficient use of testing time, the number of items should be related to the amount of time required by examinees to read and study the material about which the items are written. Careful editing and ingenuity in item development are required to produce good, efficient exercises. The suggestions given earlier for constructing multiple-choice items apply also to the items used in interpretive exercises.

Administering Multiple-Choice Tests

Multiple-choice tests can be administered with directions to examinees to mark their answers either on the test pages or on a separate answer sheet. There are advantages and disadvantages in both practices.

Having answers marked directly on the test page has the advantage of better test security, and it may reduce the time examinees, particularly young students, need to complete a test. When an examinee is leaning over a test booklet, it is difficult for his neighbors to see his answers. In addition, only one page of items is exposed at a time, and this reduces the opportunity for in-class cheating. Research on the subject of speed in taking tests suggests that marking answers on tests may be slightly more rapid for examinees than using a separate answer sheet. At the high school level the difference is not great, but for the elementary grades it is important.

The use of a separate answer sheet has a marked advantage in speed of scoring. This advantage is important when tests are long and there are a large number of examinees. The time needed to score a one-hundred-item test can be reduced significantly when separate answer sheets are used. The major disadvantage of this approach is the opportunity examinees have to look at their neighbors' answers, but this danger can be minimized by placing examinees in straight rows in the classroom and monitoring the test carefully.

Several simple and inexpensive methods exist for producing answer sheets. Two examples of easily prepared answer sheets are shown in Figure 6.1. In the first, a row of circles has been provided for each item, and the teacher would direct examinees to blacken the appropriate one. In the second, a row of letters corresponding to responses is provided, and the teacher would tell examinees to cross out the letter of their choice. For either of these formats a key could be produced by punching out the space corresponding to the keyed response for each item. An example of a key is shown in Figure 6.2. To mark the papers the teacher would place the key over the answer sheet and mark the incorrectly answered items through the key with a red pencil. The teacher should also peruse each answer sheet for multiple marks for each item.

The directions for a multiple-choice test should indicate the number of items on the test, state the time limits, provide an example of an item, describe the strategy examinees should use, and comment on any unique features the test may have. Directions should be put on the title page, and the teacher should tell examinees when they can turn the page and begin working on the test. A sample set of directions is provided in Figure 6.3.

Summary

Multiple-choice tests are flexible, efficient tools for measuring classroom achievement. The task presented—that is, the selection of the most attractive of several feasible options—parallels and reflects many real-life situations, and in this sense it provides a realistic and viable way to assess progress toward the ultimate goals of education. Skill in constructing multiple-choice tests can be developed by teachers who know the content of their courses well and appreciate the importance of their subjects within the total school curriculum.

FIGURE 6.1

Two locally produced answer sheets

```
Test  _____
Name  _____
Date  _____

      a b c d e            a b c d e

 1. 0 0 0 0 0       26. 0 0 0 0 0
 2. 0 0 0 0 0       27. 0 0 0 0 0
 3. 0 0 0 0 0       28. 0 0 0 0 0
 4. 0 0 0 0 0       29. 0 0 0 0 0
 5. 0 0 0 0 0          .
 6. 0 0 0 0 0          .
    .                  .
    .                  .
    .                  .
    .                  .
```

```
Test  _____
Name  _____
Date  _____

 1. A B C D E       26. A B C D E
 2. A B C D E       27. A B C D E
    .                  .
    .                  .
    .                  .
    .                  .
    .                  .
    .                  .
    .                  .
    .                  .
```

FIGURE 6.2

Key for tests using a separate answer sheet

```
┌─────────────────────────────────────────────┐
│                                               │
│     Test   _____           │
│     Name _____             │
│     Date   _____           │
│                                               │
│     1. A ○ C D E    25. A ○ C D E             │
│     2. A B ○ D E    26. ○ B C D E             │
│     3. ○ B C D E    27. ○ B C D E             │
│     4. A B C D ○    28. A B C ○ E             │
│     5. A B C D ○    29. A B ○ D E             │
│       .                                       │
│       .                                       │
│       .                                       │
│       .                                       │
│       .                                       │
│       .                                       │
│                                               │
└─────────────────────────────────────────────┘
```

FIGURE 6.3

Directions for a multiple-choice test

Grade 10 Literature
Second Test, November 4, 1975
Mr. Blake

Directions   This test contains 40 multiple-choice items that are to be answered on the answer sheet provided. Take out the answer sheet now and write your name and the date in the spaces provided.

You should read each item carefully and decide on the answer of your choice. Then, you should cross out the letter on the answer sheet corresponding to your choice. Be careful to keep your place on the answer sheet and mark the correct row for the item on which you are working. A sample item is provided below:

oo. Who was the author of *All the King's Men?*

a. Warren
b. Michener
c. Catton   Sample Answer
d. Snow
e. Wallace

| oo. ✗ B C D E |

You will have thirty-five minutes for the test. If you finish before the time is up, review your work; then close your test, turn your answer sheet over, and sit quietly until other members of the class have finished.

When all members of the class have finished reading the directions, you will be told to begin the test.

Exercises

1. Rewrite the following items correcting the technical flaws.

   A. How can patient needs and personnel needs be correlated in team nursing?
      1. The best qualified person is assigned to patient needs.
      *2. The qualities of the nurse and the patient's needs determine the assignment.
      3. The requests of the patient determine the assignment.
      4. The same duties are re-assigned each day so each becomes an expert.

   B. Which of the following would be best to serve as a low-cost, high-protein dish?
      1. meatloaf
      2. pork chops
      3. bacon and tomato sandwiches
      *4. peanut butter sandwiches

   C. How many glasses of milk should a ten-year-old child have a day?
      1. 1–2 glasses
      2. 2–3 glasses
      *3. 3 or more glasses
      4. 4 or more glasses

D. What was the Indians' part in the development of America?
    *1. Indians were the first real Americans.
    2. They were in the way of the pioneers.
    3. Indians were the reason it took so long for America to become the United States.
    4. They were the reason the first settlers had many hardships during their first winter in America.

E. What is the name of the water purification process during which water stands motionless while large particles settle to the bottom?
    *1. sedimentation
    2. distillation
    3. filtration
    4. aeration

F. How do Indian children today learn to read and write?
    1. from their parents
    *2. in public schools
    3. while they are playing
    4. from reading books at home

G. What is the function of a representative?
    1. speak out on the various issues
    *2. vote as the people he represents wish
    3. express his own opinion
    4. vote in case of a tie

H. What class of people seem to contribute most toward a democratic society?
    *1. middle income group
    2. low-middle income group
    3. high income group
    4. low income group

I. When voting in the House of Representatives on a *very* important bill, which method of voting should be used? Why?

    1. Viva voce—because this is the more reliable way.

    2. Rising vote—everyone is visible, making it as honest as possible.

    3. Ayes and noes—this is the most popular and expedient.

  *4. Roll-call—more accurate and it allows each individual vote to be recognized and tabulated for later reference.

J. When the Moors invaded and settled in Spain from the eighth to the thirteenth century,

  *1. they brought a much better system of education with them.

    2. they introduced feudalism.

    3. they persecuted the Christians and tried to drive them out.

    4. they fixed the capital at Madrid.

2. For a unit in your teaching field, construct five multiple-choice items that are free of technical flaws. At least two should measure ability to apply or interpret material.

3. Construct a key-list exercise with at least three items.

4. Construct an interpretive exercise with at least three items.

Suggested Readings

BLOOM, B. S., HASTINGS, J. T., and MADAUS, G. F. *Handbook on Formative and Summative Evaluation of Student Learning.* New York: McGraw-Hill, 1971: 159–223. *Suggestions for developing test items to measure application, analysis, synthesis, and evaluation items. Includes good examples of the various types of items.*

BOARD, C., and WHITNEY, D. R. "The Effect of Selected Poor Item-Writing Practices on Test Difficulty, Reliability, and Validity." *Journal of Educational Measurement* 9 (1972): 225–234. *Report on a study in which four item-writing violations were introduced into tests. Considers the effects on test difficulty, reliability, and validity.*

CASHEN, V. M., and RAMSEYER, G. C. "The Use of Separate Answer Sheets by Primary Age Children." *Journal of Educational Measurement* 6

(1969): 155–158. *A study on the ability of young school children to cope with a separate answer sheet.*

DIZNEY, H. "Characteristics of Test Items Identified by Students as 'Unfair.'" *Journal of Educational Measurement* 2 (1965): 119–121. *A comparison of items identified as unfair with other items on the same test in terms of the item difficulty and discrimination.*

MARSO, R. N. "Test Item Arrangement, Testing Time, and Performance." *Journal of Educational Measurement* 7 (1970): 113–118. *Arrangement of items was varied in terms of difficulty, similarity of content, and order of class presentation, and the effect of arrangement on performance and test anxiety was studied.*

MICHAEL, J. J. "The Reliability of a Multiple-Choice Examination under Various Test-Taking Instructions." *Journal of Educational Measurement* 5 (1968): 307–314. *Items on a multiple-choice examination were scored in three ways and the effect on reliability was studied.*

WESMAN, A. G. "Writing the Test Item," *Educational Measurement*, 2d ed. Washington D.C.: American Council on Education: 81–128. *Useful suggestions for developing test items to measure various kinds of objectives. The examples are selected from several curricular areas.*

Chapter 7

EVALUATING SKILLS,
ATTITUDES, AND INTERESTS

As a result of studying this chapter you should be able to:

1. *Recognize skills in your own field of interest which call for product or performance evaluation.*

2. *Design evaluation procedures for skills in your own field of interest.*

3. *Develop procedures to measure affective outcomes in your own field of interest.*

The techniques described in Chapters 4, 5, and 6 will suffice for the measurement of most cognitive objectives, but there are other types of classroom objectives that can be measured more adequately by different methods.

The evaluation of automobile driving provides an example of the various aspects of the measurement problem in areas which are noncognitive or only partly cognitive. How well a person operates an automobile depends on at least three factors: (1) his knowledge of traffic laws and safe driving procedures, (2) his physical skill in controlling and operating the vehicle, and (3) his attitude toward driving safety. Although the three factors are interrelated, each is important in determining the fitness of the person to operate an automobile, and each would have to be evaluated through a different measurement procedure.

The first aspect, knowledge of traffic laws and safe driving procedures, can be evaluated through the use of written tests of the type described previously. The second aspect, physical skill in controlling and operating a vehicle, can be evaluated through a road test in which the examinee drives an automobile over a prescribed course and is required to carry out specified maneuvers. Alternatively, the examinee can be tested on machines that simulate certain driving problems and conditions. Probably a combination of the machine and the road test would be most effective—for example, the examinee's vision and reaction time could be tested by specialized instruments, while his ability to parallel park could be assessed by a road test.

The third aspect, the examinee's attitude toward driving, is probably the most difficult to assess, but it is very important because it determines whether, when, and how he will use his knowledge and physical skills. While the first two aspects of driving express how well the person performs when he is trying to do his best, attitude relates to how he performs typically. The driver who habitually exceeds the speed limit, fails to yield the right of way, and spins his tires on the pavement at each start may know that these are not approved driving procedures and he may also have a high level of physical skill, but his attitude toward driving safety largely determines his usual mode of driving. The average written test and road test probably would not detect a reckless driving attitude because the individual's behavior would conceal rather than reveal his true attitude. This would be especially true if his license to drive were contingent on his ability to display approved driving habits. In current society, attitude toward driving safety is monitored primarily through arrests, warnings, and citations. Only long-term observation of a driver in a number of situations is likely to reveal much about his attitude toward driving safety.

When it is necessary to measure objectives that do not lend themselves to paper and pencil tests of achievement, the following avenues of information are available: (1) observation of the individual's behavior, (2) the products produced by the individual, and (3) what the individual reports about himself.

Evaluating Skills

A strong element of knowledge is necessary to develop most skills, but knowledge alone is not sufficient. Knowledge of football formations and rules does not insure football playing ability, nor does the ability to identify the use of woodworking tools insure ability to build a cabinet. Measurement and evaluation in the skill areas must go beyond knowledge of how to perform. Two areas which lend themselves to observation are (1) *the products of performance* and (2) *performance in progress*.

Many activities requiring skill result in some type of product; this product may serve as the primary piece of evidence for the degree of skill the individual has acquired. For example, sewing, baking, woodworking, sculpture, and painting, produce artifacts that provide direct evidence of the skill of the producer. Some other skill areas, however, result in no permanent product. Gymnastics, musical performance, automobile driving, and public speaking, require that a performance be judged as it progresses. Often an evaluation of either the process or the product will suffice. In other cases, judgment of both performance in progress and the products of performance is possible and necessary. For example, in woodworking the products made by a student are very important evidence of his ability to produce smooth, well-made pieces of furniture; but adherence to safety rules, the amount of material used and perhaps wasted, care and maintenance of tools, and speed of production are also important factors to consider in judging his performance in the workshop.

Products

Products are somewhat easier to evaluate than performance in progress because products are relatively permanent. The person judging the adequacy of a product may take the time to examine the important features of the product, may place other products beside it for comparison, and may judge the product again at some later date to check the correctness of his evaluation.

The first step in judging products of performance is to establish the criteria by which the product is to be judged. It is important to identify all the elements which are essential to an acceptable product and the deficiencies which would render the product unacceptable. The elements should be examined carefully to make sure that each is related to the overall quality of the product. Nonessentials should be disregarded. Extra time is required to judge each feature, and irrelevant or barely relevant features may detract from the rating of the essential features.

In addition to a set of elements to be judged, a set of rules must be established for judging the quality of each element. Some features may be judged as either present or absent, that is, the decision is "yes" or "no." Such elements are similar to test items which can be scored one or zero. (In the case of an undesirable feature, the scoring could be reversed; points could be awarded only if the feature were absent, or points could be deducted for undesirable features.) For example, in woodworking the squareness of corners could be judged with the aid of a trisquare, and any corner could be judged square or not square, so much out of square that it is detectable with a trisquare. Other features may fall into more than two categories or require judgment along a continuous scale of quality.

However the judgments are made, a careful record must be kept. Rating scales or check lists are valuable to the teacher in making and recording judgments. These instruments list the elements of the product that are to be considered as well as the categories to be used in making the judgments. Check lists are instruments that have only two categories for each item, such as present or absent, acceptable or unacceptable, passing or failing. Rating scales have more than two categories for judging each element; they require the evaluator to judge the place of each element on a continuum of acceptability.

A rating scale item for evaluating the ability to bake cherry pie might be stated as follows:

0. Rate the flavor of the filling.
   Excellent:_____:_____:_____:_____:_____:_____:_____:Objecti

In this item the rater would place a check mark somewhere along the line between the colons to indicate the position between excellent and objectionable that best defines the flavor of the cherry pie filling. This scale has seven positions, so the scores would range from 0 to 6 or 1 to 7.

Other types of scales are possible—for example, a three-point scale of excellent, satisfactory, or unacceptable would function for the cherry pie item, or the item could be written in the check list form with only two categories of response:

    0. Is the flavor of the filling acceptable?

         _____yes   _____no

Perhaps a more satisfactory item type is one in which the categories describe the actual condition of the element being judged rather than just rating it—for example:

    0. Which of the following statements best describes the flavor of the filling?
        _____Overly tart, sour
        _____Too sweet
        _____Too bland, very little flavor
        _____Overcooked or burned
        _____Pleasant cherry flavor, just right

Such an item is neither exactly a rating scale item nor a check list item; in some ways it resembles a multiple-choice item. One problem with the multiple-choice form is that it is difficult to score. Obviously, the last category is the most desirable, but whether there is a difference in quality among the other categories would have to be decided. One advantage of the form is that it expresses more clearly the quality of the product. If the pie is judged to have an undesirable flavor, the specific nature of the problem is readily apparent and the student will be able to correct it.

Sometimes the descriptive category form can be translated into a rating scale, which offers the advantages of numerical scoring and a description of performance. The following item might be used in woodworking:

0. Rate the smoothness of the finish.
    ____Very smooth and mirror-like, no visible bumps,
       bubbles, nicks, or streaks
    ____Very smooth, one or two minor flaws
    ____Smooth, more than two minor flaws
    ____Smooth, but with obvious bubbles or uneven color
    ____Rather rough, with obvious nicks, pits, bubbles,
       and streaks

The actual judging and scoring of products has much in common with the scoring of essay examinations, which are in themselves a special kind of product. In performing judgments of products, it is desirable to conceal the name of the student who made each one until after all judgments have been concluded. This practice will help prevent overall judgments about the individuals from interfering with the judgments of their products. Each student could write his name on a 3-×5-inch card to be placed face down beside his product. After the judging has been done, the cards can be turned over to reveal the names of the students. Judging the elements one at a time will promote effective judgment of each element.

The process described for judging products is analytic because the basis of judgment is broken down into separate elements. Other scoring schemes are possible—for example, products can be placed in ordered categories based on the overall quality of the product. In some cases, a standard or ideal product can be produced for comparison, and each student's product can be judged against the standard. These methods are effective, but analytic scoring is more likely to communicate the meaning of the overall rating to the student because the criteria for judgment are clearer.

Performance

Many important skills must be judged in progress either because no product is produced by the process or because the product does not reveal important aspects of the task. Performance in progress may be judged either in "natural" settings or under test conditions. A certain amount of observation and informal evaluation of performance in the natural setting takes place in most classrooms. From this informal observation important aspects of performance can be identified. The woodworking teacher may notice, through informal observation, that tools are being improperly used; the home economics teacher may note that a pattern is being cut improperly. Usually such problems are corrected on the spot, and evaluation and feedback are almost simultaneous. Unfortunately, by its very nature, informal observation is capricious. The teacher may observe the performance of some students hardly at all, while he may give the bulk of his attention to a few students, especially the most promising and the most troublesome. It is advisable to supplement informal observation with planned observation, in which the teacher makes a point of observing each student at work on a planned basis. In this way, the entire class can be observed over a period of time.

Although the observation of behavior in natural settings is intuitively appealing because it would appear to be relevant to "real world" performance, such observations do have a serious disadvantage. Certain important behaviors may occur quite rarely in the natural setting, and when they do occur the teacher may not be in a position to observe them. To observe such behaviors, the teacher may need to arrange a more formal situation in which the student demonstrates his command of critical skills. Such test situations have an advantage over natural situations because a larger number of critical tasks can be observed within a shorter period of time. In addition, if each examinee is required to attempt the same set of critical tasks, the performances of different examinees are easier to compare.

For example, a student's general physical fitness can be judged informally by observing his performance on the playground or in the gymnasium, but a much more comprehensive and informative appraisal of his physical fitness may be gained by observing his performance on standard tasks similar to those described by the American Association for Health, Physical Education, and Recreation:[1]

1. Pull-ups (modified for girls)
2. Sit-ups
3. Shuttle run
4. Standing broad jump
5. Fifty yard dash
6. Softball throw
7. Six hundred yard run-walk

A check list which includes the critical steps or procedures is an aid to the observer because it calls attention to the aspects of the task to be observed and provides a convenient form for recording his observations. Figure 7.1 is an example of a check list for the use of a clinical thermometer.

FIGURE 7.1

Check list for use of an oral clinical thermometer

Directions Check each of the steps as it is correctly performed.

1. Preliminaries
   _____Makes sure all materials are at hand (thermometer, wiper, soap and water)
   _____Has patient sit or lie down
   _____Shakes down thermometer to 95° or below
2. Trying the temperature
   _____Places thermometer under patient's tongue and to side of mouth
   _____Instructs patient to breathe through nose and not to bite down or talk
   _____Leaves thermometer in place for three to five minutes

[1] American Association for Health, Physical Education, and Recreation, *AAHPER Youth Fitness Test Manual* (Washington, D.C.: National Educational Association, 1958). This manual describes testing procedures for physical fitness and provides standards for boys and girls of different age levels.

_____Removes thermometer, holding firmly at top, and wipes downward with rotary motion

_____Discards wipe in waste basket

_____Reads temperature and records properly on chart

3. Cleaning the thermometer

_____Soaps thermometer thoroughly

_____Rinses thermometer thoroughly

_____Repeats soaping and rinsing

_____Dries thermometer

_____Places all used wipes in waste basket

_____Replaces thermometer in case or solution

4. Contingency if temperature change from last reading is more than 2 degrees

_____Shakes thermometer down

_____Repeats temperature trying procedure

_____Reports change to superior if second reading confirms it

5. Disqualifications

_____Drops thermometer or breaks it

_____Makes a reading or recording error of more than .2 degrees

_____Fails to shake down thermometer

_____Fails to clean thermometer properly after use

_____Fails to retake temperature if change is more than 2 degrees

_____Fails to report unusual change of temperature

_____Fails to dispose of used wipes

An added advantage of a check list is that it can serve as a training aid to clarify the desired process to the student. A check list like the one in Figure 7.1 can be used in formal performance testing, in observations of natural behavior, and even in student self-evaluation.

One problem with check lists is deciding how to score each category properly. In the check list shown in Figure 7.1, one point could be awarded for each correct action, but all actions might not be equally crucial. Wiping the thermometer *before* reading it makes the thermometer easier to read and seems sanitary, but it is not so essential as making sure the thermometer is properly shaken down and cleaned *after* use. Presumably, examinees who committed any of the errors under section 5 of the check list would receive a score of zero no matter how well they had followed the other procedures. If possible, the teacher should determine in advance the relative importance of each item on a check list and assign a weight proportionate to the importance of the item. He should also identify all crucial steps and crucial errors. The failure to include a crucial step or the commission of a crucial error should always result in failure to pass the performance test.

Another popular aid to observing performance in progress is the rating scale. The critical aspects of performance are listed on the rating scale as on the check list, but each aspect is rated for adequacy rather than being recorded as merely present or not present. For example, in public speaking, eye contact is considered important. Eye contact could be rated as follows:

   0. Eye contact

   :_____:_____:_____:_____:_____:_____:

Speaks with head down almost all the time	Maintains eye contact about half the time	Maintains eye contact almost all the time

The rater could place a mark anywhere along the scale to indicate his judgment.

It is important to use descriptive words to establish the rating scale. The following item is a poor example:

   0. Smoothness of delivery

   :_____:_____:_____:_____:_____:_____:

Excellent	Fair	Poor

This is a better scale:

   0. Smoothness of delivery

   :_____:_____:_____:_____:_____:_____:

Very smooth, never stumbled or groped for words	Stumbled over words or groped for words four or five times	Stumbled or groped for words every sentence or two

Descriptive categories of response help the rater decide how to categorize the student's performance, and they help the student understand the meaning of his ratings and what aspects of his performance need improvement.

The use of rating scales raises some of the same problems as the use of check lists. Some aspects of performance may be less crucial than others, and the teacher must decide whether high performance on one aspect of a total task compensates for poor performance on some other aspect of the task. For example, in delivering a speech, does a very smooth flow of words compensate for a complete lack of eye contact? For many tasks, it may be necessary to specify critical errors or omissions which would disqualify the examinee on the task as a whole.

Alternatively, points can be assigned to each level of performance on each aspect to be rated—for example, a seven-category scale could be assigned scores ranging from 0 to 6. The number of categories to be used on a rating scale is debatable. Generally, differences between categories should reflect perceivable differences in performance. From three to seven categories probably will suffice for most purposes.

In addition to check lists and rating scales, *rate* of work may be an important indicator of the adequacy of a person's performance. In typing and shorthand, words per minute are recognized indicators of skill because speed as well as accuracy is important in these areas.

In other instances, *frequency* is an indicator of proficiency. The frequency of errors in performance of a musical passage, the number of pull-ups a boy can do without stopping, or the number of times a student participates in a discussion can be counted and recorded, and they are viable indicators of important characteristics.

In some cases, the teacher may be interested in recording the frequency of a variety of behaviors. He may make a tally sheet which lists each classification of behavior and provides room for tallying each. An example of a sheet used to keep track of student participation during a small group discussion is shown in Figure 7.2.

FIGURE 7.2

Rating sheet for measuring class discussion

	States own ideas or opinions	Expresses agreement or disagreement with opinions of others	Asks relevant questions	Answers questions	Makes irrelevant comments
Mike	//	//	//	///	//
Barbara	/	/	//		
Jean					/
Billy	///	////		///	
Maurice	/// /	///	//	////	
Carol	////	////	///	/	
Bob	//	/	//		/
Milt	/	//	///	///	
Connie	///	///	////	///	
Curt	//	/	/		/
Laurel	////	//	///		
Gary	//	/	///	//	
Gina	/	///	/	//	
Steven	//	/	/	/	//
Audrey	/	////	//	/	

An alternative to recording frequencies is to divide the time period into brief intervals of three to five seconds each and to record the type of behavior which is going on during each interval. This procedure has been used by N. A. Flanders to analyze teaching behavior.[2]

Whatever method is used to record observed behavior, careful preparation—identifying what is to be observed, preparing usable rating scales, check lists, or recording forms—is necessary in order to obtain a proper record.

Evaluating Affective Goals

The affective domain includes objectives which deal with the feelings of students about stimuli such as school subjects, occupations, persons, groups, activities, ideas, art, or music. Stimuli that evoke feelings are called *psychological objects*. The feelings or affects experienced by individuals are called attitudes, interests, appreciations, or values.

Although affective objectives have received increased attention in recent years, educators and laymen have been concerned with affective outcomes for a long time. As D. R. Krathwohl and D. A. Payne state:

> The major efforts at test construction and curriculum building have been predominantly in the areas of achievement, yet criticism of the schools shows concern about students' "poor" attitudes, "low" motivation to achieve, slovenly work habits, and the lack of commitment to societal values.[3]

Concern for affective objectives arises because how a person behaves typically is more important than how he is able to behave on occasion, and typical behavior is not determined solely by what a person is able to do but by his feelings about what he is doing.

---

[2] Methods for obtaining and analyzing classroom interaction data are presented in N. A. Flanders, *Analyzing Teaching Behavior* (Reading, Mass.: Addison-Wesley, 1970).

[3] D. R. Krathwohl and D. A. Payne, "Defining and Assessing Educational Objectives," *Educational Measurement*, 2nd ed., ed. R. L. Thorndike (Washington, D. C.: American Council on Education, 1971), p. 31.

An assembly line worker, for example, may be perfectly capable of doing his assigned task, but his job performance may be unsatisfactory because of his feelings about the job. Perhaps the worker feels so negatively toward the job that he is chronically late to work and frequently pretends to be ill so that he can stay away. He may go so far as to sabotage the assembly line in order to avoid doing the job. Obviously his attitudes, not his skills, are the problem. In other cases, feelings may not interfere so seriously with performance, but the individual may find no satisfaction or enjoyment in an activity and thus may perform at less than his optimal ability. These problems have counterparts in school situations. Most teachers believe that learning is much easier if the student believes that what he is doing is worthwhile and if he has positive regard for learning as an activity.

The Taxonomy of Educational Objectives points out that feelings about psychological objects vary in the degree to which they are *internalized*—that is, the degree to which these feelings become a part of the personality and come to affect the person's behavior. The authors of the *Taxonomy* regard internalization as a process that takes place over time. The person begins by becoming aware of the affective stimulus, a process called *receiving*. Next, the individual begins to react to the stimulus, perhaps at first as directed by others and later by his own volition. This level is called *responding*. The person may next come to *value* the stimulus—that is, to think that it is worthwhile, to seek it out. Next he may incorporate this value into a value system, a process called *organization*. Finally, the individual's value system comes to control his behavior, called *characterization by a value or a value complex*. In this final stage the individual's behavior is very consistent with his value system and forms part of his personality.[4]

For example, a child may begin to develop a taste for classical music by hearing it on an FM radio station or by going to concerts. Becoming aware that classical music is different from other music, he may begin to turn the radio dial until he finds stations that play

---

[4] D. R. Krathwohl, B. S. Bloom, and B. Masia, *Taxonomy of Educational Objectives. Handbook II. The Affective Domain* (New York: David McKay, 1964).

classical music, and he may ask to go to concerts or buy recordings of classical music. He may try to find out more about classical music by studying its structure and learning about composers and performers, and he may desire to take music lessons. In later life, depending on how his affinity for classical music is incorporated into his value system and also upon his other values and abilities, his valuing of classical music may manifest itself in a number of ways: he may become a composer or performer, or he may pursue his liking for classical music vicariously through records, concerts, and through supporting musical societies. This value may be incorporated with other related values into a general affinity for art, literature, and music.

The categories of affective objectives make clear that much of the affective domain consists of covert changes within the individual, which may or may not be manifested in behavior. Obviously, at the later stages of development and organization, overt behavior is more likely to be controlled by and to reveal affect, but the ability to conceal rather than reveal true feeling may in itself be valued by some individuals.

Affective outcomes can be evaluated primarily through direct observation or self-report. The activities in which an individual chooses to participate—the organizations he joins, the books he reads, the hobbies and recreational activities he pursues, the television shows and movies he watches—his friends and associates, his habits, his casual conversations are all indicators of his attitudes, interests, values, and appreciations. Thus direct observation of behavior, either planned or incidental, is an intuitively attractive method of gaining information about affective outcomes. In fact, teachers probably gain most of their impressions of student attitudes and interests through informal observation. There are several disadvantages to direct observation, however: (1) the teacher's opportunity to observe may be too limited, (2) behavior may be misinterpreted, and (3) sometimes covert attitudes are not manifested in overt behavior.

Much important student behavior occurs outside the school setting. Since typical behavior, rather than optimal behavior, is the primary concern in the evaluation of affective outcomes, there should be an opportunity to sample some behaviors in nonschool settings. The teacher of health, for example, may be able to determine that a student knows *how* to brush his teeth, but the teacher is not able to observe whether the student actually *does* brush his teeth.

The child who has taken piano lessons since the age of five may not enjoy playing the piano; he may take the lessons because his mother forces him to do so. A teenager may attend church regularly, not because he is religious but because he likes to sit beside a certain girl in church.

Whether or not feelings are revealed or concealed may depend on the situation. A student may not openly express his feelings in the face of social pressure or in situations where open expression may be met with disapproval or punishment, and students may engage in some activities simply because they have no practical alternative.

If observation is to be used as a method of evaluating affective objectives, the teacher should be sure that he will be able to observe the related behaviors in an adequate variety of situations, and that the student has freedom of action to express himself and choose how he will behave.

Self-report may be obtained in a number of ways. Generally interviewing or written questionnaires are used. Direct interviews may be the only practical form of obtaining self-report from young children or from older children who are weak in reading and writing skills. In addition, interviewing allows a flexibility in the way questions are asked and an opportunity to observe the reactions of the interviewee, a flexibility not afforded by written questionnaires. However, interviews are time-consuming and the interviewer, especially if he is also a teacher, may be perceived as a threat, inhibiting honest response. Questionnaires provide the most convenient means of obtaining self-report, and if respondents are assured anonymity, their responses may be less inhibited and more honest than in direct interviews.

For overt self-report procedures to be effective, the examinee must be aware of and understand his own feelings and must report them honestly. Unless these requirements are likely to be met, little is to be gained from overt self-report techniques. This is one reason why grades are not and should not be based on student self-reports of affective outcomes. If the student believes that his grade depends on saying that he "enjoys mathematics," "studies outside class," "reads books about the subject," or "does not believe in cheating," he is likely to respond to questionnaires or interviews in a way that protects that grade no matter what his true attitudes are.

Using the correct technique for learning about student attitudes is not a simple either-or choice between observation and self-report methods. Both techniques should be used so that the teacher's hypotheses about student attitudes and interests can either be proven or disproven by independent information. The teacher should be very sure that the data obtained by any one method is consonant with other information about the student.

For many purposes, the teacher needs to examine only the results for the class as a whole. He can gain a good idea of how the class views the study of *Silas Marner* or how important students think it is to learn basic arithmetic skills by studying the responses of the whole class to questions about those subjects rather than the responses of individual students. Such information can help him make plans to improve certain attitudes and to monitor attitude shifts.

Observation

Sometimes observation of affective behavior can be aided by check lists or rating scales similar to those used in evaluating skills. At times, counting the frequency or rate of certain classes of behavior is effective. A teacher interested in playground behavior related to the objective, "The student maintains friendly relationships with peers," might summarize a series of observations of free play in several rating scale items similar to the following:

   0. Playing with other children
      _____Keeps to himself whenever possible.
      _____Usually plays with others, but likes to play alone
        sometimes
      _____Generally plays freely with others

  00. Sharing playground equipment
      _____Always willing to share with others
      _____Generally willing to share, occasionally reluctant
      _____Tries to keep others from sharing equipment, will
        give others a turn only if forced

Another teacher might keep track of playground behavior by recording and counting incidents in which the child is involved—fights, serious arguments, or occasions when the teacher himself had to intervene to urge a child to participate. Such counting procedures are relatively objective, but the teacher must be sure to observe the behavior over an adequate period of time and to record the results on the spot. This process would require carrying around a data sheet and probably a clip board, even though that might interfere with other duties.

Interviews

Interviews are of two types, *structured* and *unstructured*. Structured interviews use an interview schedule which contains set questions to be asked in a specific order. The interviewer generally does not deviate from the set format of the questionnaire, but may do so to repeat or clarify a question. The answers are either written down or coded in some way. At times the interviewer may probe to get the respondent to clarify or expand his answer. An example of some questions that might appear on a structured interview is given in Figure 7.3.

Unstructured interviews are limited to a number of key questions. The order and the exact form in which the questions are asked is not specified. The interviewer encourages the interviewee to expand on his answers and may probe some areas in great depth.

FIGURE 7.3

Questions for a structured interview

1. What is your favorite school subject?
   - _____a. art
   - _____b. English
   - _____c. home economics
   - _____d. mathematics
   - _____e. music
   - _____f. social studies
   - _____g. science
   - _____h. woodworking
   - _____i. other _____ (specify)

2. Why do you like this subject? (Check nearest correct response.)
   - _____a. teacher
   - _____b. subject matter
   - _____c. future occupational interests
   - _____d. easy work
   - _____e. other _____ (specify)

3. Which subject do you like the least?
   - _____a. art
   - _____b. English
   - _____c. home economics
   - _____d. mathematics
   - _____e. music
   - _____f. social studies
   - _____g. science
   - _____h. woodworking
   - _____i. other _____ (specify)

Presumably, the unstructured interview allows the interviewer to probe more deeply for the reasoning behind the answers. The structured interview, on the other hand, is less time-consuming and thus more topics can be covered though in less detail.

In constructing an interview schedule, close attention should be paid to the affective objectives about which information is sought. Since interviewing takes time, only the most pertinent questions should be included.

The interviewer must avoid posing a threat to the interviewee, either by argumentation or by expressing contempt or disapproval of responses. The interviewer should be aware that his facial expressions and body attitude as well as his verbal statements convey his feelings. The interviewee must be placed at ease. An unstructured interview with a student, if skillfully done, should seem like a simple conversation, not a formal interrogation.

Questionnaires

Written questionnaires resemble structured interviews because they solicit responses to set questions. Written questionnaires, unlike interviews, can be administered to large numbers of students simultaneously, which is a considerable advantage to a busy teacher. In addition, the written questionnaire removes the possibility of an interviewer inhibiting an honest response. The questionnaire can be made anonymous if only group results are needed, and this may make honest response still more likely.

Written questionnaires do lack the flexibility of interviews. There is no opportunity to probe extemporaneously or to ask a student to expand or clarify his answers. In addition, written interviews require reading and perhaps writing skill on the part of the respondent. Clear, careful wording of questions is needed to avoid misinterpretation because the questionnaire must stand by itself.

Items in questionnaires may be either open-ended or choice-type. Open-ended items are easier to construct and, like the structured interview, often yield more depth of information about the individual's feelings than do choice-type instruments. Responses to open-ended questionnaires also can provide effective alternates for the later development of choice-type questions. Open-ended items are more difficult to score and summarize, and they demand more time as well as writing skill from the respondent.

Open-ended items may take two forms. One is the direct question, for example:

0. How do you feel when it's time to do your arithmetic assignment?

_____

_____

00. Why do you feel that way?

_____

_____

Another form is the incomplete sentence:

0. When it's time to do my arithmetic assignment I usually feel _____

_____

00. I feel this way because _____

_____

A number of formats have been developed for the choice-type affective item. One form is much like the multiple-choice achievement item, for example:

0. When it's time to do my arithmetic assignment I usually feel
   a. eager to get started.
   b. anxious to get it over with so I can do something else.
   c. like putting it off until later.
   d. afraid I can't do it right.
   e. like forgetting all about it.

00. When I find an arithmetic problem I can't solve on the first try I usually
   a. keep working on it for a while, until I solve it.
   b. work on it for a while, but give up if I can't solve it.
   c. work on it for a while, but ask for help if I can't solve it.
   d. ask for help right away.
   e. just give up.

It is also possible to phrase such items in the form of a question—for example:

0. If you were watching TV and a play by Shakespeare came on the channel you were watching, what would you probably do?
   a. Watch it
   b. Watch it for a while to see if I liked it
   c. See if there was anything else on that I liked, but watch the play if there wasn't
   d. See if there was anything else on I liked, and turn off the set if there wasn't
   e. Watch anything else that was on, but not the play

00. How many western shows or movies did you watch on TV during the past week?
   a. None
   b. One
   c. Two
   d. Three
   e. Four or more

000. How much do you like news programs on TV?
   a. A lot
   b. A little
   c. Not much
   d. Not at all

Sometimes items can ask the student to compare himself with others, for example:

> 0. Compared with other people your age, how would you rate your interest in rock music?
>   a. In the top 10 percent
>   b. Above average
>   c. About average
>   d. Below average
>   e. In the lowest 10 percent

Another format is to ask the respondent to choose which of a set of statements most applies to him. In the statements below, the student is asked to indicate whether statement *a* or *b* most applies to him.

> a. A person can get ahead mainly through hard work and sacrifice.
> b. To get ahead a person needs to know the right people.

> a. Schools should teach students what to believe.
> b. Schools should teach students how to think for themselves.

Still other forms of questionnaire items resemble the true-false achievement item. For example, the following items ask the examinee to respond "true for me" or "false for me."

> T   F   0. I always do the best I can on a job.
> T   F   00. I "goof off" sometimes when I should be working.

Such items can also be designed with "yes" or "no" responses.

> yes   no   0. When you have a job to do, do you always try as hard as you can?
> yes   no   00. Do you ever "goof-off" when you should be working?

Another modification of the choice-type item is useful for examining preferences for objects or activities. The student indicates whether he likes *L*, dislikes *D*, or is unsure about *?* the activity.

L   ?   D   0. Reading books about the lives of great composers

L   ?   D   00. Watching a TV show about new scientific discoveries

L   ?   D   000. Working on a project for the science fair

A much-used form of affective item is one in which the respondent is asked to indicate his degree of agreement or disagreement with statements of belief or opinion. The responses to such items may take different forms, but most commonly the examinee indicates whether he strongly agrees *SA*, agrees *A*, neither agrees nor disagrees *N*, disagrees *D*, or strongly disagrees *SD* with the statement—for example:

SA   A   N   D   SD   0. Most students like this course.

SA   A   N   D   SD   00. If a person can't learn in school, it is generally his own fault.

SA   A   N   D   SD   000. The students in this school are too concerned with sports.

Writing items to evaluate affective objectives is similar in many ways to writing other types of items, but there are also differences. Some suggestions are:

1. Items should be written in simple, grammatical language.

2. Complex items containing several ideas should be avoided.

3. The item should be written so that respondents with different opinions will give different answers.

4. If multiple-choice items are used, the responses should be grammatically consistent with the item stem.

5. Negative statements should be avoided, especially in true-false and yes-no items.

6. Leading questions should be avoided.

If an item contains more than one idea, it may be difficult for the respondent to tell which idea is to be judged. For example, the following item contains two ideas:

SA A N D SD   0. This is a good school, but there are a lot of changes that need to be made.

Some respondents may agree that this is a good school, but they may also feel that no changes are necessary, while others may feel that this is not a good school and lots of changes need to be made. It is difficult to tell how they should respond to the item. Perhaps two items are needed to cover these ideas.

SA A N D SD   0. This is a good school.

SA A N D SD   00. A lot of changes need to be made in this school.

In some cases, students with essentially different points of view may give the same response to an item. In the following item, those students who think the teacher is very good and those who think he is terrible would give the same response:

T F   0. The skill of the teacher in this class is about average.

It would be better to phrase the item in this way:

0. Compared to most teachers, how skillful is the teacher in this class?
   a. Well above average
   b. A little above average
   c. About average
   d. A little below average
   e. Well below average

Leading questions pose a particular problem, because they expose the bias of the item writer and make honest response difficult. The leading question forces an assumption on the examinee which may or may not be tenable to him but which he must accept if he is to answer the question. Some classic examples are, "Have you stopped beating your wife?" "Why did you push that lady into the river?" and "When are you going to stop cheating on your income taxes?" More realistic examples can be found, however:

yes   no   0. Do you favor the extension of Medicare to all age groups even though this is a socialistic proposal?

SA   A   N   D   SD   00. The United States should stop its imperialist policies in Southeast Asia.

In the first item, the student is warned that the expansion of Medicare is socialism, which may have a bad connotation. In the second item the student may be opposed to "imperialist policies" but may not agree that United States policies in Southeast Asia fall into that category. In both cases, the bias of the item writer is evident.

It would be better to test the same ideas as follows:

yes   no   0. Do you favor the extension of Medicare to all age groups?

SA   A   N   D   SD   00. The United States should end its support of the present South Vietnamese government.

The writer of questionnaire items should keep in mind that the purpose of the questionnaire is to obtain student opinions, feelings, and preferences. Knowledge or command of information should not be tested by affective items, although knowledge and information presumably affect attitudes, interests, and preferences. For example:

SA   A   N   D   SD   0. The United States Postal Service employs more persons than any private corporation in the country.

This is an item which has an objective answer. No matter how the respondent *feels* about the Postal Service, his response depends only on his knowledge, not his feelings. On the other hand, the following item, which has no objectively "correct" answer, calls for the respondent's attitude toward the Postal Service:

SA   A   N   D   SD   0. Postal service would be a lot better if it were put into the hands of
private enterprise rather than left
to the United States Postal Service.

Questionnaires are sometimes scored on a single-item basis —that is, each item is tabulated separately, and no attempt is made to compile a total score. In other instances, scores are tabulated for each examinee by adding up the individual item responses. Whether or not a total score makes sense depends on the degree to which all items are directed toward the same affective stimulus. In a questionnaire of six or seven items, where one item is concerned with attitude toward arithmetic, another with interest in sports, and another with preferences for various hobbies, it makes no sense to attempt to obtain a total score. The individual item responses would be of interest, but trying to total them would be meaningless. On the other hand, a questionnaire composed completely of items related to attitude toward school and school work might yield a meaningful total score.

If single items are the main focus of attention, the data from such items may be tabulated as percentages of the group of students giving each response. For a true-false or yes-no question-naire item, the results may be tabulated easily on an extra copy of the questionnaire. The following item demonstrates the results for a class of twenty-five students. Fifteen of the students marked T and ten marked F. The number marking each response is shown below the T and F, and the percentage appears in parentheses.

T   F   0. Arithmetic is a very boring subject.
15   10
(60)   (40)

Other types of questions can be tabulated in a similar manner to give results for the whole class—for example, a multiple-choice item given to fifty students, with percentages in parentheses:

0. What are your educational plans?

    <u>3 (6)</u>   a. I want to quit school as soon as I can.

    <u>5 (10)</u>   b. I want to go to a vocational high school.

    <u>20 (40)</u> c. I want to finish regular high school, but that is all.

    <u>6 (12)</u>   d. I want to finish high school and then get some technical training.

    <u>15 (30)</u> e. I want to finish high school and then get at least some college.

    <u>1 (2)</u>   f. Other _____.

If the questionnaire is to have a total score, some way must be found to weight each response. Each item must be scored, and then the responses added. True-false and yes-no items may be weighted one and zero, but attention should be paid to the direction of the item. On a scale designed to measure favorableness toward arithmetic, one point would be awarded for a T and zero points for an F on the following item:

T   F   0. Arithmetic will be useful to me in my future life.

On the same scale, zero points would be awarded for a T and one point for an F on this item:

T   F   0. I hope I never have to use most of the arithmetic I have studied in school.

Items of the SA, A, N, D, SD type may be weighted from zero to four or from one to five. One problem in such cases is to decide how to score an omitted item. It is usually sensible to regard such an item as being undecided and to score it as if it had been marked N. Multiple-choice questionnaire items are sometimes difficult to weight sensibly, and they may not lend themselves to obtaining an overall score. If an overall score is to be obtained, each item on a questionnaire should have the same set of response categories.

The results of summed questionnaires are generally reliable. It is doubtful that single items yield reliable results for individuals, although such items may yield adequately reliable information for groups. The primary question about self-report data is their validity—that is, whether or not they reveal the true feelings of the respondent. Most questionnaires can be faked, and respondents who feel that there is an advantage in making themselves appear in a certain light may respond in a way that they think will obtain approval. It is important to make clear to respondents that all responses will be accepted without criticism and will not be used as a basis for grades. The promise of anonymity will help accomplish this purpose. It is also important to carry out promises of anonymity scrupulously if student trust is to be maintained. If possible, questionnaire data should be augmented with observation and other sources of information rather than being accepted uncritically.

Summary

Direct observation, interviews, and questionnaires provide information about skills and affective objectives which cannot be obtained from ordinary pencil and paper tests. These means of data collection should be carefully planned and coordinated with educational objectives. Data gained from these sources are a valuable addition to the total information necessary to make formative and summative evaluations.

Exercises

1. What, if any, skills in your own field of interest could be measured better by observation of student products or student performance in progress than by paper and pencil tests?

2. If you listed some skills in exercise 1, what procedures would you use to evaluate at least one of the skills? Give an example of what you would use—check list, rating scale, or observation sheet, for instance—and describe how you would use it.

3. What affective objectives pertain to your field? Give at least three questionnaire or interview items related to one of these objectives. What kinds of student behavior would you try to

observe in order to confirm or disallow the information contained in your affective items?

Suggested Readings

AMERICAN ASSOCIATION FOR HEALTH, PHYSICAL EDUCATION, and RECREATION. *AAHPER Youth Fitness Test Manual*. Washington, D.C.: National Educational Association, 1958. *An example of assessing physical fitness through representative tasks.*

BLOOM, B. S., HASTINGS, J. T., and MADUS, G. F. *Handbook on Formative and Summative Evaluation of Student Learning*. New York: McGraw-Hill, 1971. *Chapter 10 discusses the measurement of affective objectives, and chapter 23 discusses measurement in industrial education.*

EDWARDS, A. L. *Techniques of Attitude Scale Construction*. New York: Appleton-Century-Crofts, 1957. *Chapter 1 contains a highly readable discussion of attitudes, approaches for measuring attitudes, and writing attitude statements. Chapter 6 discusses summated rating scales.*

LEVINE, H. G., and MCGUIRE, C. "Role-Playing as an Evaluative Technique." *Journal of Educational Measurement* 5 (1968): 1-8. *A description of testing skills in patient interviewing, patient management, and treatment interviewing in a medical school setting.*

OPPENHEIM, A. N. *Questionnaire Design and Attitude Measurement*. New York: Basic Books, 1966. *Chapters 2 through 5 contain basic fundamentals of questionnaire design, question wording, check lists, rating scales, inventories, and attitude statements.*

ROBINSON, J. P., ATHANASIOU, R., and HEAD, K. B. *Measures of Occupational Attitudes and Occupational Characteristics*. Ann Arbor: Institute for Social Research, 1969.

ROBINSON, J. P., and SHAVER, P. R. *Measures of Social Psychological Attitudes*. Ann Arbor: Institute for Social Research, 1969. *These volumes contain instruments used in research on attitudes, interests, and values, with comments on the instruments. Many approaches to affective measurement are illustrated.*

WEBB, E. J., CAMPBELL, D. T., SCHWARTZ, R. D., and SECHREST, L. *Unobtrusive Measures: Nonreactive Research in the Social Sciences*. Chicago: Rand-McNally, 1966. *A highly interesting volume describing ways in which observation and measurement of behavior can interfere with the behavior, and ingenious methods to avoid such interference.*

PART III

The Use of Classroom
Measurement Data

A complete measurement program includes plans for the formal use of the data collected in the classroom, and the use to be made of the data influences the approach taken and the type of measurement made. The topics in this section consider the analysis and use of classroom data.

Chapter 8 presents and illustrates simple quantitative methods that are useful in the classroom. Special care has been taken to limit the topics to those that have widespread utility in a program which makes minimal use of quantitative analysis. In addition, the techniques presented are practicable for teachers in terms of time and level of mathematical expertise required to use them. Emphasis is placed on the analyses for reporting test results to students, for interpreting the results, and for examining the quality of individual items and tests for clues to ways of improving future tests.

Chapter 9 considers methods of reporting and grading. Throughout and at the close of a unit or semester, a teacher must report results to students. When testing is used in the formative stages of instruction, the information can influence decisions within the instructional process, and one set of strategies is appropriate. At these times, assigning grades is not only unnecessary and insufficient, but grades may in fact distract students from the valuable guidance that test results can provide. When the time arrives for the summative use of measurement data, a different strategy is appropriate. Teachers need to combine the information collected throughout the instructional period and dispassionately assign a grade that describes accurately the achievement level students have attained. Various grading procedures are explored in this chapter.

Many teachers express either a lack of interest in or a distaste for quantitative methods, and frequently the same teachers struggle with decisions that are viewed as subjective or arbitrary. By its nature, teaching includes making judgments, and these can be either casual, subjective interpretations of the information available or they can be formal, objective analyses of the data. In either case the final decisions are under the control of the teacher and are his responsibility. Methods of treating data well within the capability of the most unmathematically oriented teacher are available and presented in Part III.

Chapter 8

CLASSROOM QUANTITATIVE METHODS

As a result of studying this chapter you should be able to:

1. *Estimate the mean, median, and standard deviation of a group of test scores.*

2. *Convert test scores into percentile ranks and standard scores.*

3. *Construct a grouped frequency distribution.*

4. *Rank a set of scores.*

5. *Estimate the correlation coefficient between two sets of scores.*

6. *Estimate the coefficient of reliability.*

7. *Estimate the standard error of measurement.*

8. *Obtain the discrimination and difficulty indexes for test items.*

9. *Interpret group test statistics.*

10. *Interpret percentile ranks and standard scores.*

11. *Interpret reliability and standard error of measurement.*

12. *Interpret the results of item analysis.*

Many of the topics in this chapter will be familiar to teachers, and particularly the terms as they are used in everyday life. Complex treatment of classroom data is not necessary for teachers, but anyone who gives tests or works with scores soon learns that a systematic method of organizing and analyzing data is necessary if the data are to be used and interpreted in a way that benefits the teaching and learning process. The first purpose of this chapter is to present the skills and techniques necessary to interpret and use classroom data. The second purpose is to consider how basic concepts can be extended and applied in order to improve tests and test development skills. Although this chapter is divided into three sections—organization and treatment of group data, estimation of reliability and standard error, and item analysis—the techniques presented are not discrete in purpose. Both group data and information about reliability, for example, are necessary for the interpretation of a student's score, and item analysis data contribute to the teacher's knowledge of group performance and teaching effectiveness, as well as to the improvement of test quality.

Organizing and Describing Group Data

An examinee's score on a test usually is determined by the number of exercises he has answered correctly on a choice-type or short-answer test or by the number of points the teacher judges he has earned on an essay test. If the test is valid, the score represents the status of the examinee on the trait measured by the test. When a set of papers has been scored, the numbers appear in an unordered fashion, and interpretation is difficult at best. Consider, for example, the twenty scores below taken from a set of alphabetized test papers. These scores are the number of items correct for twenty examinees on a forty-item test.

```
35   21   37   38   31   25   31   29   39   28
28   34   36   35   31   33   26   27   32   36
```

With the scores presented in this way, how well can the following typical questions of interest be answered?

What are the highest and lowest scores?
What is the average score on this test?
How well did the examinee with a score of twenty nine perform compared to others in the class?

Questions such as these can be answered quite easily when the scores have been reordered from highest to lowest:

39 38 37 36 36 35 35 34 33 32
31 31 31 29 28 28 27 26 25 21.

Then it can be seen at a glance that the highest score is 39 and the lowest is 21. The average score appears to be about 32, and thus a score of 29 is slightly below the average. Probably the easiest way to put a set of scores in order is to order the test papers themselves. The time required for this simple task is balanced by the speed with which various questions of interest can be answered.

Simple ordering of scores will be sufficient and practical for most classroom tests and other single measurements. When the teacher returns test papers to students, he can help them interpret their own performance by writing the distribution of ordered scores on the chalkboard. Then each student can see how his score compares with the scores made by other members of the class.

The teacher who does not wish to present the total distribution of scores can accomplish a similar purpose by informing each student of his own rank in the class. *Ranks* are obtained by assigning the highest score a rank of 1, the next highest 2, and so on to the lowest score, as shown in Table 8.1. Tied scores are assigned the average of the ranks each would receive—for example, two scores of 36 in the table share the ranks of 4 and 5 and thus are assigned a rank of 4.5. The three 31s share ranks of 11, 12, and 13 and are assigned the average, 12.

When ranking is used, the scores written on test papers should include the number correct and the rank. The rank tells the student how many examinees earned higher scores; for example, a student with a rank of 9 knows that eight students scored higher than he.

Under certain conditions, as in determining composite scores for students in several sections of the same class, simple ordering may not be convenient. When the scores have a large range—that is, when there is a relatively large difference between the highest and lowest scores—and when a large number of scores are in-

TABLE 8.1

Ranks corresponding with scores for twenty students

Score	Rank
39	1
38	2
37	3
36	4.5
36	4.5
35	6.5
35	6.5
34	8
33	9
32	10
31	12
31	12
31	12
29	14
28	15.5
28	15.5
27	17
26	18
25	19
21	20

volved, a grouped frequency distribution can be used to simplify the subsequent use of the data.

A grouped *frequency distribution* (FD) is prepared by grouping scores into *intervals*. If the scores from the previous example are grouped into intervals containing two score points each, the distribution in Table 8.2 is obtained.

In Table 8.2 the *size* of the interval is 2: the top interval contains the score points 39 and 40, the next interval 37 and 38. After the intervals are determined, the scores in each interval are tallied. The first score in the unordered list, 35, is tallied in 35–36; the second, 21, is tallied in 21–22, and so on through all scores.

TABLE 8.2.

Grouped frequency distribution for the scores of twenty students

Interval	Tally	Frequency
39–40	1	1
37–38	11	2
35–36	1111	4
33–34	11	2
31–32	1111	4
29–30	1	1
27–28	111	3
25–26	11	2
23–24		0
21–22	1	1
		$N=20$

The tally marks are then counted and the numbers entered in the frequency column. The sum of all frequencies, N, should equal the number of scores in the collection, in this case 20.

A frequency distribution can be developed by following a few simple steps: (Data from Tables 8.1 and 8.2 are used in parentheses to illustrate the steps.)

1. Find the range of distribution of scores by subtracting the smallest from the largest score $(39-21=18)$.
2. Divide the range by 10 to obtain an estimate of the size of interval to use $(18 \div 10 = 1.8)$.
3. Select the size of interval from the numbers 2, 3, 5, 10, and multiples of 5 by taking the one next higher than the quotient found in step 2. (The interval of size 2 in the example was selected because the range divided by 10 was 1.8.)
4. Establish the highest interval to include the highest score in the collection (39–40).
5. Establish the other intervals down through the lowest interval, which contains the lowest score in the collection (21–22).

6. Tally the individual scores in each interval.
7. Count the tally marks and write the number in the frequency column (the frequency for some intervals may be zero).
8. Add the frequency column to make sure the sum equals the number of scores in the collection.

Measures of Average

The concept *average* is used widely in our society and has useful applications in the interpretation of classroom measurements. An average is used to describe the typical score and occasionally is the score selected to represent the total collection. For example, a teacher may compare this year's class with last year's in terms of the average on some measure of ability. Suppose the average IQ for this year's class is 112 and for last year's it was 104; the teacher may need to plan more instruction this year that will challenge higher ability students. The average is also used as a reference point for individual scores, and an examinee's score may be described as "well above average," or "slightly below average."

A widely used index of average is the *arithmetic mean* which is found by adding the separate scores and dividing the sum by the number of individual scores in the collection.

$$\text{Mean} = \frac{\text{sum of scores}}{\text{number of scores}}$$

The sum of the 20 scores listed in Table 8.1 is 632. Thus,

$$\text{Mean} = \frac{632}{20} = 31.6$$

The mean is the per individual share of a total. If three children decided to collect pop bottles and sell them to get the money for movie tickets costing $0.50 each, they would need to earn $1.50 or an average of $0.50 each. If they received $0.40, $0.60, and $0.65 for their bottles, the per individual share would be $1.65 ÷ 3 = $0.55. They would have enough money for all to go to the movie and each would have $0.05 left over.

For many reasons which need not be considered here statisticians find the arithmetic mean more useful than any other measure of average. The ease with which the mean can be found should encourage teachers to use it also.

A second useful measure of average that can be calculated easily is the *median*. The median is the score point which has half of the whole set of scores below it and half above it. To find the median of a set of scores, the first step is to put the scores in order from highest to lowest. If the number of scores in the set (*N*) is an *odd* number, the next step is to add one to *N* and to divide the result by 2 to obtain *a*, as follows:

$$a = \frac{N + 1}{2}$$

The final step is to begin at the lowest score and count scores upward to the *a* score. This score will be the median. For example, the median of the following seven scores when put in order—45, 45, 43, 42, 41, 38, 25—would be,

$$a = \frac{7 + 1}{2} = 4.$$

The median is found by beginning with the lowest score and counting upward to the fourth score from the bottom, which is 42.

If the number of scores is an *even* number, *a* is found by simply dividing *N* by 2 as follows:

$$a = \frac{N}{2}$$

In this case, however the median is found by adding the *a* score from the bottom to the next higher score and dividing the result by 2. For example, for following scores, in order—45, 44, 43, 43, 41, 41, 40, 21—$N = 8$, $a = 8/2 = 4$. The fourth score from the bottom is 41, and the next higher score is 43. Thus

$$\frac{41 + 43}{2} = \frac{84}{2} = 42$$

which is the median of the set of scores.

There may be some confusion about tied scores. Actually, ties are disregarded when ordering scores for the purpose of finding the median. In the example above, it makes no difference which score of 41 is regarded as being third from the bottom and which is regarded as being fourth from the bottom. In the following set of scores (48, 47, 46, 45, 45, 44, 42, 39), $a = 4$; and since either of the scores of 45 can be regarded as the fourth score from the bottom, and either 45 can be regarded as the next higher score, the median would be

$$\frac{45 + 45}{2} = 45$$

There are two primary reasons why the median is used widely in classroom work. First, it is easily found, since the teacher need only order the scores and count up through half of them. Second, the median divides the total collection in half; half of the number of scores will be above and half below the median. This characteristic of an average is intuitively understandable to examinees. To illustrate the point, consider the set: 15, 4, 3, 2, 1. The mean would be $25/5 = 5$, larger than four of the five scores in the set. The median is 3, the middle score. In this kind of distribution the value 3 is more acceptable than 5 as an indication of the average or typical score in the set.

Measures of Dispersion

An index of average such as the mean or median refers to a *level* of score within the score scale, usually the number right. For a minimal interpretation of measurements, teachers should also consider the *dispersion* or spread of scores. In the previous section a comparison of classes with average IQs of 112 and 104 was considered. While a somewhat more challenging course of study might be appropriate for the first class *on the average*, the challenge for the teacher might be greater for the second class if the range of talent were greater. For example, the lowest and highest IQs in the first class might be 105 and 120, and thus all students could use successfully and profit from learning materials of about the same level of difficulty. If, on the other hand, the IQs in the other class ranged from a low of 85 to a high of 135, much more individualization of instruction and materials would be required.

A measure of dispersion is an index that describes the extent to which scores are spread out from the average score. It describes the homogeneity (or heterogeneity) of the scores and provides a basis for comparing different collections of scores.

The easiest measure of dispersion to find is the *range*, which is simply the difference between the highest and lowest scores. In the example given in Table 8.1 the range was found to be $39 - 21 = 18$. Although the range is useful in making simple interpretations to students, it is too limited to be of much use in other ways. An index based only on the two extreme scores frequently provides an unreliable and misleading description of the variability of scores precisely because it is based on the two most atypical scores in the class. A comparison of the two sets of scores given in Table 8.3 illustrates this point. Although the range of scores in both groups is 14, four of the scores in Group I are very close together while the scores in Group II are spread across the entire range.

Only one other measure of dispersion will be recommended here, a simple estimate of an index called the standard deviation. A *standard deviation* is based on the difference between each score and the mean. The larger the differences are, the more

TABLE 8.3

Scores for two groups on the same test

Group I	Group II
15	15
4	11
3	8
2	3
1	1
Range = 14	Range = 14

spread out the scores are and the larger the standard deviation will be. A standard deviation (*SD*) is equal to:

$$SD = \sqrt{\frac{\text{Sum of each score } - \text{ the mean and squared}}{\text{Number of scores}}}$$

The estimate that is recommended here is found quite easily:

$$SD = \frac{\text{sum of highest 1/6 of scores } - \text{ sum of lowest 1/6 of scores}}{\text{half of } (N - 1)}$$

To use this formula, find the sum of the highest and sum of the lowest one sixth of the scores; then find the difference between the two sums and divide it by half the number of scores in the collection minus one.

In the earlier example, there are twenty scores. One sixth of 20 would be 3 1/3 scores, so the sum of the highest three scores and the sum of the lowest three scores are used. The formula is applied as follows:

$$SD = \frac{(39 + 38 + 37) - (21 + 25 + 26)}{1/2 \times (20 - 1)}$$

$$= \frac{114 - 72}{1/2 \ (19)} = \frac{42}{9.5} = 4.4$$

For most distributions of classroom test scores, this estimate is sufficiently accurate for the use that will be made of the index. In the preceding example the estimate of 4.4 is slightly low—the actual *SD* is 4.7—but the difference of 0.3 is not large enough to introduce serious error into the use and interpretation of the data.

There are several important uses of the *SD* in classroom work. When the same tests or comparable tests have been given to different classes, the *SD* can be used to describe the relative homogeneity of the classes on the characteristic measured by the test. For example, when the school testing program provides data concerning prior achievement or ability, *SD*s can be compared to derive an assessment of the extent to which students differ in general talent. If a teacher has had experience with a class having an *SD* of 8 and if the new class has an *SD* of 12 on the same test, the teacher can assume that individual differences exist to a greater extent in the new class. A similar application of the SD can be made when the teacher uses the same or a similar test in different sections of the same course. In this case the SDs can be compared to assess the variability of achievement in the different sections.

When two or more test scores are added to compute a composite score, such as a semester or course grade, the weight —importance—of each test in determining the composite is related to the SD of that test in relationship to the other tests in the composite. For example, if scores on two unit tests are added to obtain each student's composite, the test with the larger SD will be more important in determining a student's standing in the class on the composite obtained. Further discussion of this topic may be found in Chapter 9.

The third use of the SD is to derive comparable scores for a given class on two or more tests. This application of the SD will help the teacher describe for individual students the relative quality of performance on different tests. The SDs of different tests are not directly comparable because they are expressed in different units. One cannot assume that a unit on one test represents the same amount of achievement as a unit on another test. However, comparability on different tests is frequently defined in terms of the SD difference between a score and the mean of a distribution. Consider a class that took two tests. Test 1 has a mean of 30 and an SD of 5, and test 2 has a mean of 40 and an SD of 8. If a student earned a score of 35 on test 1, what score must he earn on test 2 to have performed at the same relative level? One way to answer this is to use the SD as a unit of distance along the score scale. The score, 35, is 5 units or the equivalent of 1 SD above mean 1. The comparable score on test 2 would be $40 + 8 = 48$. Scores expressed as SD distances from a mean are called *z-scores*.

Derived Scores

The raw score obtained by counting the number right or total points awarded on a test provides no information about the performance of a student relative to the performance of other students who took the same test. In addition, the raw scores of different tests are on different scales—that is, a unit on one test may not indicate the same increment of performance as the same unit on another test. By using information about the group as a whole, raw scores can be converted into *derived scores*, which can be interpreted more directly and are more comparable from one test to another and from one group to another.

One type of derived score is the standard score. *Standard scores* use the mean and *SD* of the test to increase the interpretability of the test scores. The *z-score*, one type of standard score, expresses a score as the distance in *SD* units the score differs from the mean. The formula for finding z-scores is

$$z = \frac{\text{raw score} - \text{mean}}{SD}$$

Using the data for test 1—mean = 30 and *SD* = 5—the formula for the scores of three students can be illustrated as follows:

Student 1. Raw score = 42, $z = \dfrac{42 - 30}{5} = 2.40$

Student 2. Raw score = 30, $z = \dfrac{30 - 30}{5} = 0.00$

Student 3. Raw score = 24, $z = \dfrac{24 - 30}{5} = -1.20$

Scores for the same students on test 2—mean = 40 and *SD* = 8—can also be converted to z-scores.

Student 1. Raw score = 46, $z = \dfrac{46 - 40}{8} = 0.75$

Student 2. Raw score = 40, $z = \dfrac{40 - 40}{8} = 0.00$

Student 3. Raw score = 36, $z = \dfrac{36 - 40}{8} = -0.50$

In actual practice the teacher who uses z-scores would convert the score of every student in the class. The values of z-scores can then be compared directly to describe the relative performances of each student on the two tests. Assume in the previous computations that the same students are involved. Student 1 has z-scores of 2.40 and 0.75. Obviously he performed much better on test 1.

Student 2 performed equally on the two tests; and student 3, though below average on both tests, performed better on the test 2. The z-score has a direct interpretation in that it indicates whether the individual's test performance is above or below the average (mean) and the distance from the mean in standard deviation units. When an entire set of scores has been converted into z-scores, the distribution will have a mean of 0 and a standard deviation of 1. Since the range of scores in a distribution is seldom more than 6 times the standard deviation, z-scores less than -3.00 or greater than $+3.00$ are very rare, and *at least* 75 percent of all z-scores will be between -2.00 and $+2.00$.

Some teachers prefer to convert z-scores to a scale using whole numbers and to avoid using negative numbers, which often cause mistakes in transcribing and are sometimes confusing to add or subtract. A commonly used scale is the *Z-score* with a mean of 50 and an *SD* of 10, and it can be obtained from z-scores by

$$Z = 10z + 50$$

For the preceding examples the Z-scores are as follows:

1. $Z = 10 \times 2.4 + 50 = 74$
2. $Z = 10 \times 0 + 50 = 50$
3. $Z = 10 \times -1.2 + 50 = 38$

1. $Z = 10 \times .75 + 50 = 57.5$ or 58
2. $Z = 10 \times 0 + 50 = 50$
3. $Z = 10 \times -.5 + 50 = 45$

The comparisons based on these Z-scores would lead to the same conclusions as those based on z-scores. The two scales provide the same information, but the units differ. The z-score has a mean or reference point of 0 and a unit of spread of 1. Z-scores have a reference point of 50 and a unit of spread of 10. Both kinds of derived scores are useful in the classroom.

A second type of derived score is based on the percentage of a class earning lower scores on any given test. A *percentile rank* reports a student's performance in terms of the percentage of his classmates that earn scores lower than his. The percentile rank is found by dividing the number of lower scores by the total number in the class, and multiplying the result by 100:

$$PR = \frac{\text{number of lower scores}}{\text{total number in class}} \times 100$$

The ordered scores from Table 8.1 are used in Table 8.4 to illustrate the computation of the percentile rank. The entries in the column titled "Number of lower scores," represent the

TABLE 8.4

Distribution of ordered scores and the number of scores lower than each score

Score	Number of lower scores	PR
39	19	95
38	18	90
37	17	85
36	15.5	78
36	15.5	78
35	13.5	68
35	13.5	68
34	12	60
33	11	55
32	10	50
31	8	40
31	8	40
31	8	40
29	6	30
28	4.5	22
28	4.5	22
27	3	15
26	2	10
25	1	5
21	0	0

number of persons making scores lower than the score in the corresponding "Score" column. Note that when scores are tied, the entry in the second column is the average of the numbers that would be obtained by simply numbering scores up from the bottom of the list. There are no scores lower than 21, so 0 is entered in column 2. Entries for 25, 26, and 27 are found by adding 1 to the lower entry. For the score of 28, the number of lower scores would be 4 and 5; so 4.5 is entered. Counting up the column, note that the three scores of 31 would have 7, 8, and 9 scores lower, so the average of 7, 8, and 9, namely 8, is entered in the second column for each value of 31.

The percentile rank for the highest scoring student is found by dividing each entry in the second column by the total number of scores, N, and multiplying the result by 100. For a student with a score of 39, the PR is:

$$PR = 19/20 \times 100 = 95$$

For the student with the score of 29, the PR is

$$6/20 \times 100 = 30$$

For each of the three students with scores of 31, the PR is

$$8/20 \times 100 = 40$$

Although this method of finding percentile ranks is slightly different from methods presented in statistics books, the simplified approach is adequate for classroom purposes and is less toilsome for teachers to use. It should also be noted that the score with a PR of 50 is not the same as the more precise median found by the procedures recommended previously. The inconsistency does not introduce serious problems for classroom work.

Percentile ranks can be explained easily to students and provide a good method for reporting test results. In some ways standard scores are more useful for teachers in maintaining records for a unit or semester. The two approaches to test-score interpretation are complementary: a standard score describes how far a student's score is from the average, and the PR describes his relative standing in the class.

Measures of Relationship

The concept *correlation* permeates everyday life and has many important applications in educational measurement. Adults frequently judge the age of a child by his size because age and size are related, at least until adolescence. Small cars are expected to use less gas per mile than large cars because of the relationship between the weight of a car and the gas it consumes. Heating bills are higher for large homes than for small ones. Bright children achieve more in less time than academically average children. The examinees with the highest scores on reading tests tend to earn the highest scores on literature tests because of the relationship between the two skills.

Measures of correlation are numerical indexes that reflect quantitatively the extent the two sets of scores or measures relate to each other—that is, the extent to which examinees hold the same relative positions on the two sets of measures. When the relationship is perfect and direct, the numerical index (or coefficient) is 1.00; when no relationship exists, the coefficient is 0; when the relationship is perfect but inverse, the coefficient is −1.00. Most correlations between measurements of interest in the classroom will be between 0 and +1.00; for example, the scores on two major tests, prior grades and current achievement, and level of interest and level of achievement. Negative relationships do exist—for example, age of students within a class and level of achievement—but will be encountered rarely in working with classroom data.

A correlation coefficient can be computed in a number of ways, but only one procedure, which is easy to apply and provides an approximate index, will be considered here. A correlation coefficient can be found when two sets of scores are available for the same group of students. Assume that a teacher has scores for a class on two major-unit tests, and he wishes to know the correlation or relationship between levels of student success on the two tests. The scores are presented in columns 1 and 2 of Table 8.5.

The calculation of the coefficient of correlation is based on the number of students who are in each of the classifications: high on

TABLE 8.5

A method for computing a correlation coefficient

Student	Score Test 1	Score Test 2	Classification Test 1	Classification Test 2
A	35	40		
B	21	23	L	L
C	37	43	H	H
D	38	47	H	H
E	25	34	L	
F	31	28		L
G	29	31		
H	39	45	H	H
I	28	27	L	L
J	36	42	H	H
K	28	35	*	
L	34	37		
M	36	30	H	L
N	35	39		
O	31	33		
P	33	41		H
Q	26	29	L	L
R	27	31	L	
S	32	40		
T	31	37		

* 28 is the fifth lowest score and there are two 28s. In such cases the teacher should flip a coin or draw a number at random to decide which of the two to include in the low group. The same principle applies if more than two scores are tied, and for the high as well as the low classification.

both tests, low on both tests, high on test 1 but low on test 2, and high on 2 but low on 1.[1] The process of obtaining these classifications is simplified by rank ordering the scores on each test

[1] This method is adapted from J. M. Wolfe, "A Simple Method of Calculating the Coefficient of Correlation," *Journal of Educational Measurement*, 8 (1971): 221–222.

separately. Then the teacher must decide how many students to include in the high and low groups; generally about one fourth of the class in each group is appropriate. In the example given in Table 8.5, there are twenty students in the class, and 5 has been selected as the number of scores in each group.

In the two columns under "classification" the letter H has been entered for the test scores that are among the highest 5 on each test and L has been entered for the 5 lowest scores. The next step is to set up a table such as the one in Table 8.6, showing the four types of classification, and to count the number of scores falling into each of the four cells of the table. In this example, student B is tallied in the lower left corner, labeled LL—low on both tests. C is tallied in the upper right corner, labeled HH, and so on for all the students in the H or L classification on either test. Note that some of the students will not tally in any of the four cells, since they were in the middle half on one or both tests. These scores are omitted from the classification.

TABLE 8.6

Classification table for finding correlation coefficient

The formula for the coefficient (r) is

$$r = \frac{(\text{sum of } HH \text{ and } LL) - (\text{sum of } HL \text{ and } LH)}{2n}$$

In the formula n is the number selected for an extreme group, in this example $n = 5$. So:

$$r = \frac{(4 + 3) - (1 + 0)}{2 \times 5} = \frac{7 - 1}{10} = \frac{6}{10} = .60$$

which is the estimated correlation coefficient.

Although examples of the use and interpretation of correlation are provided in later material, some general aspects of interpretation will be considered here. Coefficients of correlation show the extent to which high and low scores on one test are associated with high and low scores on a second test. The closer the index is to ± 1.00, the stronger the relationship. When r exceeds $\pm .90$, the relationship is quite strong. When r is between $\pm .30$, the relationship is quite weak. Scores on different tests for typical classes will generally be between .40 and .60.

Correlation coefficients do *not* show the proportion of a perfect relationship that exists; an r of .75 is not three fourths of a perfect relationship. Correlation coefficients do *not* show the proportion of high performers on one test who will score high on the second.

Teachers should consider correlation to be only a description of general tendencies—for example, with $r = .60$ between test 1 and test 2, there is a tendency for students who score high on one test to score high on the other. Exceptions certainly exist, as a review of Table 8.5 will show, but a general tendency can be observed.

Reliability and Standard Error of Measurement

Test scores should accurately reflect differences among students in their attainment of the objectives that the test was designed to measure. A test which succeeds in meeting this goal is valid for the purpose of measuring attainment of the specified objectives. One way to insure the validity of a classroom test is to use carefully a table of specifications in constructing the test so that all items will be based on course objectives and content; but even a test so derived, though apparently valid, may yield scores too inaccurate to be useful for evaluation purposes. The accuracy or precision with which a test measures whatever it measures is called reliability. Although a reliable test is not always valid—because though it measures something with accuracy, that something may not be what the teacher desires to measure—an unreliable test cannot be valid. Therefore reliability is necessary, though not sufficient, if a test is to be valid.

Test constructors strive for reliability, but they never achieve it completely, since all test scores are affected to a degree by unreliability. It is useful to conceive of a test score as consisting of two components: the *true score*—the hypothetical average of the scores a person would make if he could be measured an infinite number of times on the same test without remembering previous trials—and the *error score*—the deflection of a person's actual performance from the true score due to error of measurement. The relationship may be represented as a simple sum of the components:

$$X = T + E$$

where:

X = the observed score,

T = the true score,

E = the error score which may be either positive or negative.

The observed score X is the score that the student actually makes on the test, and it is the only score that may be known directly. Although true scores and error scores are never known for any student, their existence is inferred theoretically from the test-taking behavior of students.

First of all, it should be understood that errors of measurement are not mistakes people make in the clerical process of

handling test scores. Errors of measurement arise whenever anyone tries to measure a quantity with less than perfect measuring
instruments. Measuring instruments are all imperfect, so some
error exists in all measurement.

There are many reasons for errors of measurement. First, a
test represents only a sample of the items that could be devised to
represent the desired achievement. The particular items chosen
for a test may work to the advantage or disadvantage of an
examinee. If the test covers heavily topics which he has reviewed
recently, he may perform well. On the other hand, the test may
dwell on material presented during the two days he missed class.
A different sample of items might result in a different assessment
of his achievement. Second, a test score represents the student's
performance at one particular time. Since day-to-day performance
is affected to some extent by variations in physical health, mood,
luck in guessing, or energy level and by variations in external
conditions such as time of day, temperature, or humidity, the
estimate of a person's level of achievement at a particular time may
be atypical of his true achievement level. If the test is of the essay
type, errors of measurement occur in the scoring process. Even
under the most carefully planned, controlled conditions, scores
will depend greatly on the judgment of the person who grades the
essay test.

The difference between the student's true score and his
observed score is a reflection of the accuracy of measurement.
Ideally, this difference is zero. Then there is no error of measurement, and the true score and the observed score are identical.
Although the true score and the error score are never known for
any individual, the test scores of individuals differ from one
another because (1) there are differences among students in the
trait or traits the test measures—that is, the students have different true scores—and (2) the scores are affected by errors of
measurement. The degree to which scores differ from one another
can be described by the standard deviation of the test, SD, but the
square of the standard deviation, known as the *variance*, is more
useful for representing the relative contributions of true scores and

error scores to the apparent differences among students in their test performances.

Just as the observed score can be defined as the sum of the true score and the error score, the variance of the observed scores can be defined as the sum of the variance of the true scores and the variance of the error scores.

$$V_x = V_t + V_e$$

where:

V_x = the variance of the observed scores (the standard deviations squared, SD^2),

V_t = the variance of the true scores,

V_e = the variance of the error scores.

On an ideal test V_e will be zero and there will be no errors of measurement. This fact may be utilized to define a statistic known as the *coefficient of reliability*, which is a useful indicator of the accuracy of the scores on a test. The coefficient of reliability is defined:

$$r_{tt} = \frac{V_t}{V_x}$$

where:

r_{tt} = the coefficient of reliability,

V_x = the variance of the observed scores (SD^2),

V_t = the variance of the error scores.

Note that the coefficient of reliability is the proportion of the observed score variance which is due to true score variance. The higher this proportion, the more reliable the test. The coefficient of reliability may range from 0 to 1.00, and the nearer the coefficient is to 1.00 the more reliable the test is and the more faith the teacher may place in the accuracy of the test scores.

Unfortunately, the coefficient of reliability cannot be computed directly from the preceding formula. Several simple methods are available for estimating the reliability coefficient, but some of them are applicable only to standardized tests. Two methods which might be applied by classroom teachers are presented here.

Split-Halves Method

One procedure for estimating the reliability coefficient is the "split-halves method." This method requires that the test be scored in two separate halves. Usually the odd-numbered items are scored separately from the even-numbered items. For each examinee, then, two scores exist in addition to his total score—his score on the odd-numbered items and his score on the even-numbered items. The coefficient of correlation between the two half-tests is obtained by the procedures already outlined in this chapter. The correlation coefficient thus obtained is then used in the Spearman-Brown formula to estimate the reliability coefficient.[2] The Spearman-Brown formula is

$$r_{tt} = \frac{2r}{1 + r}$$

where:

r_{tt} = the reliability coefficient,

r = the coefficient of correlation between the two halves of the test.

Suppose eighteen students took a sixty-item test with the results shown in Table 8.7. In this example three scores are shown for each examinee: the score on the odd-numbered items, the score on the even-numbered items, and the score on the total test. The correlation between the score on the odd-numbered items and the score on the even-numbered items is estimated from the upper and lower fourths of the scores. The highest five and lowest five scores were used and were classified as shown in Table 8.8.

---

[2] Charles Spearman, "Correlation Calculated with Faulty Data," *British Journal of Psychology*, 3 (1910): 271–295; William Brown, "Some Experimental Results in the Correlation of Mental Abilities," *British Journal of Psychology*, 3 (1910): 296–322.

TABLE 8.7

Half-test and total test scores for eighteen students

	Scores		
Examinee	Odd items	Even items	Total test
1	26	27	53
2	27	25	52
3	26	25	51
4	27	24	51
5	23	24	47
6	22	23	45
7	19	22	41
8	19	20	39
9	21	18	39
10	17	18	35
11	17	18	35
12	17	15	32
13	16	15	31
14	13	18	31
15	17	14	31
16	12	18	30
17	10	19	29
18	14	12	26

Examinees 1, 2, 3, 4, and 5 scored in the highest fourth on both the odd- and even-numbered items. Examinees 13, 14, and 18 scored in the lowest fourth on both the odd- and even-numbered items. The tie among the examinees scoring 18s on the even items was settled by rolling a die. No examinees scored either both in the high fourth on the odd items and the low fourth on the even items or vice versa. Thus, five examinees scored in the high group on both half-tests, and three scored in the low group on both half-tests. These data may be displayed as shown in Table 8.9.

TABLE 8.8

Half-test scores for eighteen students classified to computation of correlation coefficient

	Scores		Classification	
Examinee	Odd items	Even items	Odd items	Even items
1	26	27	*H*	*H*
2	27	25	*H*	*H*
3	26	25	*H*	*H*
4	27	24	*H*	*H*
5	23	24	*H*	*H*
6	22	23		
7	19	22		
8	19	20		
9	21	18		
10	17	18		
11	17	18		
12	17	15		*L*
13	16	15	*L*	*L*
14	13	18	*L*	*L*
15	17	14		*L*
16	12	18	*L*	
17	10	19	*L*	
18	14	12	*L*	*L*

TABLE 8.9

Table for calculating the correlation between odd and even items for eighteen examinees

		Even items	
		H	*L*
Odd items	*H*	5	0
	L	0	3

The formula is:

$$r = \frac{(\text{sum of } HH \text{ and } LL) - (\text{sum of } HL \text{ and } LH)}{2n}$$

Since there were five scores in each fourth, $n = 5$; so:

$$r = \frac{(5 + 3) - (0 + 0)}{2(5)}$$

$$= \frac{8 - 0}{10}$$

$$= .80$$

Thus, .80 is the estimated correlation between the two half-tests consisting of the odd- and even-numbered items. This correlation is then used in the Spearman-Brown formula as follows:

$$r_{tt} = \frac{2r}{1 + r}$$

where:

$$r = .80$$

$$r_{tt} = \frac{2(.80)}{1 + .80}$$

$$= \frac{1.60}{1.80}$$

$$= .89$$

The estimated reliability coefficient is .89, which indicates that 89 percent of the variance of scores on the test is due to variations among the examinees' true scores while $1 - .89 = .11$ or 11 percent of the total score variance is due to errors of measurement.

Saupe Method

For tests on which each item is scored one or zero, an alternate method of estimating test reliability has been introduced by G. F. Kuder and M. W. Richardson,[3] but the method requires the

---

[3] G. F. Kuder and M. W. Richardson, "The Theory of the Estimation of Test Reliability," *Psychometrika*, 2 (1937): 151–160.

calculation of the proportion of examinees who pass and the proportion who fail each item. Although Kuder and Richardson presented a simplified form of their method, an even simpler formula for approximating Kuder and Richardson's formula has been presented by J. L. Saupe.[4] Saupe's formula is simply:

$$r_{tt} = 1 - \frac{.19k}{(SD)^2}$$

where:

r_{tt} = the reliability coefficient,

$(SD)^2$ = the standard deviation of the observed scores squared, or the variance,

k = the number of items on the test,

$.19$ = a constant.

To use Saupe's formula on the data shown in Table 8.7, which gave the results of a sixty-item test, the SD of the total scores must first be computed. As described earlier, the formula is:

$$SD = \frac{\text{sum of highest 1/6 of scores} - \text{sum of lowest 1/6 of scores}}{\text{half of } (N - 1)}$$

Since 1/6 of 18 scores is 3 scores, the three highest and three lowest scores are used.

The three highest total scores in Table 8.7 are 53, 52, and 51, which add up to 156, and the lowest three scores are 30, 29, and 26, which add up to 85. There are eighteen scores in all, so the formula becomes:

$$SD = \frac{156 - 85}{1/2(18\text{-}1)}$$

---

[4] J. L. Saupe, "Some Useful Estimates of the Kuder Richardson Formula Number 20 Reliability Coefficient," *Educational and Psychological Measurement*, 2 (1961): 63–72.

$$= \frac{71}{1/2(17)}$$

$$= \frac{71}{8.5}$$

$$= 8.4$$

Now the standard deviation of 8.7 is used in Saupe's formula as follows:

$$r_{tt} = 1 - \frac{.19k}{(SD)^2}$$

where:

$$k = 60 \text{ items}$$

$$(SD)^2 = (8.4)^2 = 70.56$$

thus:

$$r^{tt} = 1 - \frac{.19(60)}{70.56}$$

$$= 1 - \frac{11.40}{70.56}$$

$$= 1 - .16$$

$$= .84$$

In this case Saupe's method produces an estimate of .84 for the reliability coefficient, which is slightly lower than that from the Spearman-Brown formula.

Comparison of the Two Methods

The reliability coefficient estimated by the Saupe formula is .84, while that estimated by the split-halves method is .89. The different methods involve slightly different assumptions about the nature of the data and of reliability, and therefore diversity of results is to be expected. In general, the Saupe formula should yield lower estimates of the reliability coefficient than the split-halves method, but the two results will not differ appreciably.

The Saupe formula is not suitable for tests which are scored by any method other than that of giving one point for each correct answer and zero points for each incorrect answer, nor is Saupe's method appropriate for tests containing very easy or very difficult items. The split-halves method is strictly applicable only to tests which assign an equal number of points for each correct answer, as do many choice-type tests and attitude scales. Neither method is satisfactory for estimating the reliability of most essay tests or of tests where speed is a primary factor. Methods for calculating the reliability of tests with varying credit per item require more calculation time than is practical for most classroom teachers.[5]

The choice between the Saupe method and the split-halves method of computing reliability depends to a great extent on personal preference. The arithmetic of the split-halves method is simple, but it requires the extra trouble of obtaining scores for each half of the test, which, of course, is a good way to check on the accuracy of the scoring process. Also, when the short-cut method of estimating the correlation between halves is used, some variability in results may occur because ties must be broken randomly; such variation in results is somewhat undesirable. The Saupe formula is very easy to calculate because only the standard deviation and the number of items are needed. The standard deviation is a statistic the teacher would normally calculate in the course of summarizing a test.

For some standardized tests, coefficients of reliability are given which reflect the stability of the test scores—that is, the degree to which scores obtained at one point in time predict scores on the same measurement at a later time. Neither the Saupe method nor the Spearman-Brown method is an indication of the stability of the test scores, but that information is seldom necessary for classroom tests.

Neither of the two methods is totally satisfactory for all purposes, but because of their relative ease of computation and sufficient accuracy for practical purposes they may be useful for

---

[5]A method for essay tests is described in Robert L. Ebel, *Essentials of Educational Measurement* (Englewood Cliffs, N. J.: Prentice-Hall, 1972), pp. 419–420.

describing the reliability of classroom tests. No matter how it is estimated, the reliability coefficient must be interpreted with caution. It is only an estimate of reliability, and applies only to the group tested. The same test used with a different group of students may have very different reliability characteristics. For example, if a multiple-choice test with four choices per item is given to a class, and the mean score of the class is 70 percent of the total number of items, the reliability coefficient of the test will be much higher than it will be for a low-ability class which may make a mean score equal to 30 percent of the items. The mean score for the second class is so near that which would result from uninformed guessing (25 percent) that most students in that class must have known very few answers, and thus the differences among them are due primarily to differences in guessing luck, not real differences in performance.

The improvement of test reliability should be a serious concern of every constructor of classroom tests. Grossly inaccurate test results provide an inadequate basis for making educational decisions. If the essay test is used, reliability can be gained through the carefully planned and executed scoring procedures described in Chapter 4 and by writing items which present uniform tasks to all examinees. The reliability of choice-type tests and short-answer tests can be improved through adequate test length (in general, the more items on a test the more reliable the test) and through the quality of the individual test items. Although little or nothing can be done to improve reliability after a test has been administered, except in the case of essay tests, an inadequately reliable test may be improved for future use by lengthening it and revising or replacing inadequate items.

Standard Error of Measurement

The score that an examinee makes on a test, his observed score, is the sum of his true score and an error of measurement:

$$X = T + E$$

The variance of the observed scores is the sum of the variance of the true scores and the variance of the errors:

$$V_x = V_t + V_e$$

Although the true score and the error score for any one person cannot be known directly, the standard deviation of the error scores can be estimated, and this result can be used in interpreting individual performances. The standard deviation of the errors of measurement is known as the *standard error of measurement* and is estimated:

$$SEM = SD \sqrt{1 - r_{tt}}$$

where:

SEM = the standard error of measurement,

SD = the standard deviation of the test scores,

r_{tt} = the reliability coefficient.

For the data given in Table 8.7 the reliability coefficient was estimated to be .89 by the Spearman-Brown formula, and the standard deviation was 8.4. Applying the formula for the standard error of measurement:

$$
\begin{aligned}
SEM &= 8.4 \sqrt{1 - .89} \\
&= 8.4 \sqrt{.11} \\
&= 8.4 \,(.33) \\
&= 2.77
\end{aligned}
$$

The standard error of measurement, 2.77, means that the standard deviation of the errors of measurement on this test was 2.77. Since the square root of a decimal is difficult for some to calculate, table 8.10 is provided to aid in calculating this factor.

To calculate the standard error of measurement, first find the reliability coefficient and the standard deviation. Enter Table 8.10 with the first digit of the reliability coefficient to find the correct row and then with the second digit to find the correct column. The point where the correct row and column cross is the correct value of $\sqrt{1 - r_{tt}}$ to multiply by the standard deviation of the test. For example, the standard deviation of the previously described

TABLE 8.10

Table to find the value of $\sqrt{1 - r_{tt}}$ for calculating the standard error of measurement

		.00	.01	.02	.03	.04	.05	.06	.07	.08	.09
						Second digit of r_{tt}					
	.0	1.00	.99	.99	.98	.98	.97	.97	.96	.96	.95
	.1	.95	.94	.94	.93	.93	.92	.92	.91	.91	.90
	.2	.89	.89	.88	.88	.87	.87	.86	.85	.85	.84
	.3	.84	.83	.82	.82	.81	.81	.80	.79	.79	.78
First Digit of r_{tt}	.4	.77	.77	.76	.75	.75	.74	.73	.73	.72	.71
	.5	.71	.70	.69	.69	.68	.67	.66	.66	.65	.64
	.6	.63	.62	.62	.61	.60	.59	.58	.57	.57	.56
	.7	.55	.54	.53	.52	.51	.50	.49	.48	.47	.46
	.8	.45	.44	.42	.41	.40	.39	.37	.36	.35	.33
	.9	.32	.30	.28	.26	.24	.22	.20	.17	.14	.10

test was 8.4 and the reliability coefficient estimated by the Saupe method was .84. Entering Table 8.10 with .8, locate row .8, and entering column .04 read downward to where row .8 and column .04 cross. The value there is .40, which is $\sqrt{1 - .84}$. Thus the standard error of measurement is

$$SEM = SD \text{ (value from Table 8.10)}$$
$$= 8.4(.40)$$
$$= 3.36$$

F. M. Lord has presented an even easier method of calculating the standard error of measurement, provided the test is scored one for each correct item and zero for each incorrect item and is neither extremely easy nor extremely difficult.[6] Lord's formula is simply

$$SEM = .432 \sqrt{k}$$

---

[6] F. M. Lord, "Tests of the Same Length Do Have the Same Standard Error of Measurement," *Educational and Psychological Measurement*, 19 (1959): 233–239.

where

k = the number of items,

.432 = a constant.

Thus for the data in Table 8.7, the estimate is

$SEM = .432 \sqrt{60}$

$\qquad = .432\ (7.7460)$

$\qquad = 3.3$

The value of 3.3 is very close to that obtained by applying the first formula to Saupe's reliability coefficient and this is hardly surprising since Saupe's coefficient is based on Lord's estimate of standard error. Using Lord's formula, Table 8.11 was devised to present the standard error of measurement for tests of varying lengths.

According to test theory, errors of measurement follow the normal distribution. This theory can be used to predict that a student will score no more than two standard errors of measurement higher or lower than his true score in 95 percent of the cases,

TABLE 8.11

Table for estimating the standard error of measurement (SEM) directly from the number of items (k)

Items	SEM	Items	SEM
10	1.4	65	3.5
15	1.7	70	3.6
20	1.9	75	3.7
25	2.2	80	3.9
30	2.4	85	4.0
35	2.6	90	4.1
40	2.7	95	4.2
45	2.9	100	4.3
50	3.1	105	4.4
55	3.2	110	4.5
60	3.4	115	4.6

and his observed score will be not more than one standard error greater or less than his true score in 68 percent of the cases. Thus the standard error of measurement may be used to establish *confidence limits* for students' scores. These confidence limits establish a range of scores within which the student's true score is likely to fall, and they allow a statement of the probability that an individual with a given observed score is likely to have a true score which falls within the limits.

For example, if 3.3 is used as the *SEM* of the test described in Table 8.7, the 68 percent confidence limits for a person with a score of 51 can be found by adding and subtracting 3.3 to and from 51. The upper confidence limit is $51 + 3.3 = 54.3$, and the lower confidence limit is $51 - 3.3 = 47.7$. There are 68 chances in 100 that a person with an observed score of 51 on the test would have a true score between 47.7 and 54.3. This use of the standard error helps increase the test user's awareness of the fallibility of test scores for describing individual status.

When grades are assigned, each grading category should be at least three standard errors of measurement wide so that in terms of true score performance no examinee is likely to be misclassified by more than one grade category. Since a grade category is generally one standard deviation in width, a classroom test should have a reliability coefficient of at least .89 for all the five grade categories to be used (*A, B, C, D,* and *F*). In fact, the typical classroom test has much less reliability. A typical teacher who writes a one-hour test will do well to have a reliability of .70, but a composite score consisting of the combined results of several tests may well have the necessary reliability to justify the use of the full range of grades.

Item Analysis

Item analysis includes a number of techniques for summarizing the results for each item on a test. The purposes of item analysis are (1) to evaluate instructional effectiveness, (2) to estimate individual and group attainment through the information about performance on each item, and (3) to improve test quality by discovering defective and ineffective items so that such items may be replaced or improved for future use. Since the quality of a test depends largely on the quality of individual items, item analysis is an important ingredient in the improvement of classroom tests and the advancement of the teacher's test construction skills.

Item analysis techniques include the computation of two statistical indexes, difficulty and discrimination, and the logical inspection of item responses. The statistical indexes can be routinely computed, but interpretation requires some experience and judgment.

Difficulty Index for One-Zero Items

The *difficulty index* indicates the proportion of examinees who pass a given item. If each item is scored one point for a right answer and zero points for a wrong answer, this index may be calculated for each item by counting the number of examinees who answer the item correctly and dividing the result by the total number of examinees. For mastery tests, the difficulty index should be computed from the total group of examinees, but for discriminatory tests, adequate estimates of item difficulty may be computed by using only the examination papers of students who made high scores and students who made low scores on the total test.

For theoretical reasons, test constructors have long been advised to use the papers of the highest scoring 27 percent of the examinees and the lowest scoring 27 percent of the examinees in the item analysis process. For practical purposes, however, the classroom teacher can use the highest 25 percent and the lowest 25 percent of the papers. The middle 50 percent are not included in the item analysis unless the class size is small—less than forty. In that case, the ten highest scoring papers and the ten lowest scoring papers are analyzed. If class size is less than twenty, all papers should be used after being divided into an upper and a lower group. If there is an odd number of papers, the middle paper should be discarded. Sometimes there is a question about which paper to place in a group because of tied scores. Ties may be decided by any random procedure, such as tossing a coin or die, drawing a card, or drawing names from a hat.

Suppose a teacher has given a test to nineteen examinees and has obtained the following results:

24   38   29   25   33   36   42   15   10   28   34   49   33
43   11   41   23   42   41

He would put the test papers in rank order of performance as shown in Table 8.12. Since there are only nineteen scores, the

TABLE 8.12

Scores and ranks of nineteen students on a test

Student	Score	Rank
1	49	1
2	43	2
3	42	3.5
4	42	3.5
5	41	5.5
6	41	5.5
7	38	7
8	36	8
9	34	9
10	33	10.5
11	33	10.5
12	29	12
13	28	13
14	25	14
15	24	15
16	23	16
17	15	17
18	11	18
19	10	19

highest nine scores are included in the upper group, the lowest
nine scores are included in the lower group, and the middle score
is discarded. Two persons have made scores of 33 and are tied for
the ranks of 10 and 11. In order to decide which student's paper
with a score of 33 to include in the lower scoring group and which
one to omit from the item analysis, the teacher can toss a coin, roll
a die, or use some other random procedure. If the high scoring
and low scoring groups are established using the procedure described, the highest scoring group will include the papers with the
following scores: 34, 36, 38, 41, 41, 42, 42, 43, and 49; and the
lowest scoring group will include the papers with the lowest total
scores: 10, 11, 15, 23, 24, 25, 28, 29, and 33.

Table 8.13 shows the correct number of papers to include in
the highest and lowest groups for a representative number of class
sizes. For class sizes of forty or more, the teacher can always
determine the appropriate number of papers to include in each
group by dividing the total number of papers by 4 and rounding
the result to the nearest whole number.

Once the proper number of papers to include in the highest
and lowest scoring groups has been determined, the teacher sorts
the papers into their appropriate groups. Then the teacher com-
piles a table for each item showing the number of correct and
incorrect answers for that item in each group. Table 8.14 shows
the results for item 33 on a test taken by nineteen students.

According to the data presented in Table 8.14, the nine
highest scoring papers and the nine lowest scoring papers were
analyzed for a class of nineteen students after the middle paper
had been discarded. In the highest scoring group, seven students
answered the item correctly, and in the lowest scoring group four
students answered the item correctly. Both groups together made
a total of eleven correct answers and seven incorrect answers. The
index of difficulty may be computed by dividing the number of
correct responses in both groups by the number of papers analyzed
in both groups:

$$\text{Index of difficulty} = \frac{\text{number of correct answers in both groups}}{\text{total number of papers in both groups}}$$

TABLE 8.13

Sizes of highest and lowest scoring groups, size of combined groups, and number of papers omitted for item analysis for various class sizes

Class size	N_H Size of highest group	N_L Size of lowest group	N_C Size of combined groups	Number omitted from analysis
10	5	5	10	0
11	5	5	10	1
12	6	6	12	0
13	6	6	12	1
14	7	7	14	0
15	7	7	14	1
16	8	8	16	0
17	8	8	16	1
18	9	9	18	0
19	9	9	18	1
20	10	10	20	0
25	10	10	20	5
30	10	10	20	10
35	10	10	20	15
40	10	10	20	20
45	11	11	22	23
50	13	13	26	24
55	14	14	28	27
60	15	15	30	30
65	16	16	32	33
70	18	18	36	34
75	19	19	38	37
80	20	20	40	40

For the data in Table 8.14 the computation is as follows:

$$\text{Index of difficulty} = \frac{11}{18} = .61$$

Thus somewhat more than half the students passed the item.

TABLE 8.14

Item analysis table based on a class of nineteen students

Item 33

	High scoring	Low scoring	Total
Correct	7	4	11
Incorrect	2	5	7
Total	9	9	18

The index of difficulty is simply the proportion of students taking an examination who pass a given item, but whether or not an item is of appropriate difficulty depends on the nature and purpose of the test. The purpose of a discriminatory test is to distinguish among students on a continuum of achievment, and therefore it is desirable for a test to yield a distribution of scores with a wide variability. Variability among test scores will be greatest when each item is highly correlated with the other items on the same test.

Items which are scored right or wrong (one point for a correct answer, zero points for a wrong answer) will have maximal variances and maximal potential for correlation with other items when item difficulty is .50. In other words, .50 represents an idealized index of difficulty for all single-point items on a discriminatory test. This ideal may be tempered for choice-type tests by adding a correction for chance success to .50. This correction is .50 divided by the number of choices per item. For two-choice items (true-false) the ideal difficulty is .75; for four-choice items, .63; and for five-choice, .60. As the number of choices increases, the ideal difficulty approaches .50.

The recommended difficulty index for discriminatory test items is based on a desire to build a test with the best psychometric properties—that is, a test which maximizes differences among examinees. Strict adherence to the criterion of .50 will result in tests that are too difficult for classroom use. Better teacher-student relationships, more study effort, and more learning may result if items are somewhat easier.[7] In addition, for material which has been presented specifically in the class and which all students have studied, the teacher may find himself using many items calling for obscure achievements or requiring students to deal with excessively novel material in order to create test items that have "ideal" difficulties. The inclusion of too many fine points and too much novel material and the exclusion of many items that deal with course objectives but which are too easy may result in a test that departs from the intended specifications and loses its validity. Teachers should lean toward the somewhat easier item, with difficulties of about .70 on four- or five-choice tests. Of course, some items that are more difficult or easier are permissible when they fit the table of specifications.

The meaning of item difficulty for a criterion-referenced (or mastery) test is different from that for a discriminatory test. For such a test, differences among examinees at all levels of ability are less relevant. Only a distinction between those who pass and those who fail is important. On a criterion-referenced test the skills to be measured are generally very basic, and the teacher would expect a rather high proportion of a class to have mastered them. The ideal difficulty index for mastery test items would probably range from .80 to 1.00. Since items for a discriminatory test are generally written and selected to have a difficulty index below .80, the difficulty index for a mastery item is more nearly an indicator of teacher effectiveness than is the difficulty index of a discriminatory item. A teacher would probably discard or rewrite a discriminatory test item with a difficulty index above .80, but he should not be disturbed by a difficulty index of .80 or higher for a mastery test item. In fact, a high index of difficulty on a mastery test item

---

[7] R. N. Marso, "The Influence of Test Difficulty upon Study Efforts and Achievement," *American Educational Research Journal,* 6 (1969): 621–632.

would be encouraging to a teacher because it would indicate that a high proportion of students had mastered the skill to which the item was related and that the skill had been learned effectively by the class.

For the criterion-referenced test, items may be easy or difficult. There is no statistical basis for an ideal difficulty level since maximizing variation among examinees is not relevant to the purpose of the test. Therefore, the desired difficulty level is set by the expectations of the teacher or the school. The proportion of examinees who pass the item indicates the degree to which the concept measured by the item has been acquired and whether remedial teaching is needed.

Difficulty Index for Multiple-Point Items

The computation of indexes of difficulty for essay items, or any items which are scored on other than a two-point scale (one point for a right answer and zero points for a wrong answer) requires an alteration of the methods described in the previous section. D. R. Whitney and D. L. Sabers have described procedures for the item analysis of essay tests, and their recommendations, with some changes, are followed in this section.[8]

The initial procedures for item analysis for essay tests are identical to those for choice-type and one-zero scored tests. The teacher puts the papers into order from highest to lowest according to the total score. Then the highest scoring 25 percent and lowest scoring 25 percent of the papers are separated from the others and used for item analysis. The recommendations given in Table 8.13 may be followed for deciding how many papers to include in each group.

After dividing the papers into the high and low scoring groups, the sum of points made on each item must be calculated

[8] D. R. Whitney and D. L. Sabers, "Improving Essay Examinations III. Use of Item Analysis," *Technical Bulletin*, 11 (Iowa City: University Evaluation and Examination Service, 1970) mimeographed. See also D. R. Whitney and D. L. Sabers, "Two Generalizations of the Item Discrimination Index to Multi-Score Items," *The Journal of Experimental Education*, 39 (1971): 88–92.

for each group. Suppose that forty students took an essay test, and the total scores of the highest ten were 75, 68, 72, 60, 65, 78, 63, 69, 69, and 68; and the scores of the lowest ten were 45, 40, 35, 35, 44, 43, 45, 39, 25, and 20. Suppose that the scores on the first item of the test can range from 0 to 5, and that for the high scoring group the item scores are 5, 4, 5, 4, 4, 3, 5, 2, 3, and 3, while for the low scoring group the scores on the same item are 2, 2, 1, 1, 3, 3, 4, 3, 0, and 0. These scores may be summarized as shown in Table 8.15.

Table 8.15 shows the possible item scores for each group in the first column. The column headed F (frequency) shows the number of examinees who made each item score. For example, in the high scoring group, three examinees made scores of 5, and in the low scoring group zero examinees made scores of 5. The total of column F is the number of papers in that group, in this case ten. Each entry in the column headed FX is found by multiplying the corresponding entries in the item score column by the entries in the F column. Thus the total of the FX column is equal to the sum of the item scores for that group. The difficulty index for essay items is defined as the proportion of the difference between the highest and lowest possible item score that the average score for the class represents. The index may be calculated as follows:

TABLE 8.15

Summary of class performance on an essay item

High scoring group			Low scoring group		
Item score	F	FX	Item score	F	FX
5	3	15	5	0	0
4	3	12	4	1	4
3	3	9	3	3	9
2	1	2	2	2	4
1	0	0	1	2	2
0	0	0	0	2	0
Total	10	38	Total	10	19

$$\text{Index of difficulty} = \frac{S_H + S_L - [(n_T)(X_{min})]}{n_T(X_{max} - X_{min})}$$

where

S_H = Sum of the FX column for the high scoring group,

S_L = Sum of the FX column for the low scoring group,

X_{max} = maximum *possible* score on the item,

X_{min} = minimum *possible* score on the item,

n_T = total number of papers in the combined high and low groups.

For the item in Table 8.15, $S_H = 38$, $S_L = 19$, $X_{max} = 5$, $X_{min} = 0$, and $n_T = 20$ (the number in the high group plus the number in the low group). In terms of the formula:

$$\text{Index of difficulty} = \frac{38 + 19 - [(20)(0)]}{20\ (5-0)}$$

$$= \frac{38 + 19 - 0}{20\ (5)}$$

$$= \frac{57}{100}$$

$$= .57$$

The index of difficulty is equal to .57, which means that the class average is 57 percent of the difference between the lowest and highest possible class averages.

Discrimination Index for One–Zero Items

The index of discrimination is an important indicator of item effectiveness for any discriminatory test. Since the purpose of discriminatory tests is to distinguish as much as possible among students at all levels of achievement so that differences in achievement may be determined, an index of the contribution of each item to the discrimination process is needed. In general, an item which tends to be passed by students who have good command of the objectives measured by the total test and which tends to be failed by students who do poorly on the total test may be considered to contribute in a positive way to the ability of the test to discriminate accurately among different levels of student performance, and thus to the reliability of the test scores.

An excellent index of item discrimination may be calculated by dividing the test papers into high scoring and low scoring groups, exactly as was done for the index of difficulty, and calculating the difference between the proportion of examinees in the high scoring group who pass the item and the proportion of examinees in the low scoring group who pass the item. The formula is

$$\text{Index of discrimination} = \frac{R_H - R_L}{n_H},$$

where

R_H = the number of right answers in the high scoring group,

R_L = number of right answers in the low scoring group,

n_H = number of papers in either the high or low scoring group.

For the data in Table 8.14, $R_H = 7$, $R_L = 4$, and $n_H = 9$; therefore the calculation is as follows:

$$\text{Index of discrimination} = \frac{7 - 4}{9}$$

$$= \frac{3}{9}$$

$$= .33$$

The proportion of students in the high scoring group who passed the item was .77, while in the low scoring group it was .44. The index indicates that the proportion of students in the high scoring group who passed the item exceeded the proportion of students in the low scoring group who passed the item by .33.

The maximum possible discrimination index is 1.00 and the minimum possible is -1.00. An index of 1.00 would indicate that every examinee in the high scoring group passed the item and every examinee in the low scoring group failed the item. In such a case the discrimination between students with generally high command of the course objectives and students with low command of the objectives would be maximum.

A negative discrimination index indicates that students who made low scores on the test as a whole tended to answer the item correctly more frequently than students who did well on the test as a whole. Such a paradox may be the result of any of a number of causes. When the items are of the choice-type, negatively discriminating items often result from an error in the scoring key. Sometimes, in an attempt to obtain multiple-choice items with very homogeneous responses or to make distractors attractive, the test constructor unintentionally writes an item with two correct responses, and in such cases the test must be rescored. Occasionally, a wrong alternative is especially attractive to well-prepared students, which may indicate that a misconception has been allowed to persist.

Ambiguous or poorly written items are sometimes negatively discriminating; and if an item is so easy that students miss it only through carelessness or is so difficult that more students answer correctly by guessing than because of real achievement, the item may also discriminate negatively. Negative discrimination indexes generally indicate defective items. Therefore the cause should be sought and corrected by rewriting the item or replacing it with a better one for the next test over the same unit of work.

Since discrimination indexes calculated from the upper and lower scoring 25 percents of the papers can be 1.00 only when item difficulty is .50, discrimination indexes are generally expected to be lower for criterion-referenced items than for discriminatory test items because criterion-referenced items are passed typically by a high proportion of the examinees. Table 8.16 shows the maximum and minimum possible discrimination indexes for various levels of item difficulty when both difficulty and discrimination indexes are calculated from upper and lower 25 percents of the group. Since criterion-referenced items generally have difficulty indexes of .80 or greater, discrimination indexes above .40 are not expected, and they would usually be much lower. Therefore a

TABLE 8.16

Maximum and minimum possible indexes of discrimination for selected difficulty indexes

Item difficulty index	Maximum possible discrimination	Minimum possible discrimination
.00	.00	.00
.10	.20	−.20
.20	.40	−.40
.30	.60	−.60
.40	.80	−.80
.50	1.00	−1.00
.60	.80	−.80
.70	.60	−.60
.80	.40	−.40
.90	.20	−.20
1.00	.00	.00

revised method of calculating discrimination for criterion-referenced tests is recommended.

Since the items on a criterion-referenced test are not expected to discriminate among all levels of competence, but only to aid in making a pass or fail decision, the teacher can evaluate such items more properly by comparing the performance of students who fail the total test with that of students who pass the total test. On a good item he would expect differences in performance between students who fail the total test and those who pass the total test. Instead of basing the discrimination index on the highest and lowest scoring fourths of the examinees, he would put into the low scoring group all students who failed the total test. Thus all examinees' performances would be analyzed, and the index of discrimination would be defined as the difference between the proportion of passing examinees who answer the item correctly and the proportion of failing examinees who answer the item correctly. The formula for criterion-referenced test items is as follows:

$$\text{Index of discrimination} = \frac{R_P}{n_p} - \frac{R_F}{n_F}$$

where:

R_P = number of persons who passed the total test, and answered the item correctly,

R_F = number of persons who failed the total test, and answered the item correctly,

n_p = number of persons who passed the total test,

n_F = number of persons who failed the total test.

Table 8.17 shows the results for a hypothetical criterion-referenced test item. The test was passed by 40 students and failed by 10 students; thus $n_p = 40$ and $n_F = 10$. The item was correctly answered by 43 of the 50 examinees who took it. In the passing group 38 of 40 examinees passed the item, so $R_p = 38$; and in the failing group 5 of 10 examinees passed the item, so $R_F = 5$. The discrimination index is as follows:

$$\text{Index of discrimination} = \frac{38}{40} - \frac{5}{10}$$

$$= .95 - .50$$

$$= .45$$

TABLE 8.17

Item analysis data for a criterion-referenced item

Status on total test

		Passed	Failed	Total
Status on item	Correct	38	5	43
	Incorrect	2	5	7
	Total	40	10	50

The proportion of passing students who answered the item correctly exceeded the proportion of failing students answering correctly by .45.

For criterion-referenced tests, the discrimination is less critical than for discriminatory tests, and maximal item discrimination is not an objective. The teacher should not be much disturbed by low discrimination indexes for such items, but a negative index of discrimination would indicate that students judged generally unsatisfactory had done better on the item than students judged generally satisfactory. In such a case either the item is defective or something has gone wrong in the teaching process.

Discrimination Index for Multiple-Point Items

The discrimination index for essay and multiple-point items may be developed as an extension of the difficulty index for such items.[9] First the papers are put in order of total score and then the upper and lower fourths of the papers are identified. The item data are arranged as was done for Table 8.9, and the following formula is used for the item analysis:

$$\text{Index of discrimination} = \frac{S_H - S_L}{n_H \ (X_{max} - X_{min})}$$

where:

S_H = sum of the FX column for the high scoring group,

S_L = sum of the FX column for the low scoring group,

n_H = number of papers in the high scoring group,

X_{max} = maximum possible score on the item,

X_{min} = minimum possible score on the item.

For the data in Table 8.15, $S_H = 38$, $S_L = 19$, $X_{max} = 5$, $X_{min} = 0$, and $n_H = 10$; therefore:

$$\text{Index of discrimination} = \frac{38 - 19}{10 \ (5 - 0)}$$

---

[9] Whitney and Sabers, "Improving Essay Examinations III. Use of Item Analysis."

$$= \frac{19}{10\,(5)}$$

$$= \frac{19}{50}$$

$$= .38$$

The index represents the difference between the sums of the item scores in the high and low group as a proportion of the maximum possible difference between those sums.

Analyzing Multiple-Choice Distractors

For multiple-choice items, the indexes of difficulty and discrimination may be calculated by the methods already described, but students responses to the distractors are also of interest because they may point out weak and unattractive distractors. Ideally, each distractor in a multiple-choice item should attract several of the low scoring group. In practice, unless class size is large, this can be expected to occur only over several uses and re-uses of an item. The data for a multiple-choice item may be recorded in a table such as the one shown in Table 8.18.

TABLE 8.18
_____

Item analysis table for a multiple-choice item

		Total score		
		High 25%	Low 25%	Total
Choice	A	1	2	3
	*B	16	9	25
	C	2	2	4
	D	1	6	7
	Omit	0	1	1
	Total	20	20	40

Each row of Table 8.18 shows the number of students in the high and low scoring group who picked each alternative. The asterisk indicates that choice B was the keyed response. The difficulty and discrimination indexes were .63 and .35 respectively:

$$\text{Index of difficulty} = \frac{16 + 9}{40} = \frac{25}{40} = .63$$

$$\text{Index of discrimination} = \frac{16 - 9}{20} = \frac{7}{20} = .35$$

All the distractors attracted at least three examinees, and in no case did more high achievers than low achievers select any one distractor; one student omitted the item altogether. Since each distractor attracted one or more examinees and no distractor attracted more high scoring than low scoring students, the item functioned reasonably well, although a more even distribution of wrong answers over the distractors would have been desirable.

The analysis of another item is shown in Table 8.19. The indexes of difficulty and discrimination for the item in Table 8.19 are calculated as follows:

$$\text{Index of difficulty} = \frac{29}{60} = .48$$

$$\text{Index of discrimination} = \frac{14 - 15}{30} = \frac{-1}{30} = -.03.$$

Since the index of discrimination is only $-.03$, the item analyzed in Table 8.19 worked very poorly, choice B looks suspicious, for it was chosen by more examinees in the high scoring group than in the low scoring group; choice D was also chosen with rather high frequency. Perhaps the item was ambiguous; or perhaps choice B, choice D, or both came very close to being correct answers.

Ideally, the wrong answers to a multiple-choice item should be distributed about equally among the distractors. This seldom proves to be the case in actual practice, but distractors which do not attract any wrong answers from the low scoring group of students fail in their role of providing a plausible response for the misinformed or uninformed examinee. On the other hand, a

TABLE 8.19

Item analysis table for a multiple-choice item

	Total score		Total
	High 25%	Low 25%	
*A	14	15	29
B	8	3	11
C	0	6	6
D	6	3	9
Omit	2	3	5
Total	30	30	60

(Choice — left label for rows A, B, C, D, Omit)

distractor that attracts a great many examinees, especially those who have scored well on the total test, may be too close in meaning to the correct answer. Since the alternatives, as well as the stem, affect the difficulty and discrimination of multiple-choice items, revision of the alternatives rather than the stem is often the most effective route to improving the item. Sometimes the revision of a single defective distractor will change the characteristics of a multiple-choice item completely.

Recording choices in the item analysis of multiple-choice tests can be tedious, and a typewriter is a useful aid. In the touch-typing position, the right hand is set on the keys, j, k, l, and ;. These can be substituted for the choices A, B, C, D, or 1, 2, 3, 4 in item analysis. Table 8.20 shows an item analysis recorded for ten multiple-choice items. The responses to each item may be typed on a single line for one person without moving the right hand from the basic touch-typing position. The left hand is free to keep track of the place on the answer sheet. Each line in Table 8.20 indicates the responses for one student and each column indicates the response to a single item: the responses for item 1 are

TABLE 8.20

Item analysis data for a multiple-choice test of ten items

High scoring group	Low scoring group

```
High scoring group                    Low scoring group

j  ;  ;  k  k  l  k  ;  j  l        k  ;  k  l  l  k  ;  j  k
k  k  ;  k  l  l  k  ;  k  l        j  k  l  k  l  l  k  ;  l  j
j  ;  ;  k  l  k  k  ;  j  l        k  ;  k  k  ;  l  k  l  k  k
j  j  ;  k  l  l  j  ;  j  k        ;  ;  l  ;  l  k  j  j  l  l
j  j  k  k  l  l  k  ;  ;  l        k  j  ;  k  k  l  ;  k  k  l
k  ;  ;  ;  l  l  k  ;  j  ;        l  k  ;  ;  l  k  k  l  j  j
;  ;  l  k  l  l  k  ;  j  l        j  ;  ;  k  k  l  k  ;  k  k
j  ;  ;  k  l  k  k  j  j  ;        j  k  k  ;  ;  l  ;  ;  l  l
j  j  ;  k  l  l  k  ;  j  l        j  k  l  k  l  l  k  k  j  l
j  ;  l  k  k  ;  k  l  j  l        l  ;  l  k  k  j  j  k  j  ;
```

in the first column, the responses for item 2 in the second column, and so forth. The key is A, D, D, B, C, C, B, D, A, C (*j;;kllk;jl*). The data for item 1 of Table 8.20 are displayed in Table 8.21. The indexes of difficulty and discrimination for item 1 shown in Table 8.21 are as follows:

$$\text{Index of difficulty} = \frac{11}{20} = .55$$

$$\text{Index of discrimination} = \frac{7 - 4}{10} = .30$$

TABLE 8.21

Item analysis data for item 1 of Table 8.20

	Total score		
	High	Low	Total
*A	7	4	11
B	2	3	5
C	0	2	2
D	1	1	2
Total	10	10	20

Interpreting and Using Item Analysis Data

Item analysis techniques help to improve tests and provide thorough data on class achievement on the concept measured by the item. The discrimination index can indicate ineffective and defective items. One of the very important characteristics of item analysis is that it provides useful feedback to the test writer and helps him improve his item-writing skills.

Over a period of years the teacher should build a file of test items. Each item can be typed on a 4-by 6-inch file card along with item analysis indexes. The table of specifications showing the objective and the content can be used as a system for cross filing the cards. From semester to semester, the labor involved in preparing effective examinations will decrease as the teacher's job becomes primarily one of selecting, revising, and assembling items rather than preparing entirely new tests. Over the years the teacher's examinations will improve if careful item analysis procedures are followed. Obviously, the teacher should not yield to the temptation to use the same test time after time. Even the best examinations eventually become dated or out of keeping with the content and emphasis of the course. Even worse, no system of examination security is unbreakable, and a test which is constantly re-used will fall eventually into the hands of students, completely discrediting the fairness of the course. The teacher with a large item file who uses a little revision and a few new items can easily assemble new and effective examinations.

It is important that the test constructor react properly when an ineffective or defective item is located. It is always tempting to discard defective items, but often improvement is possible through proper attention to the rules of item writing. A study by A. Lange, I. J. Lehmann, and W. A. Mehrens indicated that revision of an item is not only likely to result in greater improvement in item discrimination than writing a new item as a replacement, but that the time required to revise an item is only about one fifth of the time needed to write a new one.[10] The test constructor should

---

[10] A. Lange, I. J. Lehmann, and W. A. Mehrens, "Using Item Analysis to Improve Tests," *Journal of Educational Measurement* 4 (1967); 65–68.

make certain that an item which has been revised still measures
the concept and objective it was intended to measure originally. If
an item is discarded, it should be replaced with one measuring the
same outcome. Otherwise, the table of specifications for the test
will be altered and the validity of the test may suffer.

Some types of items seem to have poorer item analysis
characteristics than others. Computational items typically have
good qualities of discrimination, but many easier items are relatively poor discriminators. If an item represents an important
concept but the discrimination is low, it may be appropriate to
include more items on that concept in order to give the concept
better coverage on the test as a whole. This is good procedure
because the discrimination index reflects to some degree the
importance of the item in determining the total test score.

The size of the group should also be considered in interpreting item analysis data. Item analysis techniques were developed by
those interested in standardized tests. For very large groups, item
analysis data may be expected to be relatively stable. For small
groups (and this means most classes) little reliance may be placed
on a single item analysis. However, if an item shows poor characteristics over several usages, it is probably a poor item.

Item characteristics may change drastically if the curriculum
changes. One teacher had an item with a discrimination of about
.70 and a difficulty of about .50. He decided to emphasize the
point tested by the item in a subsequent class, and the difficulty
index changed to .90 while the discrimination index dropped to
about .00. Item analysis results may be affected by changes in
teaching content or in objectives.

Although the item analysis data for an entire group, especially
an index of difficulty, may indicate objectives which have been
satisfactorily mastered by the group as a whole, the teacher should
be cautious in interpreting data from single items as indicators of
an individual student's achievement. If several items over a single
objective have been scored together as a subscore, some reliable
information about the individual may be obtained for use in
diagnosing particular strengths and weaknesses, but single items

are seldom adequate for judging the degree to which a student has attained an objective.

Summary

For every test the teacher should at least calculate the median or mean and the standard deviation and make a frequency distribution of the scores. The standard deviation will provide a convenient unit of measurement, and either the class mean, median, or the criterion (the level of performance required for a passing score on a criterion-referenced test) can serve as the point of reference for interpreting individual scores. A frequency distribution showing the performance of the whole class is useful for the teacher in the interpretation of scores and is also valuable for communication with the class about test results. A student who knows the mean or median and who can see the frequency distribution of the whole class can understand more easily the meaning of his own score. Even with criterion-referenced tests, knowledge of how others have performed on the same test can help the student understand the meaning of his own performance.

The reliability coefficient and the standard error of measurement are indicators of the accuracy of the test scores. They serve as reminders that test scores are approximations of student status, not absolutes. The degree of reliability that a test requires depends on how the scores will be used, but high reliability is one of the indications of a quality test. The methods presented in this chapter for estimating the reliability coefficient and the standard error of measurement require a minimum of computation and should be sufficiently accurate for most classroom applications.

Although item analysis requires more effort than the other quantitative methods described in this chapter, it is very important in improving the quality of future tests. Since high quality items are more likely to result from the revision of previously used items than from the writing of completely new items, the practice of saving test items and revising them for future use is highly desirable. Item analysis techniques aid the revision process by detecting weak and ineffective items. Since revising items generally requires much less time than writing new items, the time spent in item analysis will soon be repaid by the time saved in producing new tests.

Although many teachers feel that the use of quantitative methods are too much trouble, the dividends gained in test improvement and in understanding and interpreting test results are high. Much of the drudgery of statistical calculation and scoring can be avoided by using scoring machines and computers, which should become more widely available to teachers in the near future. At present, electronic calculators are available at reasonable cost, and great savings in time and improvements in accuracy can be gained through the use of these machines.

Exercises

1. What is the mean of the arithmetic test scores shown in Table 8.22? What is the mean of the science test scores?

2. What is the estimated standard deviation of the arithmetic test scores shown in Table 8.22? What is the standard deviation of the science test scores?

3. Did boys or girls do better on the average on the arithmetic test?

4. Which sex was more variable in its performance on the science test?

5. What is the grouped frequency distribution for the arithmetic scores in Table 8.22?

6. What are the ranks corresponding to each arithmetic score in Table 8.22?

7. What is the median of the arithmetic scores shown in Table 8.22?

8. What is the percentile rank of Sarah's arithmetic score? Of Joan's arithmetic score? Of Robert's arithmetic score?

TABLE 8.22

Name, sex, arithmetic test scores, and science test scores of twenty-eight students

Student	Sex	Arithmetic score	Science score
Alice	F	36	58
Allen	M	25	37
Anita	F	39	49
Bernice	F	33	42
Bert	M	51	82
Emerson	M	35	36
Ethel	F	33	49
George	M	38	37
James	M	45	55
Janice	F	38	70
Jefferson	M	37	52
Joan	F	40	20
Karl	M	41	33
Kathleen	F	50	65
Kimberly	F	34	39
Kurt	M	46	74
Laurel	F	51	77
Louise	F	53	77
Maria	F	38	37
Pauline	F	36	39
Pearl	F	32	34
Richard	M	51	76
Robert	M	54	68
Sarah	F	34	26
Stephen	M	40	54
Victoria	F	43	61
Vincent	M	40	48
William	M	33	38

9. On a test with a mean of 75 and a standard deviation of 20, what would be the z-scores corresponding to raw scores of 50, 70, 85, and 90?

10. What is the estimated coefficient of correlation between the arithmetic scores and the science scores in Table 8.22?

11. What is the estimated reliability coefficient of the arithmetic test (assuming the test is sixty items long)? Assuming one hundred items on the science test, what is the estimated reliability of that test?

12. If a test were scored in halves and the correlation between the half-test scores were .70, what would be the estimated reliability of the full length test?

13. If the science test in Table 8.22 is assumed to have one hundred items, what is the estimated standard error of measurement of that test?

14. If a certain test has a reliability coefficient of .85 and a standard deviation of 15, what is its standard error of measurement?

15. An item analysis of an essay test was carried out. The results for item 1 were as follows:

High scoring group		Low scoring group	
Item score	F	Item score	F
6	5	6	1
5	4	5	2
4	8	4	2
3	2	3	5
2	1	2	6
1	0	1	3
0	0	0	1
	20		20

Assuming the maximum possible score was 6, what is the index of difficulty for the above item? The index of discrimination?

16. What are the meanings of the two indexes computed in exercise 15?

17. The following is a summary of the results of an item analysis of a four-choice multiple-choice item for which response *B* was the correct answer:

	Upper group	Lower group
A	4	8
*B	15	6
C	6	9
D	0	1
Omit	0	1
	25	25

What is the index of difficulty for the above item? the index of discrimination?

18. Which response to the item in exercise 17 is most likely to need revision? Why?

19. Would an item with the characteristics of the one in exercise 17 be more likely to appear in a discriminatory test or a criterion-referenced test? Why?

20. Two discriminatory tests covering the same table of specifications have the following characteristics:

Test	Mean	SD	r_{tt}	SEM
A	50.5	10.3	.87	4.37
B	50.6	7.0	.73	3.64

If only one of the two tests were to be used as the sole basis for assigning grades, which test would be better? Why?

Suggested Readings

COX, R. C. "Item Selection Techniques and Evaluation of Instructional Objectives." *Journal of Educational Measurement* 2 (1965): 181–185. *This study points out that item selection on statistical grounds alone will alter the table of specifications for the test. The implication is that a defective item should be improved or replaced with an item which would fit into the same cell of the table of specifications.*

EBEL, R. L. "The Relation of Item Discrimination to Test Reliability." *Journal of Educational Measurement* 4 (1967): 125–128. *Points out that increasing the discriminating power of items increases test reliability.*

KATZ, MARTIN, ed. *Short-Cut Statistics for Teacher-Made Tests.* Evaluation and Advisory Service Series, no. 5. (Princeton: Educational Testing Service, 1964. *Presents short-cut methods for item analysis, standard error of measurement, reliability, and correlation.*

LANGE, A., LEHMANN, I. J., and MEHRENS, W. A. "Using Item Analysis to Improve Tests." *Journal of Educational Measurement* 4 (1967): 65–68. *This study concludes that item revision rather than writing new items is the preferred path to test improvement because more improvement is likely to result with less time investment.*

MASON, G. P., and ODEH, R. E. "A Short-Cut Formula for Standard Deviation." *Journal of Educational Measurement* 5 (1968): 319–320.

SABERS, D. L., and KLAUSMEIER, R. D. "Accuracy of Short-Cut Estimates for Standard Deviation." *Journal of Educational Measurement* 8 (1971): 335–339. *These two articles examine various methods for estimating standard deviation and conclude that the method presented in chapter 8 is sufficient for classroom use.*

WOLFE, J. M. "A Simple Method of Calculating the Coefficient of Correlation." *Journal of Educational Measurement* 8 (1971): 221–222. *Presents the method for estimating correlation given in Chapter 8.*

Chapter 9

GRADING AND REPORTING

As a result of studying this chapter you should be able to:

1. *Formulate an appropriate way to report formative data to students in a class you teach.*

2. *Describe a meaningful way to report the results of a midterm examination in a class you teach.*

3. *Develop a process for combining data that would be collected over a semester in a class you teach.*

4. *Explain a rationale for the weights assigned to the measures that should be combined for a summative evaluation in a class you teach.*

5. *Develop a rationale for the method of deriving grades that you will apply in your teaching.*

6. *Illustrate the use of "equal unit" and "curve" grading on data that are supplied.*

7. *Explain a rationale for your use of the F grade.*

Classroom testing serves two major, related purposes: to provide assistance to the teacher and learner that will improve the learning situation for each pupil; and to provide a reliable and valid basis for describing level of achievement for those who have the right to such information. Classroom testing may have inherent value within the total classroom instructional program—that is, teaching and learning may be improved just because tests must be constructed and taken. To realize the full value that can be derived from the assessment, however, teachers must have a plan for the use of the data collected, including a strategy for helping pupils interpret the data and use the information for effective self-direction.

This chapter will consider ways in which test data can be reported to pupils for the purpose of enhancing the teaching–learning process, and how grades or marks can be derived and reported.

Reporting Progress to Students for Formative Evaluation

The information that students should receive from classroom assessment procedures concerns three general questions: (1) how well certain concepts or processes have been mastered; (2) how well a student has progressed relative to what is possible; and (3) what each student's strong areas and weak areas are. Although the questions are obviously interrelated, they are sufficiently different to justify individual attention by teachers.

Mastery of Concepts or Processes

The first question, "How well have certain concepts or processes been mastered?" requires information based on a criterion of adequate mastery. Although professional literature in recent years has mounted a mild campaign for criterion-referenced testing and placed an emphasis on mastery learning, very few of the critical issues concerning the technology of accomplishing these strategies have been resolved. To be valid and useful, achievement tests must reflect the goals of instruction and the criteria of adequate achievement; but many elements of subjective judgment are involved in defining a skill, concept, or process, in deciding how many observations must be made to have a good assessment of

student accomplishment, and in determining what level of performance constitutes "mastery."

Even though vexing problems and many moments of frustration are in store for a teacher who attempts to define goals
precisely and to develop an effective system for assessing mastery,
there are many reasons to believe that the process will be
beneficial, that it will improve teaching and therefore student
learning. The processes referred to are essential for the effective
guidance of students toward course goals. In current literature the
term "formative evaluation" is applied to the processes used
during instruction to ascertain the progress and learning problems
of students. Formative evaluation is of primary value for the
self-direction of students and the adjustment of strategies by
teachers. Formative evaluation requires measurement that samples thoroughly the individual elements comprising the learning
task. The process of simple addition of single-digit numbers, for
example, includes knowing number combinations, knowing the
numbers up to 18, and being able to work with the zero. Measurement of skill in simple addition must include all these elements in sufficient number to allow a conclusion that mastery has
occurred.

In the preceding example the number of combinations is
sufficiently small to allow direct measurement of all possibilities.
Equally limited examples could be taken from fields other than
mathematics. In cases where such measurement is possible, the
data should be reported to students in terms of a statement that
indicates mastery has occurred—for example, "You now know this
skill and you should begin on *skill x*"—or a statement that
identifies a deficiency and a suggestion on how to correct it.

In the higher elementary grades and beyond, many of the
subjects in the curriculum do not lend themselves to a simple
analysis, and many goals are somewhat less concrete and more
complex. This fact should not dissuade a teacher from using
formative evaluation or a strategy based on mastery learning, but
less precision can be expected in the analysis of subject matter and
objectives, and measurement cannot be expected to show a one-

to-one relationship to all elements comprising a learning sequence. For every single-digit number combination, a test item could be presented; however, the application of character analyses in literature or the application of the Law of Conservation of Energy in science would not permit all possible situations to be represented on the test. Because of this situation and the attendant problems, the teacher should use a test plan to guide the development of a balanced test, one that contains a set of exercises giving appropriate emphasis to all topics and objectives.

Reporting results from tests which do not show a one-to-one relationship between items and necessary skills must differ from the process used for tests covering basic skills. For tests that do no more than sample the achievement domain, the number right usually cannot be interpreted directly as an indication of level of mastery. Item difficulty can vary greatly from test to test and teacher to teacher, and thus a given percent correct will correspond to entirely different levels of accomplishment on different tests. Since a test in areas of this kind comprises only a sample of the possible items that would be appropriate, any decision regarding the number or percent of items required for mastery is extremely subjective, with little rational or empirical evidence to support the conclusion that mastery has occurred.

Even in courses where the objectives are complex or have far-reaching implications, some goals usually can be adapted to a mastery approach. For example, in the social studies, where goals may emphasize the ability to treat social data in a rational way, some objectives relate to skills such as interpreting certain types of charts, tables, maps, and graphs. In any course, regardless of the grade level or complexity of the goals, the results of tests that relate to definable mastery should be reported. Skills or processes that appear to be mastered at the level expected should be identified for students and for those that are not mastered, suggestions for further study should be provided.

For those aspects of courses that elude the mastery approach, students and teachers should be aware of the limitations of the measurement process. Prior to the test the teacher should acknowledge that the items on the test will be representative of the possible applications of information studied and that they are pitched at what seems to him to be a reasonable level of difficulty for the course. Test results, then, should be related to the goals, and the teacher should inform each student of the qualitative assessment that can be made of the results. A useful method to use is to report a distribution of scores for the class on items related to a given objective. Verbal labels can then be assigned to various scores in the distribution. On a test with ten items related to one goal, the teacher may feel that outstanding progress is represented by scores of eight or above, average progress by scores of six to eight, and less than satisfactory progress by scores of five or less.

Since the various objectives covered by one test usually relate to a central, or at least unifying, goal, distributions of total scores on the test should be reported to the class. Labels can be applied to scores, and students can do a self-evaluation of the progress they have made and can decide whether their personal goals of excellence have been met. If they have not, students should be given additional suggestions to improve their competence with the material.

Progress in Relation to Possible Achievement

A mastery approach to teaching and testing necessarily directs the student's attention to self-development, and he may become complacent if external criteria that indicate what he should be capable of accomplishing are lacking. Self-direction and knowledge of one's achievement of specific skills and processes are undoubtedly important in personal development, and a feeling of success is a necessary part of a wholesome self-concept. Even so, maximal intellectual development seems unlikely to occur unless a challenge from some quarter exists. Of course, challenges or aspirations must be realistic so that success is experienced periodically.

Test results show the level of attainment that has been demonstrated, but test results alone do not show whether the progress made is poor, average, or outstanding. For this type of evaluation, the teacher and student must have a criterion of what is possible.

A skillful teacher will complement test scores in some way to give each student an indication of how much he has achieved compared to what he might have tried to achieve.

Some critics of testing and marking systems claim that all goals and evaluations should be individual. They claim that competition with other students is unhealthy, unnecessary, and counterproductive in terms of the important aspects of personal development. Although extreme competition and the use of a single criterion of quality unquestionably are poor practices, the arguments of the critics are less acceptable when moderation and realism prevail. How does an infant know that crawling is not the best mode of self-movement if not by observing that others around him seem to have greater freedom, more flexibility, and the potential for greater success by moving in an upright position? Is it unhealthy for an infant with the necessary physical development to try to walk in competition with older siblings and adults?

Two methods exist for reporting test results to help answer the question, "How well am I doing relative to what is possible?" One way is to let the individual know how his results compare with those of his classroom peers. An effective procedure is to report to a class the distribution of scores made by the members of the class. Though each student knows the individual score of only one person, himself, he can see how his score compares with those earned by other students who received the same instruction.

In courses in which a form of self-paced instruction and mastery units are being used, students are expected to reach a predetermined level at the close of a unit. Obviously, the report to the student is either, "You passed," or "You need to study more before starting the next unit." In such courses, students may want to know and should be told how their rate of progress compares with that of others in the class.

The second method of establishing an external criterion for what is possible is to help a student assess his accomplishments in terms of his own ability to achieve. As children progress through school, large amounts of measurement data are collected. After the first few years there are enough data—standardized test scores, teacher assessments, etc.—for a teacher to formulate a relatively accurate description of ability for each child in his class. This information, plus what the teacher has seen other students accomplish, provides a basis for helping individual students assess their achievement relative to what they may be capable of accomplishing.

There is an inherent danger in this process, namely, "typecasting" children inaccurately. A wise and perceptive teacher, realizing that all historical data are subject to error, will be alert to signs that present ability is either greater or less than the historical data suggest. Current norms of expectation should always be flexible and should be changed as new data are collected. When these cautions are observed, the process can add immeasurably to the effectiveness of learning.

Determination of Students' Strengths and Weaknesses

The extent to which an individual's abilities and accomplishments vary from field to field is well documented in educational research. Seldom are students uniformly strong or weak in all curricular fields or, in fact, in all topics within a given course. One use of classroom test results is to help students identify their strengths and weaknesses.

Since tests are developed to represent the various goals of the instruction covered, it is possible to report success on the different goals. One student may perform well on computational problems but poorly on the correct application of principles. For another student the reverse may be true. Teachers should give students an opportunity to diagnose their areas of greatest and least success. The teacher can accomplish this by indicating which items cover each of the goals and allowing students to study their marked tests. If he has time, he can report scores on each goal separately, as well as the total score.

One of the problems in comparing a student's performance on different tests or in relation to different objectives is the lack of absolute scales of measurement—that is, the number or percentage of items an examinee answers correctly on any test or part of a test depends in large measure on the difficulty of the items. A lower number right on one test may represent better achievement than a higher number correct on an easier test. Because of this problem, which is inherent in classroom testing, standard scores and percentile ranks are important tools for the teacher. Scores on all tests for a given class can be expressed as standard scores, that is, in terms of standard deviation units above and below the class average. Percentile ranks also provide an appropriate yardstick for use within a class across different tests. Changes in standard scores or percentile ranks from one test to another tell a student how well he has performed different tasks in comparison with his peers. This kind of information is useful to student and teacher in identifying areas of relative strength and weakness.

Deriving Grades for Summative Evaluation

Although some school systems have adopted a credit no-credit or pass fail system of grading, most schools still retain the use of an A-B-C grading system. The authors believe that there are appropriate uses for both systems and that the best system may include both, but the purpose here is not to argue for a particular form of grading. The fact is that teachers are required to use the system employed by the school in which they teach, and A-B-C grading is still predominant. Therefore this section will consider ways in which letter grades can be derived so that they are meaningful and accurate. Any grade is based on the composite of evidence available to the teacher, and the issues related to combining data must be resolved before the teacher can make the qualitative judgments reflected in assigning grades.

Combining Evidence of Achievement

In all classes a decision must be made concerning how test data and other evidences of achievement are to be combined to obtain a composite measure of achievement. In addition to the results of formal tests, the information available in many classes includes scores from quizzes, marks on themes and projects, and assessment of homework and recitation. These data must be combined to obtain an index that accurately reflects all aspects of a semester's activities and provides a valid composite of total achievement during the course. The method used to combine these data should be based on a consideration of the relative importance of the various measurements, their reliability, the time in the semester when they were collected, and the variability of the various scores to be combined.

The importance of any one type of measurement is a matter of subjective judgment, but several factors should be considered. Primary emphasis should be placed on the directness of the relationship between the measures and the course objectives. Homework, quizzes, and class discussion are typically more useful as learning aids than as measurement procedures. Even though these activities are important aspects of the process of obtaining knowledge and mastering concepts, they seldom provide a reliable indication of the extent to which students have developed toward course objectives.

When homework, quizzes, and class discussion measure the same achievement as that covered in formal tests, their importance in deriving the index of composite achievement should be reduced. When such activities and their assessment directly reflect course goals, and do so uniquely, they should be given an increased weight in the composite index.

The reliability of the various measures to be combined is another factor that determines the weight to be given to these measures. The value of a measure, its validity, is limited by the extent to which it is reliable, and thus greater weight should be given to the more reliable measures. Scores on formal tests usually are more reliable than marks for projects, themes, and such less formal assessments as quizzes, homework, and class participation. The scores on a well-developed test of class-period length should have a reliability coefficient near .70, and the composite of all tests should be near .90. It is extremely unlikely that any other type of measurement in the classroom would even approach this level of reliability.

The importance of measures obtained at various points in the course will vary with the nature of the course. Some course work is necessarily sequential, with new material based on that studied previously. Math courses*, languages, and to some extent science courses are of this type. In sequential courses, tests given near the end of the semester measure indirectly all the objectives of the course. Since the grade for the semester should reflect the terminal level of development in the course, it would be logical to give greater weight to the measures obtained late in the course. In some courses the material covered in different units may be relatively independent of preceding material. When this is true, the measures collected early in the course may be uniquely relevant to the assessment of total achievement and thus should be weighted in terms of the importance of the unit in the total course.

The final factor to consider is the variability of the different measures to be combined. When separate measures are combined to obtain a composite, the weight of any one measure in determining the composite scores is related to its variability in comparison with that of other measures. The more variable a set of scores, the greater will be its weight. The appropriate index of variability is the standard deviation, a measure of the extent to which the scores spread out from the average score. This index was described in the preceding chapter, but a simple illustration will indicate what happens when data are combined.

Assume that scores on two equally important tests are to be added to obtain a composite score. On test 1 the high and low scores are 80 and 70. On test 2 the high and low scores are 80 and 40. Obviously the variation of scores is greater for test 2. Assume also that one student earns the highest score on test 1 and the lowest on test 2; another student has the reverse success, the lowest on test 1 and highest on test 2. Since the tests are equally important, the composite achievement for the two students should be the same; but if their scores are simply added together the following results are obtained:

	Student 1	Student 2
Test 1	80	70
Test 2	40	80
Total	120	150

Observe that the higher total score belongs to the student who performed better on the test with more variable scores.

For a composite to reflect what the teacher wants it to reflect, the variabilities of the separate measures must be adjusted to show the appropriate relationships. This recommendation should be qualified in two ways: usually the adjustments for variability are needed only when the measures to be combined differ *markedly* in this characteristic; and the adjustments for variability are less important when the measures are highly correlated with one another. In most classes the interrelationship among various measures of achievement is close, and even though teachers should be aware of the effect of different subscore variabilities when scores are added to obtain a composite, steps to adjust are important only when differences are substantial and measurements are mutually independent.

Methods for adjusting separate measures before combining them are relatively simple to apply. If each score in a set is multiplied or divided by a constant, the standard deviation of the resulting set of scores will be more or less than the original standard deviation by the factor that was used in multiplying or dividing. For example, if each score is doubled, that is, multiplied by two, the standard deviation of the new set of scores will be double that of the original set. Similarly, if each score is multiplied by one third, which is the same as dividing by three, the new standard deviation is one third as large as the original.

A final suggestion about combining scores concerns the process. Teachers usually have a large number of scores to combine. Rather than working with each separately, the teacher should treat only major tests, themes, and projects separately and should combine all other measures as subcomposites. All quiz scores should be combined to form a quiz subtotal and all homework and recitation measures should be combined to form homework and recitation subtotal scores. Then the test scores, theme marks, and the various subtotals should be weighted according to the factors noted earlier and combined to obtain the semester or unit composite scores.

An example will clarify the process. Assume that a teacher is preparing to assign marks for a semester course. He has given four major tests during the semester and feels that the later tests should have slightly more weight than the earlier ones. In addition, he has required two major themes, has given eight quizzes, and has recorded weekly marks for assignments and for class discussion. The teacher feels that the themes and tests are about equally important and that the three less formal types of measurement should carry relatively little weight. The following table shows the standard deviations, the teacher's action, and the resultant weight.

Measure	SD	Teacher action on individual student scores	Resultant weight
Test 1	6		6
Test 2	5		5
Test 3	7		7
Test 4	10		10
Theme 1	8		8
Theme 2	5	double	10
Assignments	6	divide by 2	3
Quizzes	15	divide by 5	3
Discussion	2		2

Assigning Grades: Some Issues

Although some moves have been made in the past few years to modify traditional marking systems, the vast majority of schools still retain grades for some or all of the courses in the curriculum. The retention of some type of formal marking system indicates that there are many important reasons for maintaining a record of the quality of student progress through the school curriculum. Teachers must plan programs appropriate for the level of preparation of the students in a class; parents and children want to know the quality of the achievement that has occurred; employers want to hire a person whose past achievements fit the requirements of the position and suggest that growth will occur; admission offices for vocational schools, colleges, and universities would like to admit students who have the background to succeed.

For these and other reasons teachers are called upon to describe and record the quality of achievement that each student has demonstrated in each course. Such qualitative judgments are difficult to make, and many teachers find this aspect of their work an unpleasant responsibility. Because it is their responsibility, teachers should approach the task with good preparation, including a defensible rationale for their assessments.

Many of the criticisms of grades have been directed toward the inappropriate ways in which they have been derived and used, rather than toward their inherent characteristics. Some problems with grades can be avoided or at least minimized if teachers employ a sound rationale and have adequate data for assigning grades.

Grades should serve one primary purpose: to describe the level of achievement students have reached at the close of a unit of instruction. Grades should *not* represent the assessment of achievement level modified by deportment, and they should *not* be used as reward or punishment for cooperation, citizenship, or other similar behaviors.

By indicating the quality of achievement that has been made, grades also predict what the student is capable of achieving. A person who reads a transcript of achievement should be able to interpret the grade earned in a course as a summary of the level of achievement the student has reached and as a prediction of future achievement. The grade should reflect the knowledge the student has of the subject, his understanding of concepts, and his ability to use the information and skills included in the course.

A grade that reflects a mixture of different types of behaviors is uninterpretable. If achievement, cooperation, attitude, or interest influence the decision, a given grade could represent a high assessment of one type of factor and a low assessment of another. Then a *B* in typing might represent either outstanding ability to type by a person with a so-so attitude, or marginal ability by a very pleasant person. A grade that is supposed to be a measure of achievement should not be used to reflect nonachievement factors simultaneously.

Similar problems of interpretation arise when grades are based on estimated gain. A high grade could be assigned for a mediocre level of achievement by a student who had made good progress, but to interpret the grade as *level* of achievement would be erroneous. To expect the student to be able to start the next course in the sequence at the level indicated by the grade would also be erroneous. Although good progress should be noted by the teacher and should be rewarded, the meaning of a grade should not be compromised by basing it on growth as well as level of attainment.

The grades assigned by many teachers have been less than satisfactory as indicators of attainment, as descriptions of the capabilities of students at the close of a period of instruction. The remedy is to use grades only as measures of the level of achievement. Grades should not be treated as rewards for good behavior and they should not be reduced for poor behavior. The student's reward for learning is the improvement in his capabilities; the indication of the level of learning is the grade. Teachers should stress that reward is the realization of instructional objectives, and they should help students to avoid looking at grades as the reward or goal.

Assigning Grades: Some Methods

Teachers have a responsibility to adhere to and apply the grading policies of the school in which they are employed. Since a school system may use any one or a combination of several grading systems, this section will discuss some of the systems that are used most widely.

At one time the most popular grading system was based on percentages. Grades were recorded on a scale from 0 to 100 percent, with verbal labels attached to various ranges:

93–100	Excellent
85–92	Above average or good
75–84	Average
65–74	Poor
Below 65	Unsatisfactory, or failure

A few schools retain this system although the ranges may differ from those shown above, and in most schools the philosophy behind the system no longer regards the mark as the percentage of perfect achievement that has occurred.

Those who use a percentage grading system today recognize that even within a category, such as "excellent," there are differences. The different numbers in a category indicate where a student's achievement falls within the range—for example, if two students receive marks of 93 and 97, each has achieved very well, but the second is judged to be somewhat higher than the first.

One of the earlier problems with percentage grading was the influence it had on classroom testing. Most teachers believed that tests had to be designed so that the excellent achievers would earn grades no lower than 93 percent, above-average students no lower than 85 percent, and so on. It was assumed that the teacher could design a test that would yield results according to a predetermined and arbitrary definition of each level of achievement. In addition, the old approach encouraged the use of inefficient tests, with many items that covered insignificant achievements or that could be answered correctly by almost all students in the class.

A percentage grading system should be regarded as a numerical method for indicating five levels of achievement. The primary emphasis should be placed on obtaining sufficient evidence to assign one of the five grade categories. Since tests and other measures of achievement do not allow reliable differentiation of achievement along a one hundred-point scale, there is little reason to worry about distinctions within each category. Only when a teacher feels strongly that differences within a category are sufficiently important and reliable should different numbers be used as an approach to plus and minus grading. How many teachers, for example, could defend a decision that one student deserved a 93, another a 94, and another a 95? Generally it is most satisfactory to assign most "excellent" students the middle score of the 93–100 range, most above-average students the middle score of the 85–92 range, and so forth.

The use of five verbal labels to describe achievement on the percentage scale led naturally to the adoption of a five-point grading scale, most commonly the *A, B, C, D, F* system. This system is still the one used most widely in United States schools —in junior and senior high schools, and at the upper elementary school level in many communities. This system avoids the problems that arise in trying to describe levels of achievement in terms of a large number of categories. Whether more than five levels can be justified is a point over which much professional debate has occurred, but few would argue for the misleading system of a one hundred-point scale.

Although the *A-B-C* grading system is well established, no single approach has been adopted for deciding on the level of achievement required for each grade. Differences in the application of *A-B-C* grading have been responsible for a large share of the criticism directed at grades. Although many problems would be minimized if all teachers could agree on the standards for grades and apply those standards with equal skill, this seems an impossible goal. However, the grading process would be somewhat more systematic and the application of the principles more defensible if each teacher would consider the issues and apply measurement techniques to the process.

One approach that some teachers claim to use can be called "absolute standards" grading. This process includes the assignment of *A* grades to students who have achieved at a level judged by the teacher to be excellent. *B* grades are assigned for achievement that is good, definitely above average but not excellent. Teachers who use this approach claim to have standards based on how much is learned and how well skills have been developed, and they claim to judge each student relative to subject-matter standards, not relative to his peers.

The premise, and the weakness, of this approach is the assumption that the teacher can consistently recognize levels of excellence with which other competent judges would agree. Although the goal is that grades of A, B, and C should reflect outstanding, good, and average achievement, there is little evidence that absolute standards grading achieves that goal. Research has demonstrated that different teachers have grossly different standards and that grades are more often relative than absolute. As a result, the measurement qualities of absolute grades are quite poor and the information they convey is of questionable usefulness.

Although relative grading has frequently been criticized on some superficial grounds, the results of this approach are undoubtedly better than those obtained from absolute standards grading. Teachers generally agree quite closely on the rank ordering of a class of students. Problems of inconsistency among teachers seem to be related to the way in which the decision is made to separate the class into the categories of the grading system, to separate As and Bs, Bs and Cs, and so forth. Measurement techniques are available to assist teachers in making these decisions.

One method of relative grading is based on dividing the distribution of scores—the composite score for the class over the period for which grades are being determined—into a number of equal-sized intervals. If an A, B, C, D, F system is used, the distribution would be divided into five intervals. The unit used for dividing the distribution is the standard deviation of the scores, a measure of distance along the score scale based on the dispersion of scores from the average. A relatively simple method for obtaining an estimate of a standard deviation was presented in the preceding chapter. For most distributions of classroom composite scores the range of scores from lowest to highest might be equal to about five or six times the size of the standard deviation.

In the standard application of this approach to grading, the first step would be to determine the *C* or average grades by finding one half of the size of the standard deviation and then adding this value to and subtracting it from the mean or median score. Thus the *C* range would be one standard deviation wide, centered around the mean or median. The *B* and *D* range would also be one standard deviation wide, extending respectively above and below the *C* range. The grade of *A* would be assigned to all scores above the top score of the *B* interval, and supposedly *F*s would be assigned to all below the lowest *D*. This method is illustrated in Figure 9.1.

Figure 9.1

An illustration of the standard deviation approach to marking achievement level

Step 1 The composite measures for the class of students are derived. The set of scores given below represents the composite scores for a class of thirty students.

Composite score	
189	158
178	157
169	156
167	155
166	154
165	152
165	151
163	150
163	148
162	146
161	140
160	137
160	135
159	130
159	128

Step 2 The average score is found:

$$\text{Mean} = \frac{\text{sum of scores}}{\text{no. of scores}} = \frac{4683}{30} = 156.1$$

Figure 9.1 *continued*

Step 3 The *SD* is estimated:

$$\text{Est. } SD = \frac{\text{sum of upper 1/6} - \text{sum of lower 1/6}}{\text{half of (no. of scores} - 1)}$$

$$= \frac{(189+178+169+167+166)-(128+130+135+137+140)}{14.5}$$

$$= \frac{869 - 670}{14.5}$$

$$= \frac{199}{14.5}$$

$$= 13.7$$

Step 4 Find the *C* range: mean plus and minus 1/2 *SD*
    156.1 + 6.85 = 162.95
    156.1 − 6.85 = 149.25

Step 5 Find highest *B*: highest *C* plus 1 *SD*
    162.95 + 13.7 = 176.65

Step 6 Find lowest *D*: lowest *C* minus 1 *SD*
    149.25 − 13.7 = 135.55

Step 7 Summarize ranges for each mark

A	177 and above	D	136–148
B	163–176	F	135 and lower (tentative)
C	149–162		

For classes that approximate a cross-section of talent at their particular grade level, this approach provides a most defensible grading method. The problem, however, is that very few classes are like the mythical "average" class. When evidence exists that a given class is better or worse than the "average" class, the method should be modified. The essential element in deciding whether to use the model in Figure 9.1 or an adjusted model is the equality of *B*, *C*, and *D* intervals along the composite score scale. If a class is below average, these categories can all be shifted upward on the scale, thus producing fewer *A*s. If a class is above average, the categories can be shifted downward, producing more *A*s. In an exceptionally able class, for example, the *C* grades might extend from .75 standard deviations below the mean to .25 above. The *B* interval would then extend from .25 to 1.25 standard deviations above the mean. If a class has a preponderance of average students and few exceptionally good or poor students, the B, C, and D categories could each be made 1.2 or even 1.4 standard deviations wide.

A second way to grade on a relative basis is to assign grades in terms of a predetermined percentage distribution. The distribution of scores from a well-constructed standardized test of ability or achievement for a cross section of an age group would be bell-shaped and about six standard deviations wide. If this distribution is divided into five equal-sized intervals, 7 percent of the scores would be in the top and bottom intervals, 24 percent in the next highest and lowest intervals, and 38 percent in the middle interval. This percentage distribution can be used as the point of departure for grading classroom achievement. In an "average" class, grades would be distributed as follows:

A—highest 7 percent of the class
B—next 24 percent of the class
C—next 38 percent of the class
D—next 24 percent of the class
F—lowest 7 percent of the class

Again, adjustments can be made when a class is above or below average in achievement. If the school has given a standardized test in a subject or a general ability test, the teacher can easily tabulate scores for a given class and determine how it differs from the "average." Percentile norms are furnished with nearly all standardized tests. The teacher should determine the number of students with percentile ranks in each of the following categories:

94 and above
70–93
32–69
8–31
7 and below

He can use this tabulation, which shows how the talent in the class is distributed, as information on which to adjust from the typical distribution of grades. With this decision made, he need only count down in the distribution of composite scores to determine where the divisions between grade levels—A and B, B and C—should occur.

The Place of F in Grading Systems

Most school systems have policies that reflect local philosophy regarding failure and retention of students in school grades; however, even when a policy exists, teachers have some latitude in applying the policy; and they should give serious consideration to assigning an F. Traditionally the F grade has meant a student has achieved too little to earn credit for the work done. In the elementary grades this has meant that the student must repeat the grade. At the high school level an F means that the course does not count toward graduation, and either it must be repeated or another substituted for it to earn the credit needed.

Since an F grade usually leads to an administrative decision of great importance to the student, teachers should assign Fs with great care. They should give an F only when they have good evidence that the student's achievement level would not permit him to achieve in the next class or at the next grade level. Research on the benefit of repeating grades is not encouraging. Some schools use a process of social promotion to allow students to stay with their age group, but too often schools have employed social promotion in lieu of finding ways to help slow learners achieve up to capacity.

The F grade should never be assigned on a mechanical basis. A grading system should not require a certain number or percentage of Fs. The assignment of an F should be made only if it is in the best interest of the student on either a short- or long-term basis.

One rule of thumb might help teachers as they ponder this difficult question. If the F grade should be assigned only to students who undoubtedly learned less than those students assigned a D, the F score should be at least one standard deviation below the average D score. The teacher who is guided by this thought will be able to differentiate between D and F students.

Limiting Serious Misassignment of Grades

Errors in assigning grades probably never will be eliminated, but it is possible to avoid gross errors. Because errors affect all types of assessment, the rank order of students will contain some errors. Wherever a teacher makes the division between *A* and *B*, *B* and *C*, and other grades, he may assign some students to the wrong category; for example, he may assign a *B* to a borderline *B–C* student who really deserves a *C*.

Even though errors cannot be eliminated entirely, the measurement program can control the occurrence of errors as large as two categories. The greater the reliability of the composite score, the less often gross errors will occur. Therefore it is important to plan a measurement program that will yield a sufficiently reliable composite assessment.

Since grade intervals will be approximately one standard deviation wide, the composite should be sufficiently reliable to preclude errors equal to one standard deviation. It can be shown that the composite score must have a reliability coefficient at least as high as .89 for this to be achieved.[1]

---

[1] Every score may be affected by errors of measurement. To be confident that errors have not reduced an *A* student to a *C* grade or raised a *C* student to an *A* grade, the distance from highest *C* to lowest *A* should be equal to 3 standard errors. Since most grade intervals are about one *SD* wide, the standard error of measurement should be no larger than one third of the size of the *SD* of the scores on which grades are being based. The situation can be shown as:

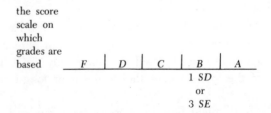

the score
scale on
which
grades are
based   *F* | *D* | *C* | *B* | *A*
                                1 *SD*
                                or
                                3 *SE*

The formula for the standard error of measurement can be used to solve for the reliability coefficient required to obtain the ratio of *SE* to *SD* that is 1:3.

Step 1. State the formula: $SE = SD \sqrt{1-r}$

Step 2. Divide both sides of 1 by *SD*: $\dfrac{SE}{SD} = \sqrt{1-r}$

Seldom will a single classroom test have a reliability coefficient greater than .75, but three well-constructed classroom tests should yield a composite with the minimum reliability required. It is clear that accurate grades can be assigned only when they are based on sufficient data.

Some Final Recommendations

In most school systems, grades need to be derived at six- or nine-week intervals for the purpose of reporting to students and parents. During these periods teachers will be collecting a variety of measures, such as tests, projects, and papers, that he will combine to provide a composite measure of achievement.

There are basically two ways to treat and combine the separate measures that are available. One is to assign a letter mark to each measure and then average them to obtain the mark for the total period. The other method is to retain the measures in numerical form, combine the numbers, and then assign the mark. The second method is recommended for several reasons.

First, each time a series of scores is reduced to fewer, more inclusive categories, some information is lost. For example, if the results of a test range from fifteen correct to sixty-five correct and if these scores are reduced to five categories—that is, A, B, C, D, and F—useful information about differences in achievement is lost. Second, the average of a series of grades would not necessarily lead to the same grade that would be assigned to the composite of the separate measures. The grade assigned to the composite measure probably is more accurate because of the information lost when separate measures are converted to marks. Third, students should be encouraged to interpret test scores and assessment of

---

Step 3. Substitute the required ratio of *SE/SD:* $1/3 = \sqrt{1 - r}$

Step 4. Square both sides of the equation: $1/9 = 1 - r$

Step 5. $1/9 = .11$: $.11 = 1 - r$

Step 6. Add r and subtract .11 on both sides of equation: $r = 1 - .11$
    $r = .89$

papers as indications of their achievement and progress toward
goals. If grades are assigned, student attention may be diverted
from the more important information the measures should convey.

Summary

Many teachers regard the grading process as the single most
difficult aspect of classroom teaching responsibilities. Some claim,
in addition, that assigning grades requires the teacher to be a
judge and that this has a counterproductive effect on the teacher-
pupil relationships essential to effective teaching.

Assigning grades will be a less noxious task if the teacher has a
satisfactory rationale and adequate data on which to base his
grading decisions. Furthermore, when teachers have provided
effective guidance and wholehearted support for each pupil, there
should be no feeling of guilt or reluctance in "telling it as it is." A
teacher does a child no favor by presenting misleading information
about the accomplishments that have been made. Expectations are
built largely on past accomplishments, and failure to reach mis-
guided expectations might be a greater blow to a pupil than
learning accurately what he has accomplished.

Marks are descriptions of levels of achievement, and teachers
should draw on measurement technology in order to assign marks
realistically and reliably. Grades are not goals; rather, they indicate how well instructional goals have been achieved.

Exercises

1. Select a class in your subject area that you intend to teach and
   describe carefully a system that can be used to report formative
   assessment data to students. Illustrate with typical results.

2. Using a typical exam for a class in your area, explain what
   different scores on the test mean in terms of mastery. Justify
   your analysis. Also indicate for selected levels of performance

how you would interpret the results to students in terms of
their relative levels of success.

3. How will you report scores on a midterm test to your class and
to individuals in your class?

4. For a goal in your area that does not lend itself to a mastery
approach, how will you report progress to your students?

5. The results for a class on the various measures collected are as
follows:

Measure	Class average	Estimated SD
Total of quiz grades	42	5
Project 1	27	3
Test 1	35	4
Test 2	47	6
Project 2	33	4
Final examination	85	14

a. If the teacher wanted to give more emphasis to measures
near the end of the semester, to weight quizzes relatively
lightly, and to give tests slightly more emphasis than projects, what weights might be assigned and how would the
teacher obtain those weights?

b. Using the scheme you developed in *a*, derive a total score
for a student who has these scores:

Quiz total	40
Project 1	30
Test 1	40
Test 2	50
Project 2	30
Final exam	90

6. Given the following scores: (a) derive equal-interval type
grades; (b) for a class that is above average in ability, indicate
the grades you would assign, using a curve grading approach.

34, 11, 4, 8, 36, 35, 42, 20,
29, 26, 30, 14, 11, 27, 23, 22,
19, 28, 22, 19, 31, 21, 16, 23, 15

7. With these scores would you assign any *F* grades? Why?

Suggested Readings

BEGGS, J. B., and BRAUN, P. H. "Models of Evaluation and Their Relation to Student Characteristics." *Journal of Educational Measurement* 9 (1972): 303–309. *A study of two ways of combining data to obtain a composite measure. Recommendations are made concerning grading practices.*

CHANSKY, N. N. "Resolving the Grading Problem." *The Educational Forum* (January 1973): 189–194. *An interesting recommendation for different grading models for different kinds of courses.*

CHANSKY, N. N. "Development of Grading Preferences in High School Students." *Education* 93 (1973): 336–338. *Reports on a study of student preferences in grades 7, 9, and 12 for various types of grading systems. An evaluation of the preferences is given.*

EBEL, R. L. "The Social Consequences of Educational Testing." *School and Society* (1965): 331–334. *Four popular aspects of this issue are analyzed. A provocative article.*

HILLS, J. R., and GLADNEY, M. B. "Factors Influencing College Grading Standards." *Journal of Educational Measurement* 5 (1968): 31–40. *A review of trends in a college. Although entering freshmen classes improved in the average aptitude score, grade distributions remained relatively constant.*

MILLMAN, J. "Reporting Student Progress: A Case for a Criterion-Referenced Marking System." *Phi Delta Kappa* 52 (1970): 226–230. *A comparison of traditional approaches and a new model. A good article that will stimulate much thought.*

TERWILLIGER, J. S. "Individual Differences in the Marking Practices of Secondary School Teachers." *Journal of Educational Measurement* 5 (1968): 9–15. *A study on the ways teachers differ in combining data obtained in a classroom and severity of grading standards.*

APPENDIX

This appendix contains answers to those chapter exercises that require specific, anticipated answers. Answers are not presented for exercises that require application of principles or development of materials for topics peculiar to various teaching fields. In some cases part of an exercise is answered here, and in other cases illustrative material is presented when the topic of the exercise suggests a general pattern for the response.

Students should complete all the exercises for a chapter before they refer to the answers so that they will have an opportunity to measure their own progress in interpreting or applying concepts. The purpose of providing the answers in the book is to give students guidance for self-measurement of achievement. The learning model implied by this process can be fulfilled only if students refer to the answers after they have completed the exercises.

Chapter 1

1. Evaluation–measurement–testing. Evaluation requires data obtained from measurement which usually includes but is not limited to information obtained from testing. Evaluation requires data from measurement, which are compared with standards. Measurement includes testing, observation, reviews of assignments, etc.

2. Although this answer will depend to some extent on your teaching field, measurement in all courses should be used to discover what kinds of problems students may be having as the class proceeds through the topic. Effective formative assessment will provide clues to both the teacher and student concerning how the learning experiences could be altered to improve each student's achievement.

3. Minimum responsibilities include collecting data at appropriate times and providing guidance to students based on an analysis of the measurement results.

4. a. formative   d. formative
   b. summative   e. formative
   c. formative   f. summative

5. a. decrease   d. improve
   b. improve   e. improve
   c. improve

6. There are many more than ten possible types of complex or compound sentences; only a sample was presented on the test. The test contains sentences representative of those a student might develop in his own writing, but the test does not measure his free-writing expertise with this punctuation skill.

Chapter 2

1. Objectives are characteristics that teachers are trying to develop in students. When stated in behavioral terms, they are specific behaviors that students can perform either because they are important in themselves or because they provide evidence of an internal characteristic of the student. Content, on the other hand, is the body of knowledge and principles which is combined with practice, demonstration, discovery, and other teaching methodologies to form the vehicle through which students acquire objectives.

2. The three levels of objectives described here are (a) school objectives, (b) departmental objectives, and (c) course objectives, They proceed from the general to the specific. School objectives are derived from the philosophy of the school and represent the characteristics the student should attain as the result of the whole schooling process, not a specific course or series of courses. Departmental objectives represent the characteristics and skills which students should develop as a result of a series of courses. Course objectives represent the goals of a single course or even a segment of a course. Examples of these objectives might be:

   School objective: Students will be able to use a logical approach to solving problems.

   Science department objective: The student will be able to apply the scientific method to analyze and solve problems.

   Science course objective: Given a description of a scientific problem, the student can derive scientific hypotheses and describe an experiment or series of experiments for testing the hypotheses.

3. Affective objectives are concerned with feelings and values. Cognitive objectives are concerned with knowledge and the application of intellectual skills.

4. Norm-referenced tests compare student performance with the average performance of some group, generally his classmates. Criterion-referenced tests compare a student's performance with a pre-established criterion. Objectives for both types of tests should be behavioral, but objectives for a criterion-referenced test should also specify a criterion of acceptable performance.

5. All objectives should be stated in terms of student behavior. The action should be made as specific as possible by an action verb. Objectives for criterion-referenced tests should contain a statement of what constitutes acceptable performance.

6. Some examples for (a) are:

   1. The student voluntarily attends classical music concerts.

   2. When given the choice of records of various kinds to play, the student selects a classical music recording.

7. Course objectives should be more specific and behavioral than school objectives. Therefore, several course objectives are usually needed for each school objective. Make sure there is a logical relationship between the course objectives and the school objectives.

Chapter 3

1. Many objectives that appear to require measurement by observation of performance can be measured in part by paper and pencil tests. For example, students can be asked questions about proper techniques, approaches, or procedures required in the performance. Frequently, the question for the teacher is whether a technique other than paper and pencil tests will do better (satisfactory reliability and better validity) than observation or product assessment.

2. Multiple measurement is justifiable when an objective is quite complex and/or extremely important. Decisions should be based on adequate information, and sometimes multiple measurement is necessary to obtain the minimal information. For example, multiple measurement could be used in English composition with a classroom test used to measure punctuation rules or with a theme used to assess how well students apply the rules in free-writing situations.

3. The measurement program for the second language class would include more frequent formative measures of the skills and knowledge required for sequential learning, would require more diagnostic measures, and would include more emphasis on factual information, such as

vocabulary. The modern authors program would probably include more emphasis on student ability to diagnose and interpret modern literature.

4.

Objectives

Topics	1 (30%)	2 (20%)	3 (10%)	4 (40%)
1 (20%)	6	4	2	8
2 (30%)	9	6	3	12
3 (40%)	12	8	4	16
4 (10%)	3	2	1	4

The number of items in whole numbers would be:

4	2	1	5
5	4	2	7
7	5	2	10
2	1	1	2

5. The topic should be specific and narrowly defined—for example, the use of commas with dependent and independent clauses or the multiplication of single-digit numbers. The criterion must specify how well an examinee must do on the test to provide reasonable assurance that the specific skill can be used in the next step of the sequence. At the present state of our knowledge, criteria must be based on part experience and a careful, rational analysis of the learning sequence requirements.

Chapter 4

1. a. The name of the tallest mountain in North America is _____.
   b. The King of England at the time of the American Revolution was named _____.

c. Discard. The topic is superficial and artificial.
d. The name of the state flower for Kansas is _____.
e. The metric volume slightly larger than a quart is the _____.

2. Check your five items against the list of suggestions provided in the chapter. For example, do the blanks appear near the end of the statement? Are the statements specific so that only the desired response can satisfactorily complete the statement?

3. a. For what product is Akron the leading producer in the United States?
   b. Discard. The item is superficial and artificial.
   c. What was the most common mode of transportation in the time of Johnny Tremain?
   d. If fewer new cars were available than could be sold, what would most likely happen to the cost of new cars?

4. The short-answer items should be checked against the suggestions for completion items in the chapter, since they apply generally to short-answer items also. Give special attention to whether only the desired response could be made by examinees. To check your questions further, make sure you can prepare a scoring key for the items.

5. A test plan, table of specifications, should be prepared and each item written specifically to cover some aspect of the table. The questions should require as little writing as necessary, and the test should include as many items as practicable.

6. Add a statement concerning how the ten points would be distributed across the characteristics of the answer to be scored. For example, three points will be awarded each for noting the major domestic and international factors, and four points will be awarded for analyzing the way in which the program responded to the factors.

   Key: Domestic factors
       1. Restless youth with humanistic motives and no formal way to participate in building world peace
       2. A shortage of domestic employment opportunities

   International factors
       1. Decline of American prestige
       2. Assertions of imperialistic American motives
       3. Shortage of skilled people in emerging nations

   Responsiveness
   Provided support for youth in helping emerging peoples; helped Americans learn more of other cultures; provided needed assis-

tance to nations without sending government or political officials
to other countries.

7. Answers will vary.

Chapter 5

1. Samples:

    a. The pistil of a flower produces pollen. (F)

    a. Pollen is produced by the anthers of a flower. (T)

    b. A forced air furnace heats a house by convection. (T)

    b. A forced air furnace heats a house by radiation. (F)

    c. If demand is constant and less wheat will be produced next
       year than was produced this year, the price of wheat will
       probably rise. (T)

    c. If demand is constant and more wheat will be produced next
       year than was produced this year, the price of wheat will
       probably rise. (F)

2. a. The item contains the negative *not*
       Better: Toads are reptiles. (F)

    b. The item is partly true and partly false.
       Better: Mt. McKinley is located in Colorado. (F)
         or: Mt. Ranier is the highest mountain in North America. (F)

    c. The word "every" is a clue to the falseness of the item, and
       the item is too sweeping.
       Better: More than 90 percent of the children in the United
       States have television sets in their homes. (T)

    d. This is merely a textbook statement. Besides, it would be more
       important to know the rules and be able to apply them than
       to merely know how many rules there are.
       Better: A fifty-item true-false test will be generally more reli-
       able than a fifty-item multiple-choice test. (F)

3. Sample response:

    a.

	Function	Organ
<u>B</u>	1. Removes waste products from the blood stream	A. heart
<u>A</u>	2. Pumps blood to the body	B. kidney
<u>E</u>	3. Transfers oxygen to the bloodstream	C. large intestine
		D. liver
		E. lung

<u>D</u>	4. Regulates blood sugar level	F. small intestine
<u>F</u>	5. Transfers nutrients from the digestive tract into the blood stream	G. spleen
<u>D</u>	6. Produces bile	

b. Vitamin   Condition prevented

<u>D</u>	1. Niacin	A. Rickets
<u>E</u>	2. Thiamine	B. Night blindness
<u>B</u>	3. Vitamin A	C. Pernicious anemia
<u>F</u>	4. Vitamin C	D. Pelagra
<u>A</u>	5. Vitamin D	E. Beriberi
		F. Scurvy

4. There are no headings to the columns. Both stimuli and responses are heterogeneous. There are equal numbers of stimuli and responses. In general, only one response is a relatively sensible answer to each stimulus. Probably several homogeneous item sets or a different item form would be better for these items.

5. Most fields have at least some knowledge that can be measured by true-false items. True-false items often can be used to test the correct application of principles and generalizations.

6. Matching items are particularly useful for testing the ability to distinguish among terms and concepts and to find relationships between concepts and ideas.

7. For true-false items, be alert for textbook statements taken out of context, items made false by merely placing a negative in a true sentence, items partly true and partly false, trivial items, imprecise terms, and words such as "all" and "none." Try to write interpretive exercises, and use underlining in longer sentences to distinguish which part of the item is to be judged true or false. For matching items, be alert to long, heterogeneous matching sets; look for stimuli with no plausible incorrect responses. Improve matching items by shortening the sets of stimuli, labeling stimuli and responses, and adding extra incorrect responses.

Chapter 6

1. The following revisions of the items avoid the serious problems of the originals.

   a. The distractors do not follow the stem—that is, they are not examples of "correlating" patient and personnel needs. The problem could be eliminated by developing new distractors or by rephrasing the stem. For example: "On what basis are individual assignments made to members of a nursing team?"

b. The cost of the products depend to a significant extent on the geographic location. The problem can be eliminated by specifying a location. For example: "In the United States Midwest which of the following would provide the best, low-cost, high protein dish?"

c. The responses overlap. They should be rewritten, such as:

    a. 1–2
    b. 3–4
    c. at least 4
    d. at least 5

d. There are several problems: the intent of the item is not made clear in the stem; the keyed response is inappropriate to the stem; and distractors are of questionable appropriateness to the stem. Two alternate solutions would be: (1) draft an item on the apparent intent, that Indians were the first Americans, or (2) use each response as the basis for a True-False item. An example of the former could be:

When did Indians arrive in North America?

    *a. Before the Pilgrims
    b. With the Pilgrims
    c. During the Civil War
    d. With the Spanish explorers

e. The approach is inverted, and the term should be in the stem. For example: Which of the following best describes the process of sedimentation as it is used in water purification?

    *1. Heavier-than-water particles settle from undisturbed water.
    2. Large impurities are removed as water passes through some porous material.
    3. Impurities are removed as precipitates that form when chemicals are added to the water.
    4. Bacterial impurities are killed when large amounts of air are mixed with the water.

f. The stem asks "how" but the distractors and keyed response tell "where."

g. The intent of the item is unclear; but even so, the word "represents" in the keyed response gives a clue to the correct answer as the stem is presented. Assuming that this item is for students just beginning to learn about government, it could be revised to:

On what bills does a representative have the right to vote?

   a. Only those that affect the region he represents
   b. Only those introduced by someone from his state
   c. Only those already passed by the Senate
  *d. All bills brought before the House of Representatives

h. The item is controversial and probably does not clearly suggest the knowledge that the teacher wishes to measure. Depending on intent, the stem could be:

Which group of people pay the largest share of the annual income tax collected by the federal government?

or

People from which group are most active in the processes that must function in a democratic society?

i. An actual rather than theoretical approach should be taken in the stem. Also, the keyed response may be too attractive because of its relative length. The stem and d could be revised to:

What method of voting is used in the House of Representatives on extremely important bills? Why?

   d. Roll-call. It is the most accurate method and votes are permanently recorded.

j. No question is posed in the stem.

Which of the following did the Moors introduce into Spain during their settlement there in the eighth to thirteenth centuries?

  *a. A better educational system
   b. Feudalism
   c. Persecution of Christians
   d. Efficient methods of farming   •

2. Check your items against the suggestions given for developing stems, keyed responses, and distractors. For each item make sure that a specific and important question is asked clearly and concisely. Can the

question be inferred from the keyed response? Do distractors appear to be misunderstandings and misconceptions?

3. The responses for the key-list exercises should be homogenous, such as a group of colors, elements, generals, or legumes. Every response should be a feasible answer for each question.

4. The suggestions for constructing items should be applied against the items you developed. In addition, does the passage, graph, or chart require a reasonable amount of time for reading or studying in terms of the number of items asked? This form of testing can be inefficient if the response time required is relatively long per item included in the exercise.

Chapter 7

1. Answers will vary. Some fields may have no important objectives in this category, but most fields have at least some. For example, in chemistry and biology correct laboratory procedures and use of equipment should be demonstrated; in language courses oral skills must be demonstrated; in a subject such as arithmetic, it is helpful sometimes to have the student explain his procedures and reasoning orally as he works out a problem.

2. Answers will vary. Describe your evaluation plan as completely as possible. Describe the elements necessary to adequate performance in the skill and any features that would be undesirable or cause disqualification. The rules for scoring or making a pass–fail decision should be described. Make sure all critical features are considered.

3. Answers will vary. Most fields have at least some affective objectives, and some affective objectives tend to apply to most fields since all fields should contribute to the general goals of the school. The items may be of different types. An attempt should be made to get at the same idea from different angles. For example, the following items might pertain to a student's enjoyment of science as a subject:

SA   A   N   D   SD   O. I enjoy studying about science.

OO. When it is time to study about science, I feel

_____

_____.

OOO. Observation: When checking the students' library cards, the teacher noted that only three of the thirty-five children in the class had checked out at least one book about science during the second six weeks of school.

Chapter 8

1. 40.2; 51.2

2. 7.70; 17.55

3. Boys; their mean is 41.2 while the mean for girls is 39.3.

4. Girls; their standard deviation is 20.6 while the boys standard deviation is 14.8.

5.
Interval	tally	f
53–55	//	2
50–52	////	4
47–49		0
44–46	//	2
41–43	//	2
38–40	₩ //	7
35–37	////	4
32–34	₩ /	6
29–31		0
26–28		0
23–25	/	1
		28

Other intervals are possible.

6.
Raw score	Rank	Raw score	Rank
36	19.5	34	22.5
25	28	46	7
39	14	51	4
33	25	53	2
51	4	38	16
35	21	36	19.5
33	25	32	27
38	16	51	4
45	8	54	1
38	16	34	22.5
37	18	40	12
40	12	43	9
41	10	40	12
50	6	33	25

7. 38.5

8. 20; 57; 96

9. -1.25; $-.25$; $.50$; $.75$

10. .57 or .64 depending on how tied scores were decided.

11. .81; .94 by Saupe's method.

12. .82 by the Spearman-Brown Formula.

13. 4.3 from Table 8.11.

14. 5.85

15. .60; .30

16. The difficulty index indicates that the average student made a score on item 2 which was 60 percent of the possible score. The discrimination index indicates that the difference between the upper and lower groups in average score on the item is 30 percent of the maximum possible difference. In general, the indexes indicate that the item was of appropriate difficulty for the group and that it did contribute positively to discriminating between students who had command of the material and those who did not.

17. .42; .36

18. Choice D; since it attracted only one person from the low scoring group and none from the high scoring group, it may not be plausible even to poorly informed students.

19. Discriminatory test; the item does discriminate well and hopefully more than 42 percent of a class would master a basic skill at a minimum level.

20. Test A, because of its higher reliability.

Chapter 9

1. The system for reporting progress to students must reflect the nature of the course, but common features and principles apply to most courses. In many cases, formative assessment will be reported orally and discussed with each student. In some cases comments will be written on tests, projects, or themes. Adequate progress and correct approaches should be noted, and when errors are found, the teacher should indicate what the student should do to eliminate the problem.

2. Many students will learn from the exercise just how difficult it is to apply a mastery analysis to typical tests. The process in most courses will be almost entirely subjective. However, you might be able to say that some score, for example 8 out of 10 correct, should indicate ability

to pursue the next step in the process. On the same test, 6 or 7 correct might suggsest the need for some review before the student starts the next step. Scores of 5 or below might indicate the need for a thorough review and an additional test on the topic. Relative success could be reported by means of rank in class or by reporting the class average so students could see how well classmates did on the test.

3. A good way to report midterm test results is to show the class the distribution of scores on the test and encourage individuals to see how they compared to the extreme and average scores. Ask students to compare their results with their personal standards of expectation. Verbal labels—for example, "very good," "satisfactory," "review is needed"—could be made for different score ranges.

4. Most teachers have a good idea of how well a class should be able to perform on a test, basing this prediction on past experience and the difficulty of the test. Verbal labels can be assigned to different levels of success.

5. a.

Measure	Class average	Estimated SD	Action	Final Relative weight
Quiz Total	42	5	leave alone (or ÷ 2)	5 (2.5)
Project 1	27	3	double scores	6
Test 1	35	4	double scores	8
Test 2	47	6	double scores	12
Project 2	33	4	double scores	8
Final Exam	85	14	leave alone	14

b.

Original score	Adjusted score
40	40 (or 20)
30	60
40	80
50	100
30	60
90	90
Total	430 (or 410)

6. a. 42 36 35 34 31 30 29 28 27 26 23 23 22 22 21
      20 19 19 16 15 14 11 11   8   4

$$\text{mean} = \frac{566}{25} = 22.64$$

$$\text{est. } SD = \frac{(42 + 36 + 35 + 34) - (11 + 11 + 8 + 4)}{12}$$

$$= \frac{147 - 34}{12} = \frac{113}{12} = 9.4$$

$$C \text{ range} = 22.64 + 4.7 = 27.34$$
$$22.64 - 4.7 = 17.94$$
$$\text{highest } B = 27.34 + 9.4 = 36.74$$
$$\text{lowest } D = 17.94 - 9.4 = 8.54$$

Thus
- A 37 and above
- B 28–36
- C 18–27
- D 9–17
- F 8 and below (tentative)

b. If the class is above average in ability, the curve could be modified as:

- A 35 and above
- B 26–34
- C 16–25
- D 6–15
- F 5 and below (tentative)

7. Only two scores, 8 and 4, could be considered as possible F grades. The lowest score is less than 0.5 SD below the D range, and a teacher should require supporting evidence before assigning a grade that will require a student to repeat the unit or course. If the unit or course is part of a sequence, remedial work for at least the two low-scoring students would be appropriate.

INDEX

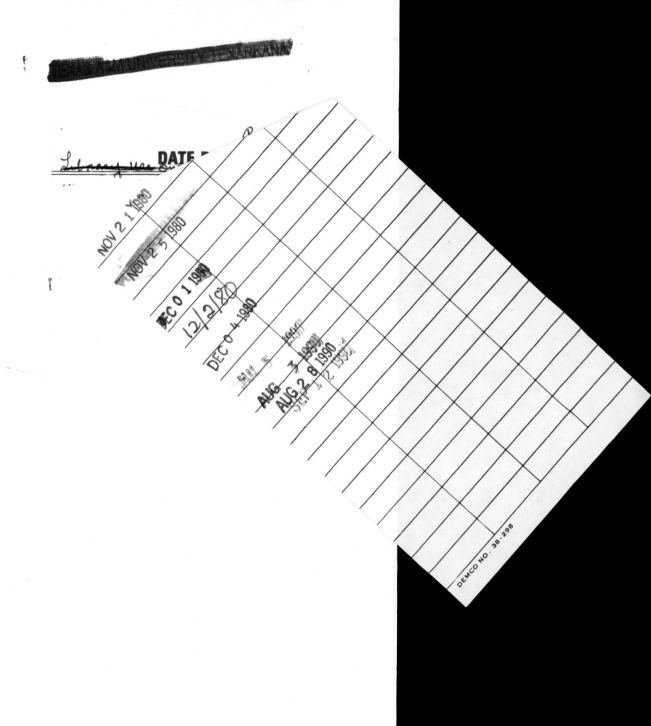